Yazoo County Mississippi

1850 U.S. Census and Marriages

Compiled and
Transcribed

by

Diane Fyans Roos

HERITAGE BOOKS
2019

HERITAGE BOOKS
AN IMPRINT OF HERITAGE BOOKS, INC.

Books, CDs, and more—Worldwide

For our listing of thousands of titles see our website
at
www.HeritageBooks.com

Published 2019 by
HERITAGE BOOKS, INC.
Publishing Division
5810 Ruatan Street
Berwyn Heights, Md. 20740

International Standard Book Number
Paperbound: 978-1-55613-343-5

FOREWORD & ACKNOWLEDGEMENTS

This book was started with the intention of transcribing the 1850 Census for Yazoo County, Mississippi. As I was working on it I noticed many names for which I already had much information because several of my ancestral lines are from Yazoo County. I believe that the maternal lines are often neglected and felt it would be beneficial if I listed the maiden names of the wives where I knew them. Then I couldn't stop myself. I checked to see if I could find the marriages for others in the census in order to establish maiden names, or at least previous names (from other marriages). I only checked the marriages in Mississippi. Depending on the response I receive, I may continue to search for the missing marriages in other states. I subsequently checked the families against 5-6 sources. I was able to find many mistaken names and spellings by checking with other sources. I have tried to make this as accurate as possible, but I am sure there are still a lot of mistakes. I didn't check to make sure that the marriages were indeed the people listed. If I found a marriage of John Doe to Jane Smith and John Doe's wife's name was Jane in the Census, and the time and place were right, I made the assumption that her previous name was Jane Smith. On most of the families I was able to verify this with other sources, but not all. The copy I was working with was dark and I am sure there are mistakes with the initials L & S as they are very similar in the original. Please be aware of this if this applies to your family. I tried to copy the original Census as it was written, even though there were obvious mistakes in the original document. From checking with other sources, I found many names which where written phonetically by the census taker, i. e. Mayner which in other records is Manor. Check the index carefully for possible other spellings of your name. By checking the census with the 1860 Census, I find that the ages varied a great deal. One was 51 in the 1850 Census and was only 55 by the 1860 census. So bear this in mind when establishing whether these people are your ancestors. The ages are very misleading. There was a lot of duplication of people in the census also. They often gave different information in the same census. When I had a previous name or spouse, and there was not enough room, I left out some of the census information, such as real estate value. I hope this will be useful to you.

I would also like to thank and acknowledge several people who have been important in the completion of this work. First of all by mother, Leone Slater Fyans, who has spent a lifetime in collecting and organizing family history. Her example has instilled in me a love of those who have gone before me and the sacrifices that they made. But, I decided early on, that I was not going to waste my life thinking about dead people. It was the patient devotion of my dear friend Karen Clifford who changed all of that. If she had not taught me the skills necessary to make genealogy an exciting quest that was intellectually stimulating, I would never have changed my position. She is a professional genealogist who trained me as an apprentice while I worked for her business. It was not an easy conversion! But she persisted. I would also like to thank my sister, Renee Christiansen for her financial and emotional support. My brothers Jack & Joe Fyans and their wives, Beth and Laurie, have also been supportive, although I sense that they aren't going to waste their lives with dead people either. To my children, Stacey, Deborah & Kathryn, I give my thanks for their loving support and for letting me show them what I was doing and for them acting interested even though they didn't understand what I was doing or the importance of it. To my husband, Gerard, I give special thanks for all the freedom to do what ever makes me happy, as long as he doesn't have to do it too! He has put up with a lot of mess with note books and printouts all over our room and bed. He has encouraged me to get it done and has been supportive of my efforts.

I am grateful for the new sources and computer equipment that has helped to keep our ancestors straight. I never would have done any of this if it had not been for the new computer software and word processing tools that are now available. I would also like to thank the staff and supporters of the Monterey County Family History Center located in Seaside, California. All of the resources of the library have made much of the work easier. The unselfish devotion of the staff in keeping the library open and funded has been most impressive.

When you find a name enclosed in ( )'s, it is showing a (maiden or previous name). When you find a name enclosed in { }'s, it is showing a (previous or future spouse).

SOURCES

1840 US Census for Yazoo County, MS as indexed in <u>Yazoo - Its Legends & Legacies</u>, by Harriet DeCell and JoAnn Prichard, (Yazoo Delta Press, 1988)

1850 US Census for Yazoo County, MS (Original Microfilm FHL)

1860 US Census for Yazoo County, MS (Original Microfilm FHL)

Mississippi Marriages as extracted on to the INTERNATIONAL GENEALOGICAL INDEX (IGI) (On microfiche FHL)

<u>Marriages & Deaths from Mississippi Newspapers, Vols. I-IV</u>, by Betty Couch Wiltshire, (Heritage Books, Inc., 1987-1990)

<u>Yazoo-Its Legends & Legacies</u>, by Harriet DeCell and JoAnn Prichard, (Yazoo Delta Press, 1988)

Cemetery Records of Yazoo County, MS, unpublished by Linda Crawford, Yazoo County Historical Society (1989)

```
#1    HOOTER, James N.        29  M  LA  Planter      800
      HOOTER, Annesse M       24  F  MS  (POTTER, Annie M.)
      HOOTER, Cyntha J         5  F  MS
      HOOTER, Sarah E          4  F  MS
      HOOTER, Massie          21  F  MS
      WINDHAM, William        18  M  MS  Laborer

#2    MANSFIELD, William A    21  M  MS  Planter      200 {PEERS, Mary}

#3    BAINS, Moses            35  M  NC  Planter       60
      BAINS, Cyntha           40  F  MS  (POTTER, Cynthia)
      SHORTER, Susan          25  F  MS  Blind

#4    POTTER, John            42  M  MS  Planter     1200
      POTTER, Elizabeth       30  F  LA
      POTTER, John C          17  M  MS  Laborer
      POTTER, Caleb           13  M  MS
      POTTER, Thomas           9  M  MS
      POTTER, James            7  M  MS
      POTTER, Polly            5  F  MS
      POTTER, Joseph           3  M  MS
      POTTER, John Jr.         1  M  MS

#5    SMITH, Austin P         43  M  MS  Planter     1600
      SMITH, Sarah C.         41  F  MS  (COOPER, Sarah)
      SMITH, James            14  M  MS
      SMITH, Malissa E        13  F  MS
      SMITH, William Z.        8  M  MS
      SMITH, George E          6  M  MS
      SMITH, Theophilus        1  M  MS

#6    WASSON, Elihu           38  M  NC School Teacher   600
      WASSON, Sarah T         28  F  VA  (COOPER, Sarah)
      POND, Walter A          11  M  VA
      POND, Sidney A           9  M  VA
      POND, Thomas             4  M  VA
      WASSON, Lucius E         3  M  MS
      LUMLEY, Joseph S        21  M  MS  {MARTIN, Nancy Catherine}

#7    COWAN, Hugh             50  M  TN  Planter       50
      COWAN, Sarah            52  F  VA
      COWAN, Matilda O        20  F  MS
      COWAN, Rebecca          18  F  MS
      COWAN, Sarah J          10  F  MS
      PERRY, Ann              59  F  TN

#8    WOODARD, Frances        25  F  MS  {SHAFER, Jacob}
      WOODARD, Margaret C      5  F  MS
      EISHAM, Margaret        53  F  KY
```

```
#9    HILDERBRAND, Philip      56   M   MS   Planter      1404
      HILDERBRAND, Rachel      47   F   MS   (HAMBERLIN, Rachel)
      HILDERBRAND, Philip      17   M   MS   Laborer
      HILDERBRAND, Thomas      16   M   MS   Laborer
      HILDERBRAND, Rachel A    14   F   MS   in school
      HILDERBRAND, Mary F      12   F   MS   in school
      HILDERBRAND, Louisa S    10   F   MS   in school
      HILDERBRAND, David        7   M   MS   in school
      HILDERBRAND, Joseph       3   M   MS
      COODY, Warren            21   M   MS   Overseer (RUNDELL, Sally)

#10   ANDERSON, William E      40   M   SC   Planter      400
      ANDERSON, Mary J         19   F   MS   (HAMBERLIN, Mary Jane)
      ANDERSON, David M         3   M   MS
      ANDERSON, William W       9   M   MS

#11   ERWIN, William C         42   M   MS   Planter      700
      ERWIN, Margaret A        35   F   MS   (ANDERSON, Margaret A)
      ERWIN, David             15   M   MS
      ERWIN, Daniel            12   M   MS
      ERWIN, Henry F            6   M   MS
      ERWIN, Archibald          3   M   MS
      YOUNG, Joseph            25   M   LA   Laborer

#12   ERWIN, David C           34   M   MS   Planter
      ERWIN, Margaret          37   F   MS

#13   RICE, Joel C             52   M   TN   Physician
      RICE, Joel W             21   M   TN   Medical Student
      RICE, Lewelyn            19   M   TN   Medical Student
      RICE, Cornelius A        16   M   KY   Student
      RICE, Noland S           13   M   MS   in school

#14   SAYRE, William K         37   M   PA   Waggon Maker  100
      SAYRE, Sarah             31   F   MS   (HOOTER, Sarah S)

#15   CALVITT, Charles         42   M   MS   Planter      4000
      CALVITT, Elizabeth       32   F   MS
      CALVITT, Ada             10   F   MS   in school
      CALVITT, Mary             7   F   MS   in school
      CALVITT, Martha A        21   F   MS
      CALVITT, John            26   M   MS   Planter

#16   HARRIS, Jonathan M       31   M   MS   Planter      2000
      HARRIS, Joseph F         20   M   AL   Laborer

#17   MARTIN, James            30   M   TN   Planter      400
      MARTIN, Lucretia         21   F   GA   (COLLUM, Lucretia A)
      MARTIN, Mary              3   F   MS
      MARTIN, William A      1/12   M   MS
```

```
#18   ROBINSON, James H      32    M   MS   Planter      800
      ROBINSON, Mary E       30    F   MS   (STURDIVANT, Mary E?)
      PEERS, Minerva         31    F   MS
      GRISHAM, Martin V B    12    M   MS   (RODGERS, Francis M}

#19   COODY, Zephemiah       36    M   MS   Planter      349
      COODY, Eliza J         24    F   MS   (IRWIN, Elizabeth?)
      GILBERT, Maria A       48    F   LA
      COODY, Warren           8    M   MS   in school

#20   CLARK, Jethro B        50    M   NC   Planter      2271
      CLARK, Delany          40    F   AL
      BAKER, Lutilda         21    F   NC   {McFARLAND, Andrew)
      CLARK, John             9    M   MS   in school
      CLARK, Susannah         8    F   MS   in school
      CLARK, David            1    M   MS

#21   McKEE, Copeland        53    M   GA   Planter
      McKEE, Anna R          56    F   SC                 8000
      GUINN, Charles E       21    M   MS   Planter {CASSELS, Hester)
      GUINN, Morris M        16    M   MS   Planter (HEWTON, Sarah R?}
      SEAGER, James P        20    M   TN   Laborer

#22   STURDIVANT, Ransom     20    M   MS   Planter      960
      STURDIVANT, Mary A     18    F   MS   (HOWARD, Mary A. G)
      STURDIVANT, Ann E    6/12    F   MS

#23   PEERS, William N       35    M   VA   Planter      800
      PEERS, Sarah A         26    F   MS   (STURDIVANT, Sarah Ann)
      PEERS, Mary E          11    F   MS   in school
      PEERS, John W           8    M   MS   in school
      PEERS, Nancy A          3    F   MS

#24   PEERS, Samuel P        48    M   VA   Planter      500
      PEERS, Catherine       45    F   MS   (KING, Catherine){HAMBERLIN}
      PEERS, William         18    M   MS   Laborer
      PEERS, Elizabeth       16    F   MS   in school
      PEERS, Marion          13    M   MS   in school
      PEERS, Samuel          11    M   MS   in school

#25   SMITH, James           42    M   SC   Overseer
      SMITH, Celia A         28    F   MS
      LOWRY, John R          14    M   TN   in school{DUFFEY, Elizabeth E}

#26   WILES, W W             24    M   MS   Planter      2500
      WILES, Elizabeth L     21    F   MS   (GWINN, Elizabeth L)
      WILES, Morris G         1    M   MS
```

```
#27   HOOTER, Michael          59   M   LA   Planter      3150
      HOOTER, Sarah A          38   F   MS   (POTTER, Sarah Ann)
      HOOTER, Mary             13   F   MS   in school
      HOOTER, John S            9   M   MS   in school
      HOOTER, Margaret          5   F   MS   in school
      HOOTER, Michael Jr.       3   M   MS
      BRANNEN, Joseph          18   M   GA   Planter
      BRANNEN, Harrison        17   M   MS   Planter

#28   STURDIVANT, Henry        60   M   NC   Planter      600   {Ann}
      BRADSHAW, Sarah          70   F   TN

#29   DILLEY, Samuel           48   M   PA   Saw Miller
      DILLEY, Lemenda H        33   F   MS   (USHER, Charlotte Lemenda Hinds)
      DILLEY, Lucy A           13   F   MS   in school
      DILLEY, Sarah C          11   F   MS   in school
      DILLEY, Joseph A          9   M   MS   in school
      DILLEY, Robert W          7   M   MS   in school
      DILLEY, Samuel U          6   M   MS
      DILLEY, Eugene P          4   M   MS
      DILLEY, Abraham T         2   M   MS
      DILLEY, Benjamin R      5/12  M   MS

#30   SCREWS, James H          32   M   TN   Planter      300
      SCREWS, Latitia          25   F   MS   (BRADSHAW, Letetia){LESTER}
      SCREWS, Archibald         6   M   MS   in school
      SCREWS, John              5   M   MS   in school
      SCREWS, Celia A           3   F   MS
      SCREWS, James             1   M   MS

#31   MARCHBANKS, C. W.        37   M   AL   Overseer {LILLYBRIDGE, Susan}
      MARCHBANKS, Elizabeth    30   F   AL

#32   HERRIN, John             36   M   MS   Planter
      HERRIN, Rhoda            33   F   MS
      HERRIN, Mary             14   F   MS
      HERRIN, Saline           13   F   MS
      HERRIN, William          11   M   MS
      HERRIN, John W            9   M   MS
      HERRIN, Edward            7   M   MS
      HERRIN, Charles           5   M   MS
      HERRIN, Robert            3   M   MS
      HERRIN, Isaac             2   F   MS
      HERRIN, Stephen         1/12  M   MS

#33   HAMBERLIN, Catherine S   43   F   MS   1300 (USHER, Catherine S)
      HAMBERLIN, Monroe        21   M   MS   Planter
      HAMBERLIN, Thomas        16   M   MS
      HAMBERLIN, Elvira        13   F   MS   in school
      HAMBERLIN, Catherine     10   F   MS   in school
      HAMBERLIN, Isaac          8   M   MS   in school
      HAMBERLIN, Sarah         25   F   MS   (FOSTER, Archer H}
```

```
#34   HAMBERLIN, John W         19    M   MS   Planter
      HAMBERLIN, Anne M         17    F   MS   md this yr (HOOTER, Anne)

#35   MARTIN, William           54    M   NC   Planter     200
      MARTIN, Susannah          53    F   NC   (HARRIS, Susannah)
      MARTIN, Elisha A          20    M   TN   Laborer
      MARTIN, Nancy C           22    F   TN   (LUMBLEY, Joseph S)
      MARTIN, Sampson A         18    M   TN   Laborer
      MARTIN, Jesse W           15    M   TN
      MARTIN, Joseph J          11    M   MS   twin/in school
      MARTIN, Susan I           11    F   MS   twin/in school
      MARTIN, Isaac W            8    M   MS

#36   MARTIN, William P         28    M   TN   Planter     200
      MARTIN, Rebecca           20    F   MS   (FLETCHER, Rebecca)
      MARTIN, James W            3    M   MS
      MARTIN, Benjamin F         2    M   MS

#37   LUMLEY, William W         26    M   MS   Carpenter (Lucy below)
      LEWIS, Lucy J             20    F   NC   (md 18 Dec. 1850)

#38   HUNT, Thomas              33    M   VA   Planter
      HUNT, Cenia               34    F   NC
      HUNT, Thomas J          1/12    M   MS
      SMITH, Cyntha             60    F   NC

#39   HARROLD, James            26    M   SC   Planter
      HARROLD, Amanda           21    F   MS
      HARROLD, William        5/12    M   MS
      BELLOW, Elisha            26    M   MS   Laborer

#40   ERWIN, Hugh C             52    M   GA   Planter     2000
      ERWIN, Elizabeth          45    F   TN   (SIBLEY, Elizabeth)
      ERWIN, William W          24    M   MS   Laborer
      ERWIN, Frances            20    F   MS
      ERWIN, Elizabeth          15    F   MS   in school
      ERWIN, Mary               11    F   MS   in school
      JAGGERS, Martha E          9    F   MS
      JAGGERS, Lucinda A         5    F   MS
      BILES, James              28    M   AL   Laborer

#41   McCLURE, John             46    M   KY   Planter
      McCLURE, Anne             50    F   MS
      McCLURE, Thomas           13    M   MS   in school
      CRAIG, John               20    M   MS   Laborer
      GLOVER, Daniel            21    M   MS
      CRAIG, David              26    M   MS   Laborer
```

```
#42   SIBLEY, Asa                29  M  MS   Planter
      SIBLEY, Mary A.M.          28  F  MS
      SIBLEY, William H.H.        8  M  MS
      SIBLEY, John C              5  M  MS
      SIBLEY, Samuel W            2  M  MS
      SIBLEY, Susan A             3  F  MS
      SIBLEY, Nancy G             7  F  MS

#43   STUBBLEFIELD, Stephen P  25  M  AL   Overseer
      STUBBLEFIELD, Eliza P     17  F  MS   md this yr (RUSSELL, Eliza)

#44   WHELESS, Frederick W       38  M  NC   Planter      5000
      WHELESS, Elizabeth A       27  F  MO   (DORSEY, Elizabeth Ann)
      WHELESS, Quesney            6  M  MS
      WHELESS, Ada                4  F  MS
      WHELESS, Falba              3  F  MS
      WHELESS, Kossuth            1  M  MS
      DORSEY, Ellen D            17  F  MO

#45   HODGES, Jesse              31  M  TN   Overseer     3300

#46   WILSON, Robert             42  M  NH   Merchant/4000/md this year
      WILSON, Margaret           30  F  MS   (PARKS, Margaret)
      FINNUCANE, Dawson W        21  M  MS   Physician
      ALVERSON, William          23  M  MS   Merchant Clerk

#47   FOSTER, A.Y.               29  M  SC   Carpenter
      FOSTER, Chana              17  M  SC   Laborer
      FOSTER, Martha             17  M  MS
      BAKER, Benjamin            23  M  NC

#48   MILES, Deut H              52  M  MD   Planter      12000
      MILES, Virginia            18  F  MD
      MILES, Mary J              16  F  MD
      MILES, Elizabeth            6  F  MS
      MILES, Sheridan             4  M  MS

#49   HIRSH, Samuel              20  M  GERMARNY         Merchants Clerk
      BELL, Lucius G             34  M  NY   Tailor

#50   MARBLE, Rinaldo D          25  M  MS   Planter {CHAMBERS, M.A.}
      MARBLE, B.F.               21  M  MS   Painter {EVERETT, Sarah}

#51   DOUGLAS, Henry             39  M  IRELAND  Merchant [LYLE, Susan]
      LYLE, William H            12  M  TN   in school  (ROBINSON, Lucy}
      SCHAFER, J.                42  M  MD   Carpenter
      REAGAN, Thomas J           19  M  AL   Laborer

#52   RILEY, William W           32  M  AL   Laborer
      RILEY, Harriet E           18  F  MS   (REICE, Harriett Elizabeth)
      RILEY, Martha P. A.         8  F  AL   in school
      RILEY, William E            1  M  MS
```

```
#53   BALLARD, John          59     M   NC   Planter      100
      BALLARD, Andrew J      14     M   MS   in school
      BALLARD, Sarah R       10     F   MS   in school

#54   COODY, Lydia           35     F   MS
      COODY, Henry C          5     M   MS
      COODY, Robert           4     M   MS

#55   SPIARS, Robert F       25     M   MS   Planter
      SPIARS, Mary C         24     F   MS
      SPIARS, Robert K P      6     M   MS
      SPIARS, John            2     M   MS
      SPIARS, Frances A       3     F   MS
      RUSSELL, Mary A        11     F   MS   in school

#56   SPIARS, Robert         57     M   MS   Planter      20,000
      SPIARS, Gracy          45     F   MS
      SPIARS, John C         24     M   MS   Planter
      SPIARS, James          17     M   MS   Student      in school
      SPIARS, Levi            8     M   MS   in school
      SPIARS, William         4     M   MS

#57   CALVITT, Thomas        57     M   MS   Planter 400
      CALVITT, Priscilla     40     F   MS   (MITCHELL, Priscilla)
      CALVITT, Samuel        22     M   MS   Planter
      CALVITT, Frances J     13     F   MS   in school
      CALVITT, Mary          11     F   MS   in school
      CALVITT, George         6     M   MS   in school

#58   EDMUNDSON, James W     47     M   SC   Planter      600
      EDMUNDSON, Louisa      40     F   SC
      EDMUNDSON, William     20     M   SC
      EDMUNDSON, Sarah       14     F   SC
      EDMUNDSON, George      12     M   MS
      EDMUNDSON, Atlantic     6     F   MS
      EDMUNDSON, Josephus     3     M   MS
      EDMUNDSON, Mary         1     F   MS

#59   GALE, James B          26     M   LA   Planter      4,500
      GALE, Mary F           22     F   TN
      GALE, Inez F        10/12     F   MS
      BEAUMIN, James W       20     M   MS   Overseer

#60   HODGES, John H         22     M   KY   Overseer

#61   PEYTON, William H      24     M   TN   Overseer (ALLEY, Emily May)

#62   PRITCHETT, Sarah M     40     F   MS                1,800
      PRITCHETT, Robert J S  19     M   MS   Overseer  in school
      PRITCHETT, Henry M     15     M   MS   in school
      PRITCHETT, Georganna    7     F   MS   in school
      PRITCHETT, William P    4     F   MS
```

```
#63   WOODBERRY, George W      39    M    NH   Physician (SPIERS, Martha Jane)
      WOODBERRY, Robert S       4    M    MS
      WOODBERRY, George W       2    M    MS

#64   CARMAN, Richard          28    M    MS   Bricklayer (NEWBAKER, Martha)
      CARMAN, Missouri         21    F    MS   (HAMBERLIN, Missouri)

#65   STAMPLEY, Absalom        42    M    MS   Overseer
      STAMPLEY, Harriet S      21    F    TN   (LYLE, Harriet S)
      STAMPLEY, John S          3    M    MS
      WILBORN, Joseph          24    M    AL   Laborer
      STUBBLEFIELD, David A    24    M    MS   Laborer

#66   McLEOD, Alexander        39    M    NC   Planter 1,000 (MILES, Virginia)
      McLEOD, Cordelia         25    F    MS   (SPAIN, Cordelia)
      McLEOD, Richmond          9    M    MS   in school
      McLEOD, Emma J            3    F    MS
      McLEOD, Jane M         4/12    F    MS
      McLEOD, Nancy            80    F    NC
      SPANE, Nancy             65    F    NC

#67   VANCLEAVE, Jonathan      52    M    KY   Overseer

#68   FOX, Daniel N            31    M    OH   Planter (DAVIS, Martha J)
      BARTON, Daniel J         23    M    LA   Carpenter

#69   BONNEY, Caleb D          45    M    VA   Planter (HALL, Indiana Catharine)

#70   CARPENTER, Robert S      32    M    TN   Overseer      2,000

#71   STAMPLEY, Richard        50    M    MS   Planter       2,500
      STAMPLEY, Abbygen        48    F    MS   (SMITH, Abigail)
      STAMPLEY, Sarah A        18    F    MS
      STAMPLEY, Jesse S        19    M    MS   Merchants Clerk in school
      STAMPLEY, John           17    M    MS   Student in school
      STAMPLEY, Jefferson      15    M    MS   in school
      STAMPLEY, Malvinia       13    F    MS   in school
      STAMPLEY, Richard        11    M    MS   in school
      STAMPLEY, Leonidas        9    M    MS   in school

#72   STAMPLEY, David          21    M    MS   Planter
      STAMPLEY, Sarah          16    F    MS   (FLOWER, Sarah)

#73   BRAZEALE, Davis          51    M    SC   Planter       9,000
      BRAZEALE, Niaha?         41    F    SC
      BRAZEALE, Elliott F      38    M    MS   Planter
      CARMAN, Delanson         20    M    MS   Overseer (NEWBAKER, Mary)
      ERWIN, David C            5    M    MS
```

```
#74   EWING, Martin W         51   M   KY   Planter     17,000
      EWING, Ann              44   F   SC   (BYNUM, Ann S.)
      EWING, Robert W         15   M   MS
      EWING, Ann B            13   F   MS   in school
      EWING, Benjamin B       10   M   MS   in school

#75   BONNEY, Moses H         33   M   VA   Planter     8,000
      BONNEY, Laura E         23   F   MS   (STOWER, Laura)
      BONNEY, Edward           5   M   MS
      BONNEY, Sarah            4   F   MS

#76   WILDY, William W        41   M   VA   Planter     8,000
      WILDY, Laurena          31   F   AK   (HALL, Laurena Matilda)
      HALL, William           21   M   AK   Law Student in school
      CHILDRESS, William G    14   M   AK   in school
      CHILDRESS, Samuel       12   M   AK   in school
      WILDY, Matilda           9   F   MS   in school
      WILDY, H                 5   M   MS
      WILDY, Sally             2   F   MS   (HOLLOMAN, William Emery)
      WILDY, Ada               1   F   MS

#77   MABIN, Joseph W         24   M   MS   Planter 30,000 (MARLEY, Mary R)

#78   UTLEY, John W           29   M   TN   Overseer
      UTLEY, Louisa           20   F   MS   (HART, Louisa G)
      WADLINGTON, Ferdinand   18   M   MS   Laborer
      ALBETS, Andrew          40   m   GER  Laborer

#79   CLARK, Council          49   M   NC   Planter
      CLARK, Sally            50   F   NC
      CLARK, Jethro           20   M   NC   Laborer (HART, Minerva)
      CLARK, Reuben            7   M   MS   in school

#80   LAVENDER, Joseph P      45   M   TN   Planter
      LAVENDER, Saber         44   F   KY   (HART, Sabra)
      LAVENDER, Jerome P      11   F   MS   in school
      LAVENDER, Ferdinand W    9   M   MS   in school
      LAVENDER, Elizabeth      7   F   MS   in school
      LAVENDER, Henry C        6   M   MS   in school

#81   HART, John              20   M   MS   Planter     in school
      HART, Minerva           14   F   MS   in school (CLARK, Jethro)
      HART, Mississippi       12   F   MS   in school

#82   MARLEY, Samuel          56   M   NC   Planter     50,000
      MARLEY, Nancy           45   F   KY   (DAVIS, Nancy)
      MARLEY, Robert H        21   M   MS   Planter     500
      MARLEY, Walter S        19   M   MS   Student     in school
      MARLEY, Nancy C         17   F   MS   in school
      MARLEY, Amelia          15   F   MS   in school
      MARLEY, Samuel P        13   M   MS
      MARLEY, Wesley A.       11   F   MS   in school
      WALKER, Semitha         25   F   VT
```

```
#83   CALLIHAM, George W          37   M   MS   Planter
      CALLIHAM, Harriet           28   F   VA   (PARISH, Harriet)
      CALLIHAM, Robert             8   M   MS   in school
      MABIN, Lauretta A           19   F   MS

#84   HOLLIMAN, Abner S           42   M   TN   Planter
      HOLLIMAN, Pamelia           26   F   KY
      HOLLIMAN, Thomas L           8   M   MO   in school
      HOLLIMAN, Elijah D           6   M   MO   in school
      HOLLIMAN, Pamelia H          1   F   MO
      MATIAR, William B           38   M   IRE  school teacher

#85   SLATER, Launer M            23   M   MS   Planter      1,500

#86   MABIN, Robert M             38   M   MS   Planter      1,440  {Eliza}
      MABIN, Mary J               29   F   TN
      MABIN, Benjamin F            1   M   MS

#87   DICKSON, John L             33   M   SC   Planter      1,680
      DICKSON, Marian L           24   F   MS
      DICKSON, Ann R               8   F   MS
      DICKSON, Arabella O        9/12  F   MS

#88   CLARK, William              36   M   NC   Planter
      CLARK, Nancy J              20   F   MS   (CLARK, Jane?)
      CLARK, Elizabeth            11   F   NC
      CLARK, Reuben               10   M   NC
      CLARK, Mary M              7/12  F   MS

#89   HOLLIMAN, Thomas R          31   M   MO   Planter      15,000
      HOLLIMAN, R A               20   F   MS   (COOK, Rebecca Ann)
      HOLLIMAN, Fielding C         3   M   MS
      HOLLIMAN, Mary A             2   F   MS
      SLATER, The. A.             13   M   MS   in school
      HAMBERLIN, Mississippi      17   F   MS   (SLATER, Mississippi)
      HAMBERLIN, William          22   M   MS   Overseer

#90   MABIN, Thomas S             31   M   MS   Planter      3,600
      MABIN, Nancy A              19   F   MS
      MABIN, Mary E                4   F   MS
      MABIN, William               2   M   MS
      MABIN, Andrew S              1   M   MS
#91   MABIN, Warren I             36   M   MS   Planter      50
      MABIN, Elizabeth             6   F   MS
      MABIN, Mary A                4   F   MS
      MABIN, Charity              21   F   NC

#92   COODY, Archibald            50   M   GA   Planter      1,500
      COODY, Eliza                42   F   SC   (HAINING, Eliza)
      COODY, Archibald, Jr.       14   M   MS   in school
      COODY, Emily                11   F   MS   in school
      COODY, Joseph A              6   M   MS   in school
      COODY, Silas W               1   M   MS
```

```
#93   NEWBAKER, John            38   M   MS   Planter
      NEWBAKER, Penimia         24   F   MS   (COODY, Penninah){GALLOWAY, J}
      NEWBAKER, Marshall H       6   M   MS
      NEWBAKER, Benson           2   M   MS

#94   HAMBERLIN, James          26   M   MS   Planter      200
      HAMBERLIN, Mary J         22   F   MS   (COODY, Mary Jane)
      ISENHOOD, William         18   M   MS   Laborer

#95   REYNOLDS, E R M           39   M   TN   Planter
      REYNOLDS, Lucy R          39   F   TN
      REYNOLDS, Mary C          12   F   TN   in school
      REYNOLDS, Wiliam H H       9   M   TN   in school
      REYNOLDS, James C J        6   M   TN   in school
      REYNOLDS, John R           1   M   MS

#96   NEWBAKER, Catherine       60   F   MS   1,200 (FENHOOD, Catherine)
      NEWBAKER, Lucinda         29   F   MS
      NEWBAKER, David S         27   M   MS   Planter      800
      NEWBAKER, Thomas          25   M   MS   Planter
      NEWBAKER, Mary            18   F   MS   twin
      NEWBAKER, Martha          18   F   MS   twin

#97   HAMBERLIN, Moses          43   M   MS   Planter      1,440
      HAMBERLIN, Frances        22   F   MS   (ISONHOOD, Frances)
      HAMBERLIN, Stephen L      16   M   MS   Student      in school
      HAMBERLIN, Roland M       15   M   MS   in school
      HAMBERLIN, John A         11   M   MS   in school
      HAMBERLIN, Ann             8   F   MS   in school
      HAMBERLIN, James D         2   M   MS   (IRWIN, Julia Helen)

#98   HART, Harrison H          36   M   MS   Planter      9,500
      HART, Eliza A             38   F   MS   (BUFORD, Eliza Ann)
      HART, Mary A              17   F   MS
      HART, James               14   M   MS   in school
      HART, Georgana            12   F   MS   in school
      HART, Susan E              5   F   MS
      HART, Eliza J              1   F   MS
      HART, Delilah             70   F   SC

#99   HALL, Archibald C         58   M   TN   Planter      800
      HALL, Mary B              47   F   TN   (HAMILTON, Mary B)
      WALLACE, Elvira           22   F   TN   (HALL, Elvira){BRADSHAW, James}
      HALL, Samuel S            17   M   TN   Student
      HALL, Octavia E           13   F   TN   in school
      HALL, Laurina M           10   F   TN   in school
```

```
#100  SMITH, Benjamin          55   M   SC   Carpenter     480
      SMITH, Ann L             43   F   VA
      SMITH, James M           17   M   TN   Planter
      SMITH, William B         15   M   MS   in school
      SMITH, Susan A           13   F   MS   in school
      SMITH, Joseph B          12   M   MS   in school
      SMITH, Edward H          10   M   MS   in school
      SMITH, Tennesse           8   F   MS   in school
      SMITH, Mary R             6   F   MS   in school
      SMITH, Louisa H           4   F   MS

#101  ADAMS, Benjamin F        30   M   TN   Planter       1,500
      ADAMS, Phebe             26   F   MS   (RUNDELL, Phebe E)
      ADAMS, Caroline F         6   F   MS   in school
      ADAMS, Nancy A            4   F   MS
      ADAMS, Gerrizein M        1   F   MS
      McLAIN, Alfred           19   M   MS   Overseer

#102  YANKEY, William A        47   M   VA   Planter
      YANKEY, Edney C          39   F   MS   (OLDHAM OR WILLIAMS, E. C)
      OLDHAM, John             17   M   MS
      YANKEY, Mary E           13   F   MS   in school
      OLDHAM, Sarah A          13   F   MS   in school
      OLDHAM, James            10   M   MS   in school
      OLDHAM, Minerva           8   F   MS   in school
      OLDHAM, Moses             6   M   MS   in school
      YANKEY, Mary J            2   F   MS   (ERVIN, M. J.)
      YANKEY, Jonathan          1   M   MS

#103  HARROLD, William S       34   M   SC   Blacksmith    500
      HARROLD, Lydia           23   F   MS
      HARROLD, John             5   M   MS
      HARROLD, Mary             2   F   MS
      HAMBERLIN, William A     18   M   MS   Blacksmith (REAVES, Jane)
      FOSTER, Archibald H      46   M   VA   Waggon Maker   380

#104  EDMONDSON, William S     38   M   VA   Waggon Maker
      EDMONDSON, Mary F        21   F   AL
      EDMONDSON, Samuel S       3   M   AL
      EDMONDSON, Angeline B     2   F   MS
      EDMONDSON, William P   5/12  M   MS
      DESMOND, Council         33   M   NC   Planter (KING, Mary L)

#105  FOSTER, J H              35   M   MS   Planter       3,100
      FOSTER, Rebecca          29   F   MS   (OGDEN, Rebecca)
      FOSTER, Samuel M         10   M   MS   in school
      FOSTER, Mary A            9   F   MS   in school
      FOSTER, Margaret E        7   F   MS
      FOSTER, Martha            5   F   MS
      FOSTER, Lucy M            3   F   MS
      FOSTER, Isaac J           1   M   MS
      FOSTER, Thomas O       4/12  M   MS
      SLATER, T. A.            14   M   MS
      CARMAN, Valentine P      26   M   MS   Pilot
```

```
#106  HOOTER, James          50    M   LA   Planter      320
      HOOTER, Nancy          39    F        birthpl unkn (SMITH, Nancy)
      HOOTER, John W         11    M   MS   in school
      HOOTER, Minerva A       5    F   MS

#107  HOOTER, William L      24    M   MS   Planter
      HOOTER, Maria L        19    F   MD   (HOWARD, Maria Louise)
      HOOTER, James A         2    M   MS
      HOOTER, John L       8/12    M   MS
      HOWARD, Phebe          50    F   MD

#108  JOHNS, William         53    M   PA   Planter    1,410
      JOHNS, Sarah           39    F   KY
      JOHNS, William O       10    M   MS   in school
      JOHNS, George W         7    M   MS   in school
      JOHNS, Ellen            3    F   MS   {HARDWICK, Jeff}

#109  NEWBAKER, James        39    M   MS
      NEWBAKER, Mary A       21    F   TN   (GRIZZAND, Mary A)
      NEWBAKER, James Jr.     2    M   MS
      NEWBAKER, John W        1    M   MS

#110  SISSON, Henry          37    M   MS   Planter
      SISSON, Mary J         22    F   MS
      SISSON, Oliver         13    M   MS
      SISSON, James E        10    M   MS
      SISSON, Annes E         3    F   MS

#111  REED, Matthew          47    M   TN   Blacksmith  125
      REED, Jane             24    F   MS   (HOOTER, L. J.)
      SIMMS, Rebecca         12    F   MS
      REED, Mary A            5    F   MS
      REED, Virginia          3    F   MS
      REED, John              1    M   MS

#112  BLANKS, Richard        39    M   NC   Planter
      BLANKS, Elizabeth      23    F   MS
      BLANKS, James           5    M   MS
      BLANKS, John            3    M   MS
      BLANKS, Mary J          2    F   MS
      BLANKS, Elizabeth    6/12    F   MS
      ISENHOOD, Martha       20    F   MS

#113  CARSON, George         36    M   MS   Planter      300
      CARSON, Margaret J     23    F   MS   (COOPER, Margaret J)

#114  BRIGMAN, Thomas        40    M   SC   Carpenter
      BRIGMAN, Elizabeth     45    F   VA   (POOL, Elizabeth P)
      DOUGHARTY, Sarah A     10    F   IRE
      DOUGHARTY, Charles      7    M   IRE
```

```
#115 JACKSON, Cavill          25  M  VA    Planter
     JACKSON, Mary            24  F  MS
     JACKSON, Martha E         4  F  MS
     JACKSON, Henry C          2  M  MS    twin
     JACKSON, William C        2  M  MS    twin

#116 JUDKINS, John F          38  M  VA    Overseer
     JUDKINS, Martha J        38  F  VA
     DREWRY, Frances H        16  F  VA    in school

#117 REGAN, William           30  M  MS    Planter      11,000
     REGAN, Mary A            28  F  MS    (THOMSON, Mary A)(BUTLER, Mary)
     REGAN, William L          4  M  MS
     STINNETT, James L        12  M  MS

#118 NUNNIMAN, Joseph         32  M  GERMANY         Gardener

#119 WASHBURN, A. W.          38  M  VT    Physician    4,080
     WASHBURN, Leonora        28  F  AL
     WASHBURN, George W        1  M  MS

#120 SHIRLEY, Thomas          31  M  GA    Planter      250
     SHIRLEY, Martha A        29  F  MS
     SHIRLEY, Robert          11  M  MS    in school
     SHIRLEY, John             6  M  MS
     SHIRLEY, William          2  M  MS

#121 EVERETT, John            54  M  NC
     EVERETT, Lavina          28  F  MS
     EVERETT, Benjamin        17  M  MS    Student  in school
     EVERETT, James           15  M  MS    in school
     EVERETT, Agnes           12  F  MS    in school
     EVERETT, John Jr.         9  M  MS    in school
     EVERETT, Eliza            7  F  MS
     EVERETT, Henry C          3  M  MS

#122 PENDER, John             43  M  NC    Planter      200
     PENDER, William B        28  M  NC    Planter      200
     PENDER, Helen            33  F  NC
     PENDER, Nancy            31  F  NC
     PENDER, Amanda           14  F  NC
     PENDER, James W          10  M  NC
     PENDER, Helen            60  F  NC

#123 RUSSELL, Elijah          33  M  SC    Overseer
     RUSSELL, Eliza           23  F  MS
     RUSSELL, Mary F           5  F  MS
     RUSSELL, Abner R          3  M  MS
     RUSSELL, Reuben           1  M  MS

#124 MILLER, Joshua           41  M  KY
```

```
#125  WRENN, William R        34   M   VA   Planter       500
      WRENN, Catherine        25   F   MS
      WRENN, William           7   M   MS   in school
      WRENN, Robert            2   M   MS
#126  ROWE, Elizabeth         39   M   MS
      ROWE, Sarah             12   F   MS   in school

#127  POWELL, Richard B       26   M   VA   Planter      5,200
      POWELL, M. J.           22   F   MS   (DYER, Mary Jane)
      POWELL, Edward B         7   M   MS   in school
      POWELL, Martha A         4   F   MS
      POWELL, Alice C          2   F   MS
      CHAMBERS, M. A.         25   F   MS   (MARBLE, Rinaldo D)
      DYER, Leana             10   F   MS   in school

#128  ALFORD, Jackson         36   M   TN   Planter (ELLISON, Elizabeth)
      ALFORD, William         48   M   TN   Planter       360
      ALFORD, Missouri        16   F   MS
#129  HALL, Elizabeth         19   F   AL
      HALL, Tenesse            1   F   MS

#130  DENTON, Solomon G       55   M   VA   Planter       320
      DENTON, Frances         48   F   GA   (ALFORD, Fannie)
      DENTON, Solomon         11   M   MS

#131  McGIBONEY, James        37   M   NC   Carpenter   200
      McGIBONEY, Mary         20   F   MS   (DENTON, Mary Neel)
      McGIBONEY, James         4   M   MS
      McGIBONEY, Mary          2   F   MS

#132  EDMONDSON, John S       50   M   SC   Overseer
      EDMONDSON, Mary         34   F   AL
      EDMONDSON, Mississippi  12   F   MS
      EDMONDSON, Mary         10   F   MS   twin
      EDMONDSON, Sarah E      10   F   MS   twin
      EDMONDSON, John J        8   M   MS
      EDMONDSON, William C     7   M   MS
      EDMONDSON, Druscilla S   5   F   MS
      EDMONDSON, America       4   F   MS

#133  REVELL, James           21   M   SC   Overseer

#134  CALVITT, Joseph         30   M   MS   Planter

#135  GARDNER, Lewis          37   M   MS   Overseer
      GARDNER, Elizabeth      28   F   MS
      GARDNER, Seaborn        10   M   MS   in school
      GARDNER, Sarah J         8   F   MS   in school
      GARDNER, Mary A          6   F   MS   in school
      GARDNER, William J       4   M   MS
      GARDNER, Martha E        2   F   MS
```

```
#136 RAY,   Elijah              44   M   TN   Planter      400
     RAY,   Emily               33   F   TN
     RAY,   Frances M           17   M   MS   Laborer
     RAY,   James J              9   M   MS
     RAY,   Mary J               7   F   MS
     RAY,   Hernando D           5   M   MS
     RAY,   George N             3   M   MS

#137 HAGAN, Henry               45   M   SC   Planter    2,500
     HAGAN, Elizabeth           44   F   MS
     HAGAN, Sarah A             15   F   MS
     HAGAN, James               13   M   MS
     HAGAN, William H            9   M   MS
     HAGAN, George S             7   M   MS
     HAGAN, Eugenia              6   F   MS
     HAGAN, Mary E               4   F   MS

#138 CARSON, John Jr.           28   M   MS   Planter
     CARSON, Lavitius           18   F   MS
     CARSON, Mary E              5   F   MS
     CARSON, Jasper              3   M   MS

#139 CALVITT, Alexander         32   M   MS   Planter      460
     CALVITT, Elizabeth         50   F   MS

#140 PERKINS, Robert S. G.      45   M   VA   Lawyer       200
     PERKINS, Judith N          37   F   MS   (HURST, Judith Nutt)
     PERKINS, Mary              18   F   MS
     PERKINS, Amanda            15   F   MS   in school
     PERKINS, Susan             11   F   MS   in school
     PERKINS, Martha             9   F   MS   in school
     PERKINS, Julia              7   F   MS   in school
     PERKINS, Kate               6   F   MS   in school
     PERKINS, Lucy               3   F   MS
     PERKINS, Charles            1   M   MS

#141 GRAYSON, Sarah R           33   F   MS   (CHEW?, Sarah R) 24,070
     GRAYSON, Thomas T          16   M   MS   Student      in school
     GRAYSON, Francis T         37   M   TN   Lawyer
#142 RAWLINGS, Caroline H       35   F   MS
     RAWLINGS, Daniel           14   M   MS   twin
     RAWLINGS, Emma J           14   F   MS   twin

#143 SALE, Eveline R            28   F   MS   1,760 (SWAYZE, Richard)
     WHITTEN, Eliza             10   F   MS

#144 FRIEDLANDER, Samuel        38   M   GERMANY    Merchant  5,500
     FRIEDLANDER, Lear          30   F   GERMANY
     FRIEDLANDER, Sarah          5   F   MS
     FRIEDLANDER, Henry          3   M   NY
     FRIEDLANDER, Nancy          1   F   MS

#145 CHEATHAM, William          33   M   VA   Planter    2,000
```

```
#146 INGRAM, Nathaniel      30   M   SC   Planter
     INGRAM, Susanna        50   F   SC                    5,000
     INGRAM, Richard        21   M   SC   Planter    in school
     INGRAM, Moses          18   M   SC
     INGRAM, Hannah         16   F   SC

#147 BARKSDALE, Harrison    35   M   TN   Overseer
     BARKSDALE, Laura       30   F   TN
     BARKSDALE, Fountain L  10   M   MS   in school
     BARKSDALE, Samuel L     8   M   MS   in school
     BARKSDALE, Lycurgus     6   M   MS
     BARKSDALE, William      4   M   MS
     BARKSDALE, Harrison     1   M   MS

#148 RUSSELL, Abner         39   M   SC   Planter (MORTON, Catherine)
     RUSSELL, Gaton D        8   M   MS   in school
     RUSSELL, William J      6   M   MS   in school
     RUSSELL, Sarah C        4   F   MS

#149 BUTTON, William S      32   M   TN   Negro trader

#150 ANDERSON, Isaac A      33   M   TN   Gin wright

#151 COOK, Nathan P         49   M   SC   Minister    2,130
     COOK, Elizabeth A      28   F   MS   (CESSNA, Elizabeth Ann)
     COOK, Thomas B         16   M   MS   Laborer    in school
     COOK, Amanda            8   F   MS   in school
     COOK, Margaret          6   F   MS
     COOK, Culbertson        4   M   MS
     COOK, Milton W          2   F   MS
     COOK, John W         1/12   M   MS

#152 LEWIS, Thomas C        49   M   VA   Planter     540
     LEWIS, Elizabeth       36   F   MS
     ALFORD, Frances        13   F   MS
     ALFORD, Sarah          12   F   MS
     LEWIS, Isabella         5   F   MS
     LEWIS, Elizabeth        3   F   MS

#153 WALKER, Alfred         46   M   GA   Chair maker
     WALKER, Sarah          41   F   MS
     WALKER, Asa            17   M   MS
     WALKER, Mary J         14   F   MS
     WALKER, Robert F. M    11   M   MS
     WALKER, Alfred Jr.      6   M   MS
     WALKER, Moses E. N.     2   M   MS

#154 CARRUTH, Samuel O      40   M   MS   Planter
     CARRUTH, Jane          32   F   MS   (ADAMS?, Martha)
     CARRUTH, Eveline        7   F   MS
     CARRUTH, Thomas         5   M   MS

#155 BUNCH, William         32   M   GA   Overseer
```

```
#156  PERRY, James Jr.        28   M   TN   Planter
      PERRY, Mary             22   F   TN   (O'DONALDSON, Mary)
      PERRY, Nathaniel         1   M   MS

#157  McCORMACK, Benjamin T   36   M   AL   Laborer

#158  JENKINS, Elijah         43   M   GA
      JENKINS, Caroline       36   F   GA
      JENKINS, George         15   M   GA
      JENKINS, Mary           13   F   GA
      JENKINS, Henry          11   M   MS
      JENKINS, John            9   M   MS
      JENKINS, Maria           7   F   MS
      JENKINS, Emma            4   F   MS
      JENKINS, Edward          1   M   MS

#159  BRIGMAN, James W        25   M   MS   Laborer
      REESE, John             23   M   MS   Laborer

#160  SHERRARD, Joel          40   M   GA   Planter
      SHERRARD, Elinore       36   F   MS   (BUCKLEY, Eleanor) 3,200
      SHERRARD, Joel Jr.       8   M   MS
      SHERRARD, Mary E         6   F   MS
      SHERRARD, Frances V      3   F   MS
      SHERRARD, Thomas W       5   M   MS
      GREEN, Eliza            37   F   MS

#161  SHERRARD, William       36   M   GA   Planter      960
      SHERRARD, Minerva A     27   F   MS
      SHERRARD, William Jr.    7   M   MS
      SHERRARD, Benjamin       5   M   MS
      SHERRARD, John L         3   M   MS
      SHERRARD, Richard        1   M   MS
      LOTT, Elizabeth         24   F   MS

#162  SHERRARD, John R        30   M   GA   Planter      480
      SHERRARD, Emily         22   F   VA   (McGEE, Emily)
      SHERRARD, Sarah          5   F   MS
      SHERRARD, Martha         3   F   MS

#163  ALTON, George A         53   M   MD   Planter      200
      ALTON, Cynthia          30   F   LA
      ALTON, William I         9   M   MS
      ALTON, Henry C           7   M   MS
      ALTON, Gustavus          5   M   MS

#164  STUBBLEFIELD, Marlin    32   M   AL   Planter      480
      STUBBLEFIELD, Almira    19   F   AL   (McCORMACK, Almira)
      STUBBLEFIELD, Sarah A    3   F   MS

#165  ANDERSON, Sidney        65   M   MS   Planter    1,400
      ANDERSON, William       22   M   MS
```

```
#166 ANDERSON, John N          30   M   MS   Overseer
     ANDERSON, Mary            26   F   VA   (ANDERSON, Mary Jane)
     ANDERSON, Lauretta         3   F   MS
     ANDERSON, William          2   M   MS

#167 RILEY, Robert            28   M   MS   Physician

#168 MOREY, William S         30   M   NY   School Teacher

#169 JACKSON, Jesse H         42   M   TN   Brick Mason
     JACKSON, Martha          29   F   AL
     JACKSON, Jane             9   F   AL
     JACKSON, Druscilla        7   F   AL

#170 WATERS, Needham          30   M   GA   Planter       393
     WATERS, Lucinda          22   F   AL
     WATERS, John W            2   M   MS

#171 PARISH, Anderson         57   M   VA   Planter     1,920
     PARISH, Archibald A      23   M   VA

#172 McCORMACK, John C        56   M   GA   Planter     2,500
     McCORMACK, Amanda        38   F   GA   (BELCHER OR PEARCE, Amanda)
     McCORMACK, Amanda        17   F   AL
     McCORMACK, Robert P      18   M   GA   Laborer
     McCORMACK, Elizabeth     15   F   GA
     McCORMACK, Robert        13   M   AL
     McCORMACK, Elizabeth     12   F   AL   in school
     McCORMACK, Joseph        11   M   AL   in school
     McCORMACK, Franklin       9   M   AL   in school
     McCORMACK, George         7   M   MS   in school

#173 MARSHALL, Thomas S       41   M   GA   Planter
     MARSHALL, Milley         35   F   GA
     MARSHALL, Charles        16   M   GA
     MARSHALL, Frances        14   F   GA   in school
     MARSHALL, William        11   M   GA   in school

#174 YOUNG, Lavina            48   F   SC
     YOUNG, Thomas D          18   M   AL   (HILL, Cynthia A)
     YOUNG, Rachel            16   F   AL
     YOUNG, Keziah            13   M   AL   twin
     YOUNG, Samuel            13   M   AL   twin
     YOUNG, Mary A            10   F   AL

#175 McCORMACK, James C       25   M   AL   Planter
     McCORMACK, Elizabeth     26   F   AL
     McCORMACK, Sarah A        3   F   AL
     McCORMACK, John H         1   M   AL
```

```
#176  STEVENS, Tolbert        36   M   VA   Planter
      STEVENS, Martha         35   F   GA
      STEVENS, Robert H        8   M   MS
      STEVENS, Elizabeth       6   F   MS
      STEVENS, James F         3   M   MS

#177  WALLER, Elizabeth       23   F   MS   (SORRELS, John L}
      WALLER, James S         13   M   MS
      WALLER, Susan           10   F   MS
      WALLER, William          5   M   MS

#178  CHEW, William S         73   M   MD   Planter
      CHEW, Thomas R          25   M   MS   Physician
      CHEW, Robert E          22   M   MS   Law Student

#179  PURVIS, Henry A         41   M   NC   Planter      5,440
      PURVIS, Eveline         26   F   MS   (ALDRIDGE, Eveline)
      PURVIS, James R          5   M   MS
      PURVIS, Philip G         3   M   MS
      PURVIS, Sarah F          1   F   MS
      ALDRIDGE, Mary A        21   F   MS

#180  PURVIS, Edward W        46   M   NC   Planter

#181  CAMPBELL, Augustus      31   M   NC   Overseer
      CAMPBELL, Angeline      25   F   KY   (EDGAR, Angeline)
      CAMPBELL, Emily          2   F   MS

#182  HUDUALL,  William W     60   M   VA   Laborer

#183  PURVIS, John W          46   M   NC   Planter      4,000
      PURVIS, Sarah           46   F   KY
      BARDGES, Henry          11   M   MS   in school
      DAVIS, Margaret S       18   F   MS
      BOSWELL, Thomas R       31   M   NC   Gin wright

#184  HOLMES, Benjamin R      27   M   MS   Physician    5,950
      HOLMES, Louisa          26   F   TN
      HOLMES, Laura            6   F   MS
      HOLMES, Adrian D         4   M   MS
      HOLMES, John P           2   M   MS
      BASS, Alfred            25   M   TN

#185  SHELL, Thomas H         60   M   SC   Planter
      SHELL, Mary             42   F   SC
      SHELL, George H         23   M   SC   Merchants Clerk
      SHELL, Maria C          19   F   SC
      SHELL, Thomas W         12   M   MS   in school
      SHELL, Peter J           8   M   MS   in school    twin
      SHELL, Ira B             8   M   MS   in school    twin
      SHELL, Emily             5   F   MS
```

```
#186 COOPER, Edward W        38   M   NC   Planter        960
     COOPER, Martha E        23   F   SC
     COOPER, Jonathan         8   M   MS   in school
     SHELL, Sarah            11   F   MS   in school

#187 LUSE, Richard H. M.     25   M   MS   Planter

#188 SWAYZE, Budd            27   M   MS   Planter   Md this yr
     SWAYZE, Octavia S       19   F   MS   (KING, Ocatvia)
#189 SWAYZE, Alfred          25   M   MS   Planter   Md this yr
     SWAYZE, Sina            18   F   MS   (BOYD, Sinah A)

#190 BARROW, Nancy           46   F   GA
     BARROW, Samuel          27   M   LA   Planter

#191 PINKSTON, Felix G       37   M   GA   Planter   100
     PINKSTON, Susan         23   F   LA   (ANDERSON, Susan Annie)
     PINKSTON, John S         8   M   MS
     PINKSTON, Elizabeth      7   F   MS
     PINKSTON, Mary J         5   F   MS
     PINKSTON, Anderson       4   M   MS
     PINKSTON, Margaret       2   F   MS

#192 CARSON, Alfred T        30   M   AL   Overseer
     CARSON, Laura           24   F   KY   (EDGAR, Laura)
     CARSON, Robert           4   M   MS
     CARSON, Charles          2   M   MS
     EDGAR, Martha E         14   F   MS

#193 FARLEY, John J          27   M   MS   Overseer   200
     FARLEY, Mary F          27   F   TN
     FARLEY, William          5   M   MS
     FARLEY, James            3   M   MS

#194 BURRUS, Addison         39   M   MS   Planter   1,680
     BURRUS, Rebecca I       25   F   MS   (OGDEN, Rebecca Irion)
     BURRUS, James            8   M   MS   in school
     BURRUS, Lucy M           6   F   MS
     BURRUS, Mary A           4   F   MS
     BURRUS, Enos H           3   M   MS
     QUINNE, William         20   M   MS   (BOVARD, Mary J. F.)
     BURRUS, William A     4/12   M   MS

#195 RUSSELL, Susanna        60   F   SC              1,000
     RUSSELL, Nixon          29   M   SC   Planter
     RUSSELL, Margaret E     21   F   MS
     RUSSELL, Zachary F       4   M   MS
     RUSSELL, James D         3   M   MS
     RUSSELL, Ann A        1/12   F   MS

#196 GREEN, John F           22   M   MS   Medical Student
```

```
#197 KING, William L          34  M  TN  Overseer
     KING, Ann                22  F  MS  (SPELL, Ann)
     KING, Aaron               8  M  MS
     KING, Elias               5  M  MS

#198 KING, John H             35  M  TN  Overseer

#199 GRIFFIN, B. Harvey       23  M  MS  Overseer  (PENNY, Mary E)

#200 McCARTY, T.C.R.          36  M  GA  Overseer
     McCARTY, Catherine       29  F  SC
     McCARTY, Matilda          5  F  MS

#201 YORK, John B             24  M  TN  Overseer  (SPELLS, Martha)

#202 EVERETT, Thomas          47  M  NC  Planter
     EVERETT, Jane            38  F  NC
     EVERETT, Rebecca A       21  F  NC
     EVERETT, Lucy J          19  F  NC
     EVERETT, Agnes C         17  F  NC
     EVERETT, William D       14  M  NC  in school
     EVERETT, Mary E          12  F  NC  in school
     EVERETT, Thomas Jr.       9  M  TN  in school
     EVERETT, Mary E           7  F  MS
     EVERETT, Henry H          3  M  MS

#203 SWAYZE, William          37  M  MS  Planter     2,600
     SWAYZE, Mary A           34  F  ENG (COUSINS, Mary Ann)
     SWAYZE, Solomon           9  M  MS  in school
     SWAYZE, Emma              7  F  MS
     SWAYZE, Mary              5  F  MS
     SWAYZE, Frances           4  F  MS
     SWAYZE, Agnes             3  F  MS
     SWAYZE, Virginia          1  F  MS

#204 SWAYZE, Richard          40  M  MS  Planter {SOJOURNER, Mary}
     SWAYZE, Emily            16  F  MS  (LUSE, Nathan)
     SWAYZE, Belinda          14  F  MS  in school
     SWAYZE, Prentiss         11  M  MS  in school
     SWAYZE, Hardy             9  M  MS  in school
     SWAYZE, Orange            7  M  MS
     SWAYZE, Missouri          5  F  MS
     LUSE, Nathan H           26  M  MS  School Teacher

#205 KING, Douglas S          43  M  MS  Planter {DAVIS, Letitia}
     KING, Maria              26  F  MS
     KING, Thomas S           18  M  MS  Planter
     KING, William P          14  M  MS  in school
     KING, James D            11  M  MS  in school
     KING, Maria E             9  F  MS  in school
     KING, Frances E           6  F  MS
     KING, John D              4  M  MS
     KING, Letitia             2  F  MS
```

```
#206  SELSER, Hiram              30   M   MS   Planter
      SELSER, Margaret          34   F   MS   2,800 (BOWMAN, Margaret)
      O'REILLY                  17   M   MS   (prob John Bowman O'Reilly)
      NOLAN, Maria L             2   F   MS
      WALKER, William O         26   M   VA   Overseer

#207  BRIDGFORTH, Robert F      62   M   VA   Planter      3,240
      BRIDGFORTH, Martha        59   F   VA   (CABANISS, Martha)
      BRIDGFORTH, Eliza A       30   F   VA
      BRIDGFORTH, Amanda C      20   F   VA
      BRIDGFORTH, Mary A        16   F   VA   in school
      BRIDGFORTH, William M     15,  M   VA   in school
      WORTHINGTON, George H     48   M   VA   Overseer

#208  BRIDGFORTH, James C       39   M   VA   Planter
      BRIDGFORTH, Robert M      28   M   VA   Planter
      BRIDGFORTH, Maria         24   F   VA

#209  NELSON, Elzira            35   F   LA                960
      NELSON, T. J. L.          15   M   MS   in school
      NELSON, Franklin H        13   M   MS   in school
      NELSON, Elizabeth E       10   F   MS   in school
      NELSON, Bernard H          6   M   MS

#210  ROSS, Elizabeth           33   F   MS   (ROSS, John P?)
      ROSS, Richard             14   M   MS   in school
      ROSS, Thomas J            12   M   MS   in school
      ROSS, William K           10   M   MS   in school
      ROSS, Mary L               7   F   MS   in school

#211  ROBERTS, George W         23   M   MS   Planter      480
      ROBERTS, Martha           23   F   MS
      ROBERTS, Orville R       1/12  M   MS

#212  ROBERTS, Mary             30   F   AL
      ROBERTS, Thomas B         12   M   MS   in school
      ROBERTS, Levi R            9   M   MS   in school
      ROBERTS, John W            4   M   MS
      ROBERTS, Elmira M          2   F   MS
      ROBERTS, Charles W        24   M   MS   Planter
      ROBERTS, Lewis R          22   M   MS   Planter
      ROBERTS, William          30   M   MS   Planter      400

#213  HADDICK, Allen            28   M   TN   Planter
      HADDICK, Sophia           24   F   AL
      HADDICK, Sarah C           3   F   MS
      HADDICK, Eliza A         6/12  F   MS
```

```
#214  CUNNINGHAM, Moses B      33   M   AL   Planter      640
      CUNNINGHAM, Mary         34   F   MS
      CUNNINGHAM, Charles      15   M   MS   in school
      CUNNINGHAM, William      13   M   MS   in school
      CUNNINGHAM, Elizabeth    11   F   MS   in school
      CUNNINGHAM, Caroline      9   F   MS   in school
      CUNNINGHAM, Mary A        5   F   MS
      CUNNINGHAM, Eliza         3   F   MS
      CUNNINGHAM, Catherine     1   F   MS

#215  WHITE, John              25   M   AL   Planter
      WHITE, Louisa            20   F   AL
      WHITE, Emily              1   F   MS

#216  CASON, John A            27   M   MS   Planter      1,200
      CASON, Jane              53   F   TN   (CARNES?, Jane)
      CASON, Jane E            17   F   MS
      CASON, Pennington        11   M   MS

#217  DOOLING, Thomas J        35   M   IN   Planter      1,200
      DOOLING, Clarissa        29   F   MS
      DOOLING, Susan            2   F   MS
      NOONAN, Thomas           55   M   IRE  Laborer

#218  YANDELL, Burton          36   M   TN   Physician    2,220
      YANDELL, Malvina         30   F   VA
      MAYS, Laura A            25   F   MS   (ECHOLS, William A)

#219  RABB, William            45   M   MS   Planter      2,520
      RABB, Hester J           41   F   MS   (LUSE, Hester Ann)
      RABB, Matilda            14   F   MS   in school
      RABB, Rachel              6   F   MS
      RABB, William F           3   M   MS
      RABB, Harriet J         6/12  F   MS
      ELLISON, James           25   M   MS   Overseer

#220  BERRY, James C           24   M   MS   Planter      400
      BERRY, Margaret E        21   F   LA   (JACKSON, Margaret E)

#221  BOYD, Robert D           42   M   MS   Planter  (JEFFERSON, Elizabeth)
      BOYD, Nancy A            32   F   GA
      BOYD, Thomas J           14   M   MS
      BOYD, Frances E           5   F   MS
      BOYD, M. E.               3   F   MS

#222  McGEHEE, Edward S        35   M   VA   Physician
      McGEHEE, Nancy           32   F   GA
      McGEHEE, Augustus        15   M   GA
      McGEHEE, James E          9   M   MS
```

```
#223 JOHNSON, Frances          50   F   SC
#224 RICHARDSON, George W       24   M   SC   Laborer
     RICHARDSON, William J      22   M   SC   Laborer
     RICHARDSON, Joseph S       20   M   SC   Laborer
     RICHARDSON, Winston B      18   M   SC   Printer or Painter
     RICHARDSON, Sarah J         4   F   MS
     RICHARDSON, Frances E       1   F   MS

#225 RICHARDSON, Robert J       17   M   MS   Planter(LUCIUS, Lucinda)
     RICHARDSON, Thomas C       15   M   MS
     JOHNSON, Lafayette         11   M   MS

#226 BANKS, Winston            40   M   SC   Lawyer       1,000

#227 COX, George A             39   M   TN   Planter
     COX, Sarah A              30   F   MS                4,200
     COX, Virginia E           14   F   MS   in school
     SHEPPARD, Eliza           11   F   MS   in school
     COX, Elvira               41   F   VA

#228 FUGATE, Vincent H         34   M   MO   Physician   2,500
     FUGATE, Emeline R         20   F   MS   (HENDRICKS, Emeline R)
     FUGATE, Middleton          2   M   MS

#229 RUSSELL, George W         30   M   VA   Physician   200
     RUSSELL, Sarah A          29   F   VT   (RUSSELL, Sarah Ann)
     RUSSELL, Cornelia C        1   F   MS

#230 LEMMONS, Cornelius        38   M   MS   Planter     200
     LEMMONS, Caroline         35   F   MS
     LEMMONS, William          14   M   MS   in school
     LEMMONS, David            13   M   MS   in school
     LEMMONS, Sarah            11   F   MS   in school
     LEMMONS, Margaret          9   F   MS   in school
     LEMMONS, John              7   M   MS   in school
     LEMMONS, James             5   M   MS
     LEMMONS, Malcomb           3   M   MS
     LEMMONS, Andrew M          1   M   MS

#231 SPIARS, John W            49   M   MS   Planter     800
     SPIARS, Lydia             37   F   MS
     SPIARS, Sarah             13   F   MS
     SPIARS, Gracy              7   F   MS
     SPIARS, Robert            10   M   MS
     SPIARS, John               8   M   MS
     SPIARS, Theophilus O       5   M   MS
     SPIARS, Charles C          1   M   MS
```

```
#232 LEMMONS, Malcomb        47   M   NC   Planter      1,800
     LEMMONS, Mary           48   F   KY
     LEMMONS, Jane           16   F   MS
     LEMMONS, Martha         15   F   MS
     LEMMONS, Nancy          10   F   MS
     LEMMONS, Daniel         18   M   MS   Laborer
     LEMMONS, Levi           11   M   MS

#233 BEALE, William C        37   M   VA   Planter      1,000
     BEALE, Maria T          23   F   VA
     BEALE, Margaret T        9   F   MS

#234 HERROD, John            45   M   TN   Planter      1,200
     HERROD, Sabora          30   F   MS   (Deborah in 1860 Census)
     HERROD, Joseph          15   M   MS
     HERROD, Herry H          5   M   MS

#235 COMPTON, Mabrella       37   F   TN
     COMPTON, John           14   M   TN   in school  (HUGHS, Margaret)
     COMPTON, Henry          10   M   TN   in school

#236 NICHOLS, Daniel         27   M   GA   Laborer
     NICHOLS, Eliza A        18   F   OH
     NICHOLS, William         2   M   AL
     NICHOLS, James        6/12   M   MS

#237 GANDY, Harriet          25   F   MS
     GANDY, John H            5   M   AL
     GANDY, William E         1   M   MS
     GANDY, Elliot         3/12   M   MS

#238 HARRIS, Thomas          21   M   Unknown          Laborer
     HARRIS, Henrietta       14   F   AL   (DENSON, Henrietta)

#239 TRUNK, John             29   M   GER  Planter      300
     TRUNK, Catherine        30   F   GER  (WESSELL, Catherine)
     TRUNK, Rosina         9/12   F   MS

#240 MARTIN, Caroline        25   F   FRANCE

#241 WALKER, Edward          33   M   TN   Laborer      220
     WALKER, Frances         25   F   NC   (SECRIST, Francis)
     WALKER, John L           5   M   MS
     WALKER, Sherwood         2   M   AR

#242 ALFORD, Thomas F        24   M   MS   Laborer      50
     ALFORD, Rachel J        18   F   MS   (VANCE, Rachel)
     ALFORD, Josephine     3/12   F   MS   (HAGAN, Wm. B.)

#243 GILLIAN, Leslie         28   M   NC   Laborer      50
     GILLIAN, Eliza L        23   F   MS
     GILLIAN, Susan E         2   F   MS
     GILLIAN, Endora       3/12   F   MS
```

```
#244 THAMES, Redding        45    M   MS   Planter     125   [THOMAS]
     THAMES, Elizabeth      36    F   MS   (MARBLE, Elizabeth)
     THAMES, Virginia        3    F   MS
     THAMES, Elizabeth    2/12    F   MS

#245 BELL, David M          47    M   NC   School Teacher   200
     BELL, Rachel           40    F   SC
     BELL, Cornelius        18    M   LA   Laborer
     BELL, Robert           15    M   LA   in school
     BELL, Elizabeth        10    F   MS   in school
     BELL, Eliza             8    F   MS   in school
     BELL, Jane              5    F   MS
     BELL, Endora            3    F   MS
     BELL, Asa               1    M   MS

#246 ROWLEY, John R         30    M   LA   Laborer
     ROWLEY, Matilda        20    F   LA
     ROWLEY, Cornelia        5    F   MS
     ROWLEY, Ophelia         3    F   MS

#247 CHAMBERS, Solomon G    42    M   NC   Planter     700
     CHAMBERS, Catherine    29    F   TN   (McCAFFREY, Catherine M)
     CHAMBERS, Mary E       11    F   MS
     CHAMBERS, E. B.         6    F   MS
     CHAMBERS, H. F.         2    F   AR

#248 BARFIELD, Mary         47    F   SC               400
     BARFIELD, Simeon       17    M   MS   Planter
     BARFIELD, Susan        14    F   MS   in school
     BARFIELD, Andrew       12    M   MS   in school
     BARFIELD, George       10    M   MS   in school
     BARFIELD, Nancy         7    F   MS

#249 DYER, Absolom          56    M   SC   Planter     500
     DYER, Elizabeth        51    F   MS
     DYER, Francis B        18    M   MS   Laborer
     DYER, Harriet E        10    F   MS   in school

#250 LUCIUS, J              38    M   SC   Overseer
     LUCIUS, Martha A       36    F   SC
     LUCIUS, J. B.          17    M   SC
     LUCIUS, Barboam E      14    F   SC   in school
     LUCIUS, E. C.          11    F   SC   in school
     LUCIUS, Lucinda C       5    F   SC
     LUCIUS, Catherine       4    F   MS
     LUCIUS, Thomas J        2    M   MS
     LUCIUS, Sarah E      3/12    F   MS

#251 BROWN, Miles I         33    M   VA   Planter   1,000
     BROWN, Susan           23    F   MS   (POWELL, Susan)
     BROWN, Frances          4    F   MS
     BROWN, Charles          2    M   MS

#252 FORDEN, William        31    M   IRE  Laborer
     FORDEN, Richard        28    M   IRE  Laborer
```

```
#253 BALLANCE, James          52  M  TN  Planter      4,000
     BALLANCE, Eliza          40  F  MS  (ADAMS, Eliza)
     BALLANCE, Caroline       19  F  MS  in school
     BALLANCE, Mary A         14  F  MS  in school
     BALLANCE, Charles W      11  M  MS  in school

#254 DENNIS, John M           30  M  MS  Overseer(BENTLEY, Elizabeth)

#255 HUNTER, H. W.            29  M  MD  Overseer

#256 PRICE, Amos              37  M  VA  Overseer

#257 ARMSTRONG, Christopher   34  M  MS  Planter       600
     ARMSTRONG, Sibley        67  F  NC

#258 GALTNEY, J. J.           36  M  MS  Overseer    2,000
     GALTNEY, Clarissa        31  F  MS  (FRISBY, Clarissa)
     GALTNEY, Olivia          13  F  MS  in school
     GALTNEY, Indiana         10  F  MS  in school
     GALTNEY, Thomas           8  M  MS  in school
     GALTNEY, Victoria         6  F  MS  in school
     GALTNEY, Albert           4  M  MS
     GALTNEY, Martha           2  F  MS

#259 BROOCKS, James A         39  M  VA  Planter     5,000
     BROOCKS, Elizabeth       34  F  MS
     BROOCKS, Martha A        11  F  MS  in school
     BROOCKS, James P          9  M  MS  in school
     BROOCKS, Joab F           5  M  MS
     CLARK, Ellen             16  F  VA  in school

#260 WRIGHT, J. M.            25  M  GA  Overseer

#261 LAUGHORN, Elias M        28  M  NC  Carpenter

#262 JOHNSTON, William B      30  M  MS  {CLARK, Mary Elizabeth Eleanor}
#263 ARMSTRONG, William       13  M  MS
     ARMSTRONG, Thomas        11  M  MS
     ARMSTRONG, John           9  M  MS
     ARMSTRONG, Mary           7  M  MS
     ARMSTRONG, George         5  M  MS
     ARMSTRONG, Lucinda        3  F  MS

#264 LASSITER, Brown          45  M  GA  Planter     9,000
     LASSITER, George A       13  F  MS  in school
     LASSITER, Walter         11  M  MS
     LASSITER, James F         7  M  MS
     LASSITER, Wesley M        3  M  MS
     LASSITER, Avery A         1  F  MS
```

```
#265 JACKSON, Upton          44    M  VA  Planter      500
     JACKSON, Ailsey         25    F  NC
     JACKSON, Matthew         6    M  MS
     JACKSON, Flemming        4    M  MS
     JACKSON, Mary A       6/12    F  MS

#266 COOPER, Benjamin        54    M  SC  Planter      400
     COOPER, Mary            47    F  SC  (HOGAN, Mary)
     COOPER, Mary A          13    F  MS
     COOPER, Eveline         10    F  MS
     COOPER, William H.H.     5    M  MS
     COOPER, Soloman B        2    M  MS
     HAGAN, Martha            7    F  MS

#267 TAYLOR, Green B         33    M  TN  Planter    1,000
     TAYLOR, Mary            30    F  MS
     TAYLOR, William L       10    M  MS  in school
     TAYLOR, George W         6    M  MS
     TAYLOR, Mary             1    F  MS

#268 THOMPSON, Preston S     30    M  MS  Planter      500
     THOMPSON, Jane          25    F  MS  (CALVIT, Jane)
     THOMPSON, Amanda         2    F  MS

#269 BUCKHANAN, Sarah        60    F  TN               200
     BUCKHANAN, William      25    M  MS  Overseer
     BUCKHANAN, David        20    M  MS  Overseer
     BUCKHANAN, Daniel       21    M  MS  Laborer
     BUCKHANAN, Thomas       19    M  MS  Laborer
     BUCKHANAN, Nancy        27    F  MS

#270 NORMAN, William D       33    M  MS  Laborer
     NORMAN, Lavina          31    F  MS
     NORMAN, James R          4    M  AR
     NORMAN, Nancy L          3    F  MS
     NORMAN, Andrew J      8/12    M  MS
     SPELLS, Z.D.             9    M  MS
     SPELLS, Mary E           8    F  MS

#271 BENTLEY, William J      40    M  SC  Planter    1,200
     BENTLEY, John S         11    M  MS  in school
     BENTLEY, Samuel A        8    M  MS  in school
     BENTLEY, Julia J         6    F  MS
     BENTLEY, Nancy           3    F  MS

#272 THARP, Abraham          26    M  MS  Planter
     THARP, Mary A           20    F  MS  (SISIL, Mary Ann)
```

```
#273  ROBINETT, Nathan        56   M   GA   Planter      1,500
      ROBINETT, Elizabeth     48   F   MS   (GARDNER, Elizabeth)
      ROBINETT, Lewis         26   M   MS   Planter       100
      ROBINETT, John          21   M   MS   Laborer
      ROBINETT, Martha        15   F   MS
      ROBINETT, Susan         12   F   MS
      ROBINETT, Margaret      10   F   MS
      ROBINETT, Jane           9   F   MS
      ROBINETT, William        7   M   MS
      ROBINETT, Catherine      4   F   MS

#274  JOHNSTON, Walter L      34   M   MS   Planter      3,850
      JOHNSTON, Mary          29   F   MS   (O'NEAL, Mary)
      JOHNSTON, M.S.A.         6   F   MS
      STARK, Jane             7   F   MS
      EDMONDSON, Zachery       3   M   MS
      EDMONDSON, Union       6/12  F   MS   (CHANDLER, J. H)

#275  GILL, Jeremiah N        48   M   SC   Planter       375
      GILL, Frances S         33   F   AL
      GILL, Magnus R          16   M   MS   Laborer
      GILL, Mary J            14   F   MS
      GILL, Martha F          11   F   MS
      GILL, John R             9   M   MS
      GILL, Elizabeth          7   F   MS
      GILL, Jeremiah A         5   M   MS
      GILL, Margaret A         3   F   MS
      MATHIS, Mary A          17   F   MS

#276  RODGERS, Moses H        22   M   AL   Planter
      RODGERS, Martha A       19   F   MS   (BURNS, Martha Ann)
      RODGERS, Sarah E         1   F   MS

#277  RODGERS, Theron H       28   M   AL   Overseer
      RODGERS, Frances A       7   F   MS

#278  LONG, Jesse G           35   M   NC   Planter       600
      LONG, Martha L          32   F   NC   (KING, Martha L)
      LONG, Elizabeth          8   F   AL   in school
      LONG, Sarah              6   F   MS   in school
      LONG, Charles            4   M   MS
      LONG, Malvina            2   F   MS
      LONG, William            1   M   MS
      LONG, A. V.             37   M   NC   Planter

#279  BOYD, Richard           38   M   MS   Planter       800

#280  WORD, William M         29   M   TN   Planter
      WORD, Mary P            22   F   TN   (PHIPPS, Mary Pauline)
      WORD, Elizabeth          4   F   TN
      WORD, Adelia             3   M   TN

#281  MATHIS, W. F.           19   M   MS   Laborer
      WILLIAMS, B. R.         35   M   TN   Laborer
#282  CARSON, John            70   M   SC   Planter      2,500
```

```
#283  FRILEY, Martin M       36   M   TN   Planter        500
      FRILEY, Tabitha C       30   F   VA
      FRILEY, William         12   M   MS   in school
      FRILEY, Louisa F        10   F   MS   in school
      FRILEY, John L           8   M   MS
      FRILEY, James            6   M   MS
      FRILEY, Joseph           3   M   MS
      FRILEY, Venitia          1   F   MS

#284  HUFFMAN, John           35   M   MS   Planter
      HUFFMAN, Margaret       33   F   MS   (CARRADINE?, Margaret) 400
      HUFFMAN, Elizabeth      14   F   MS
      HUFFMAN, Mary            9   F   MS
      HUFFMAN, Caroline        4   F   MS

#285  COX, Hampton            41   M   MS   Planter 1,500
      COX, Clarissa R         27   M   KY   (WOOD, Clarissa R)
      COX, Mary E             11   F   MS   in school
      COX, Josephine           5   F   MS
      COX, David              35   M   MS   Planter
      COX, William            25   M   MS   Planter

#286  BURKHEAD, J. C.         25   M   SC   Carpenter

#287  FRILEY, Sarah           60   F   GA   320
      FRILEY, David           22   M   MS   Planter
      FRILEY, Emily           19   F   MS
      MATHIS, Lucy            10   F   MS

#288  WILKINSON, Albert       38   M   VA   Planter        5,000
      EUESTES, Jacob          15   M   MO   in school

#289  BROWN, Abner            51   M   SC   Planter        1,280
      BROWN, Katura           51   F   GA   (KEITH, Katury)
      BROWN, Buksaule         25   M   MS   Laborer
      BROWN, Bandon           17   M   MS   Laborer
      BROWN, Sarah K          15   F   MS

#290  PENNY, George W         20   M   MS   Overseer (MOORIS, Mary)

#291  JOHNSON, James          56   M   TN   Planter
      JOHNSON, Nancy          30   F   TN   (PITTMAN?, Nancy)
      JOHNSON, Jehu           15   M   MS
      JOHNSON, Hiram          12   M   MS
      JOHNSON, Frances        10   F   MS
      JOHNSON, Miles           8   M   MS
      JOHNSON, Elizabeth       7   F   MS
      JOHNSON, Ann E           5   F   MS
      JOHNSON, John            3   M   MS
      JOHNSON, Laura           1   F   MS
```

```
#292 JOHNSON, Caleb          32   M   MS   Laborer
     JOHNSON, Miranda        28   F   MS
     JOHNSON, Oliver         10   M   MS
     JOHNSON, Thomas          9   M   MS
     JOHNSON, Mary            8   F   MS
     JOHNSON, Abner           6   M   MS
     JOHNSON, James           4   M   MS
     JOHNSON, Sarah           2   F   MS
     JOHNSON, William         1   F   MS

#293 DIXON, Benujah?         30   M   NC   Planter
     DIXON, Mary             20   F   NC

#294 NESBITT, Moses E        43   M   TN   Physician

#295 MORTON, Joseph W        30   M   TN   Planter (POWERS, C.A.)
     MORTON, Fanny E         20   F   TN   Md this year (PHIPPS, Fanny E)

#296 FOULKS, Tapley          46   M   VA
     FOULKS, Emiline         21   F   VA
     FOULKS, Milissa         18   F   VA
     FOULKS, Thomas          17   M   VA
     FOULKS, Rebecca         13   F   VA   in school
     FOULKS, William          8   M   VA

#297 RICHMOND, George O      33   M   TN   Planter
     RICHMOND, Martha H      31   F   LA
     RICHMOND, Joseph J?      9   M   KY
     RICHMOND, Mary Ann       5   F   KY

#298 FRUZIER, Robert P       36   M   NC   Planter      2,000
     FRUZIER, Sarah          29   M   TN
     FRUZIER, Julia           8   F   MS   in school
     FRUZIER, Robert         2?   M   MS   in school
     FRUZIER, Sarah A         7   F   MS   in school
     FRUZIER, Mary           76   F   NC

#299 CARRAWAY, John          23   M   MS   Planter      1,000

#300 HOLLIDAY, Dixon         32   M   TN   Planter      2,100
     HOLLIDAY, Charlotte     25   F   TN   (OWENS, Charlotte)

#301 BARFIELD, Thomas C      45   M   NC   Planter
     BARFIELD, Mercy L       33   F   MS   (WHITE, Mercy Leonard)
     BARFIELD, Rebecca       12   F   AR   in school
     BARFIELD, Mercy         10   F   AR   in school
     BARFIELD, Nathan L       8   M   MS   in school
     BARFIELD, John           6   M   MS
     BARFIELD, Louisanna   6/12   F   MS

#302 GUICE, Ephraim          52   M   MS   Planter (BURK, Amelia)
     GUICE, Alexander        10   M   MS
     GUICE, Augusta          12   F   MS
```

```
#303 FERRIS, William D        23   M   KY   Planter
     FERRIS, Amanda           20   F   MS   (GUICE, Amanda C)
     FERRIS, Colombus          1   M   MS
     FLOWERS, Benjamin L      19   M   SC   Laborer
     HARMON, Hezekiah         36   M   SC   Laborer

#304 HENRY, Dixon            51   M   SC   Planter      2,000
     HENRY, Eleanor          40   F   MS
     HENRY, Jefferson D      13   M   MS   in school
     HENRY, Franklin B       11   M   MS   in school
     HENRY, James M           9   M   MS   in school
     HENRY, Milton L          6   M   MS
     HENRY, Mary L            4   F   MS
     HENRY, Harriet C         2   F   MS

#305 LEWIS, Benjamin E       46   M   SC   Planter      1,200
     LEWIS, Mary             42   F   TN   (BRADFORD?, Mary)

#306 JOHNSON, Benjamin F     30   M   VA   Physician

#307 FERGUSON, Andrew J      43   M   NC   School Teacher
     FERGUSON, Emeline       32   F   NC   (PETER, Emeline W)
     FERGUSON, Alexander      2   M   MS

#308 GRAYSON, Mary J         28   F   VA
     GRAYSON, Frances A      12   F   MS   in school
     GRAYSON, Mary           10   F   MS   in school
     GRAYSON, Robert C        7   M   MS   in school

#309 HELM, William J         56   M   MA   Physician    1,200
     HELM, Lucretia C        36   F   VA
     HELM, William W         18   M   VA   Laborer
     HELM, Samuel            16   M   MS   in school
     HELM, Fanny B           13   F   MS   in school
     HELM, Lucretia B         4   F   MS   in school

#310 BRUMFIELD, Charles      55   M   SC   Planter 960
     BRUMFIELD, Harriet      46   F   GA   (KNIGHT, Harriet)
     BRUMFIELD, Lucy         16   F   MS   in school
     BRUMFIELD, Thomas A     14   M   MS   in school
     BRUMFIELD, George W     11   M   MS   in school
     BRUMFIELD, Oscar         9   M   MS   in school
     BRUMFIELD, Jesse         7   M   MS   in school

#311 WHITE, Rebecca          60   F   MS   1,920  (HARMON, Rebecca)
     WHITE, Nathan H         21   M   MS   Planter
     WHITE, Louisianna       21   F   MS
     WHITE, Francis E        18   F   MS
```

```
#312 GARTLY, William          49  M  LA     Planter      19,840
     GARTLY, Elizabeth O      33  F  MS     (DAVIS, Elizabeth O)
     GARTLY, Margaret         19  F  MS
     GARTLY, Julia            17  F  MS     in school
     GARTLY, William F        15  M  MS     in school
     DAVIS, Eugenia R         15  F  MS     in school
     DAVIS, William H         13  M  MS     in school
     DAVIS, Robert V          10  M  MS     in school
     DAVIS, Mary E             8  F  MS     in school

#313 KIERNON, Frank           40  M  IRELAND  Ditcher
     HALEY, William           55  M  IRELAND  Gardner

#314 MURRAY, Robert           30  M  SC     Overseer

#315 COLLINS, Lemuel P        34  M  MD     Overseer      2,000
     COLLINS, Phoebe J        24  F  MS     (WHITE, Phebe Jane)
     COLLINS, Adolphus        14  M  MD
     COLLINS, Samuel           5  M  MS
     COLLINS, Sewell F         1  M  MS

#316 ROSE, James              40  M  VA     Planter       4,000

#317 MOSELY, Joseph R         35  M  VA     Planter      18,430
     MOSELY, Lucina? J        33  F  MS
     MOSELY, Josephine         8  M  MS     in school
     MOSELY, Edwin             6  M  MS
     MOSELY, Ann E             3  F  MS
     BROWN, John              40  M  TN     Overseer (BURNS, Mary L)

#318 DAVIS, Franklin          64  M  NY     Planter       2,200
     DAVIS, Margaret          65  F  GA

#319 WILLIAMS, Tuy?           30  M  MS     Overseer
     WEST, Augustus           24  M  LA     Laborer

#320 STREET, John P           43  M  SC     Planter       1,200
     STREET, Eliza A          45  F  SC
     STREET, James A          16  M  LA     in school
     STREET, John W. F.       13  M  LA     in school
     STREET, Francis M        11  M  LA     in school
     STREET, Samuel A          7  M  MS     in school

#321 JOHNSON, John            55  M  SC     Planter      18,000
     JOHNSON, Loranne         41  F  GA
     JOHNSON, Louisa          10  F  MS     in school
     JOHNSON, John             8  M  MS     in school
     JOHNSON, Robert E         5  M  MS
```

```
#322 McCORKNEY, J. D.        38    M   SC   Overseer
     McCORKNEY, Sarah J      23    F   SC
     McCORKNEY, Evéline      13    F   AK
     McCORKNEY, Maben         8    M   MS
     McCORKNEY, Jesse         5    M   MS
     McCORKNEY, Julia         3    F   MS
     McCORKNEY, George     6/12    M   MS

#323 STREET, William         38    M   TN   Planter
     STREET, Malissa A       26    F   LA
     STREET, Martha          10    F   LA
     STREET, Mary             6    F   MS
     STREET, John             4    M   MS
     STREET, David            2    M   MS

#324 FERRIS, Josiah H        36    M   KY   Planter
     FERRIS, Dozia           27    F   TN
     FERRIS, Martha F         7    F   TN
     FERRIS, George F         6    M   TN
     FERRIS, Susan S          5    F   TN
     FERRIS, Sarah E          3    F   MS
     FERRIS, Caroline A       1    F   MS

#325 MARTIN, Martha          50    F   TN
     MARTIN, Caroline        21    F   TN
     MARTIN, Rebecca         16    F   TN   in school
     MARTIN, Louisa          15    F   TN   in school
     LOVETT, Thomas           4    M   MS

#326 ROBINETT, John R        27    M   MS   Planter
     ROBINETT, Margaret R    19    F   MS

#327 CLARK, Elijah J         17    M   VA   Laborer {JOHNSON, Sarah A}
     CLARK, Travis R         15    M   VA   {YOUNG, Laura}
     CLARK, Charles H        12    M   VA

#328 BERRY, Young            62    M   SC   Planter 640 {IVOY, Nancy}
     BERRY, Effie A          33    F   MS
     BERRY, Samuel           17    M   MS   Overseer
     BERRY, Israel           14    M   MS
     BERRY, Elizabeth        11    F   MS
     BERRY, Susana           10    F   MS
     BERRY, Thomas A          7    M   MS
     BERRY, Joseph C          6    M   MS
     BERRY, Julia R        6/12    F   MS

#329 McDUFFIE, John          26    M   MS   Planter
     McDUFFIE, Martha J      19    F   MS   (BERRY, Martha J)

#330 ANDING, Celeste         51    F   MS   3,600  (DUNN, Celeste)
     ANDING, Martin          13    M   MS   (McGEE, Louisiana Indiana)
```

```
#331 CAUSEY, Jesse          28    M   MS   Planter        500
     CAUSEY, Celeste        26    F   MS   (BELL, James R)
     CAUSEY, William         6    M   MS
     CAUSEY, Charles         1    M   MS
     WILLIAMS, Susan        24    F   MS
     DUNN, Charles          20    M   MS

#332 BAIN, Robertson       38    M   VA   Overseer
     BAIN, Mary            38    F   VA
     BAIN, Elinor          10    F   AK
     BAIN, Walter           6    M   MS

#333 BLACKMAN, Henry G     31    M   PA   Planter      14,000
     BLACKMAN, Mary J      25    F   MS   (BALFOUR, Mary J)
     BLACKMAN, Bettie       5    F   MS
     BLACKMAN, Isabel       3    F   MS
     BLACKMAN, Susan        1    F   MS

#334 MILLS, Buford B       30    M   KY   Overseer

#335 GARNOTT?, John B      24    M   NC

#336 LUCUS, John           30    M   GA   Laborer
     LUCUS, Nancy          29    F   AL
     LUCUS, William         5    M   MS

#337 HEARD, W. Farkney     22    M   MS   Planter

#338 SCOTT, Burnwell       55    M   GA   Planter
     SCOTT, Mary           60    F   NC
     BELL, Mary R          17    F   MS   in school
     BELL, Rayford         19    M   MS   in school     Planter
     CAUSEY, Cornelius     16    M   MS   in school     Student
     COTTER?, Caroline     12    F   MS   in school

#339 McCANN, Rachel N      45    F   SC   4,000
     McCANN, Patrick N     24    M   AL   Justice of the Peace
     McCANN, Susan         18    F   AL
     McCANN, Robert        17    M   AL   in school
     McCANN, Martha J      20    F   AL
     McCANN, James         14    M   AL   in school
     McCANN, Emma          12    F   AL   in school
     McCANN, Mary          10    F   AL   in school

#340 ADAMS, Washington J   32    M   MS   Overseer
     ADAMS, Harriet        26    F   MD
     ADAMS, Thomas          6    M   MS
     ADAMS, James         3/12   M   MS
```

```
#341  THOMPSON, Mary            56   M   NC
      THINS, Margarie           22   F   MS
      THOMPSON, Mary J           5   F   MS
      THOMPSON, Levi             3   M   MS
      THOMPSON, Oliver G        19   M   MS   Planter

#342  MOORE, Ezekiel            36   M   IRELAND   Pedler
      MOORE, Mary A             33   F   IRELAND
      MOORE, Ezekiel, Jr.       12   M   NY
      MOORE, Elizabeth           9   F   NY
      MOORE, William J           6   M   IL
      MOORE, Jane                3   F   IL

#343  DUNN, David               50   M   MS   Planter    2,723
      DUNN, Lavinia G           33   F   MS   (GLASSBURN, Lavinia)
      DUNN, Richard L           15   M   MS
      DUNN, Rebecca M           13   F   MS   in school
      DUNN, Averey? G           11   M   MS   in school
      DUNN, William              9   M   MS   in school
      DUNN, David J              7   M   MS
      DUNN, John B               5   M   MS
      DUNN, Celeste A            2   F   MS

#344  GARY, Benjamin C          50   M   VA   Blacksmith  240
      GARY, Mary                44   F   KY   (DAVIS, Mary)
      GARY, Malinda A           13   F   MS   in school
      GARY, Mary A               9   F   MS   in school
      GARY, Eliza                6   F   MS
      GARY, Robert               3   M   MS
      GARY, Josephine            1   F   MS

#345  WRIGHT, Robert            21   M   TN   Overseer (SPIARS, Sidney)

#346  HOOKER, Samuel N          40   M   TN   Planter
      HOOKER, Sarah             35   F   AL
      HOOKER, Elizabeth         20   F   AL
      HOOKER, Jackson           16   M   AL   Laborer
      HOOKER, Samuel            14   M   AL
      HOOKER, Easter A          12   F   AL
      HOOKER, Jutha E           10   F   AL
      HOOKER, Melissa A          8   F   AL
      HOOKER, Robin              6   M   AL
      HOOKER, John               5   M   MS

#347  WILLIAMS, Tabitha J       22   F   AL   (HOOKER, Tabitha)
      WILLIAMS, Sarah E       8/12   F   MS

#348  THARP, John W             26   M   MS   Laborer
      THARP, Margaret           18   F   MS

#349  THARP, Abraham            26   M   MS   Laborer
      THARP, Mary A             21   F   MS   (SISIL, Mary Ann)
```

```
#350  WARMACK, Jeanot          48  F  NC
      WARMACK, Effie J         22  F  MS
      WARMACK, Bennet          14  M  MS   in school
      WARMACK, Mary A          11  F  MS
      WARMACK, Apolonia         7  F  MS

#351  WILLIAMS, Jemima         55  F  MS                     641
      WILLIAMS, William M      20  M  MS   in school  Laborer
      WILLIAMS, David F        18  M  MS   in school  Laborer

#352  MAYNER, Lavina           40  F  VA   (JARRET, Lavina)
      MAYNER, Thomas           25  M  TN   Planter
      MAYNER, John             20  M  TN   Laborer
      MAYNER, Levi             18  M  TN   Laborer

#353  O'NEAL, Joab             42  M  TN   Planter
      O'NEAL, Eveline          22  F  TN   (MANOR, Evelina C)
      O'NEAL, Mary              1  F  MS

#354  MAYNER, Sanders          26  M  TN   Planter
      MAYNER, Margaret         20  F  SC   (SWAIN, Margaret J)
      MAYNER, William           2  M  MS
      MAYNER, Levi              1  M  MS

#355  GERRARD, Jesse           54  M  OH   Planter      240
      GERRARD, Tabitha         47  F  OH
      GERRARD, Lydia C         22  F  MS
      GERRARD, William         20  M  MS   Laborer
      GERRARD, Elizabeth       16  F  MS
      GERRARD, Abner F         11  M  MS
      GERRARD, Robert G         8  M  MS
      GERRARD, Benjamin A       5  M  MS
      ARNOLD, Mary             60  F  MS

#356  NEELY, Emily             40  F  LA   300 (ERWIN, Emily)
      NEELY, William           20  M  MS
      NEELY, Jane T            18  F  MS
      NEELY, Nancy S           16  F  MS
      NEELY, Susan             13  F  MS   in school
      NEELY, Minerva           11  F  MS   in school
      NEELY, Martha             8  F  MS   in school

#357  HOWELL, Robert W         23  M  AL   School Teacher

#358  BROWN, Clasus? A         29  M  AL   Gun Wright
      BROWN, Simeon F          32  M  OH   Carpenter (FOSTER, Lucy)

#359  PHIPPS, M. B.            23  M  TN   Stage Driver
```

```
#360 RUSSELL, William G        42    M   SC   Planter
     RUSSELL, Elizabeth        35    F   MS   (MOORE, Elizabeth)
     RUSSELL, Sarah A          14    F   MA
     RUSSELL, Napoleon B       10    M   MS
     RUSSELL, Columbus          8    M   MS
     RUSSELL, Elizabeth         6    F   MS
     RUSSELL, Mary              3    F   MS
     RUSSELL, Reuben C       6/12    M   MS

#361 STEWART, Felix G          40    M   TN   Planter       200
     STEWART, Nancy A          32    F   MS
     STEWART, James            13    M   MS
     STEWART, Charles          11    M   MS   in school
     STEWART, Seth              8    M   MS   in school
     STEWART, Adeline           6    F   MS

#362 BRUCE, Thomas J           45    M   TN   Planter
     BRUCE, Catharine          24    F   MS   (HERRIN, Catherine M. J)

#363 BROOKS, Thomas            71    M   VA   Planter
     BROOKS, Elizabeth         67    F   VA
     BROOKS, Charles H S.      28    M   VA   Laborer
#364 BROOKS, Hugh              26    M   VA   Planter     1,000
     BROOKS, Mary              30    F   MS
     GUTHREY, Andrew            7    M   MS   in school
     GUTHREY, Eliza             3    F   MS

#365 STEWART, Samuel V         34    M   TN   Constable    500
     STEWART, Mary M           29    F   TN
     STEWART, Andrew M         11    M   MS
     STEWART, Samuel G          9    M   TN
     STEWART, Washington D      7    M   MS
     STEWART, Margaret E        5    F   MS
     STEWART, Hannah            2    F   MS

#366 KAYES, Michael            47    M   Ireland  Planter
     KAYS, Mary A              40    F   MS   (McDUFFIE, Mrs. Mary)
     KAYS, Patrick H            6    M   MS   in school
     KAYS, O Daniel             4    M   MS
     KAYS, Martha J             2    F   MS
     McDUFFIE, Norman L        12    M   MS   {DUNN, Rebecca M}

#367 BAILEY, Pleasant B        45    M   KY   Minister
     BAILEY, Maria T           45    F   TN
     BAILEY, Thomas K          23    M   AL   School Teacher
     BAILEY, John W. C.        18    M   AL   in school   Planter
     BAILEY, Mary J            16    F   AL   in school
     BAILEY, Martha E          11    F   AL   in school
     BAILEY, Missouri           8    F   AL   in school
```

```
#368 SWAYZE, H. A.            27  M  VT  Physician
     SWAYZE, Charles         30  M  VT  Planter      3,000
     SWAYZE, Nancy A         18  F  MS  (PENDER, Nancy Ann)
     SWAYZE, Clara E          1  F  MS

#369 POWERS, Benjamin        43  M  LA  Planter      2,800
     POWERS, Cynthia A       32  F  LA

#370 ANDREWS, James H        41  M  NY  Dentist
     ANDREWS, Caroline       39  F  NY

#371 BATTAILE, William       30  M  VA  Lawyer       5,000
     BATTAILE, Mary          26  F  MS  (HENDRICKS, Mary J)
     BATTAILE, Edmonia        3  F  MS
     BATTAILE, Charles        1  M  MS
     LAMKIN, Thomas          24  M  GA  Overseer

#372 JONES, Daniel           48  M  VA  Lawyer
     JONES, Eliza            40  F  VA  (WORTHINGTON, Eliza)
     JONES, Samuel W          9  M  MS

#373 VAUGHAN, Henry          50  M  SC  Planter     55,000
     VAUGHAN, Emma M         40  F  GA  (REECE, Emma)
     VAUGHAN, Mary S         22  F  SC
     VAUGHAN, Margaret A     20  F  SC
     VAUGHAN, Henry          17  M  SC  in school    Student
     VAUGHAN, Charles B      13  M  MS  in school
     VAUGHAN, Hugh R         11  M  MS  in school
     VAUGHAN, James           8  M  MS  in school
     VAUGHAN, Alice A         6  F  MS  in school
     VANGHAN, Emma            3  F  MS
     VANGHAN, Frances         1  F  MS

#374 MORTON, Alexander       51  M  NY  Lawyer       500
     MORTON, Elenor H        46  F  MD  (HALE, Elenor)   1,000
     MORTON, Ellen S         20  F  LA
     MORTON, Cornelia        18  F  LA
     MORTON, Catherine L     16  F  LA
     MORTON, Alice L         12  F  LA
     MORTON, Alexander       10  M  MS
     MORTON, William          8  M  MS
     MORTON, Augustine        5  M  MS

#375 HANCOCK, George M       45  M  VA  Raftsman {BROWN?, Melissa}
     HANCOCK, John H         55  M  VA  Gin Wright (WRIGHT, Delphine)

#376 ALFORD, Henry           51  M  GA  Planter
     ALFORD, Annis           45  F  SC  (COTTINGIN, Annie)
     ALFORD, Tennessee       16  F  MS
     ALFORD, Missouri        14  F  MS  in school
     ALFORD, Henrietta       10  F  MS  in school
     ALFORD, Robert           6  M  MS
```

#377 GILL, Harrison   37   M   MS   Planter   800
     GILL, Lydia   31   F   MS
     GILL, William J   11   M   MS   in school
     GILL, Susanna   8   F   MS   in school

#378 TILLEY, Calvin   34   M   NC   Planter
     TILLEY, Sarah   23   F   MS
     TILLEY, Nancy   4   F   MS
     CONNELLY, Nancy   54   F   NC

#379 FISHER, John   41   M   TN   Laborer
     FISHER, Holley   21   F   MS   (HERROD, Holley)
     FISHER, Andrew J   5   M   MS
     FISHER, Francis E   4   F   MS
     FISHER, Ellen M. A.   9   F   MS
     FISHER, Amanda D   1   F   MS

#380 SPENCER, J. W.   27   M   OH   Engineer

#381 MERCHANT, Alfred   42   M   MD   Laborer
     MERCHANT, William   5   M   MS

#382 STEWART, Hiel   38   M   NC   Wood Chopper 1,100
     STEWART, Rosana   26   F   SC
     McMASTERS, John   15   M   SC   (LANGFORD, Mary C}
     McMASTERS, Jefferson   12   M   SC   (CRIPPEN, Jane)
     STEWART, James   8   M   MS
     STEWART, Mary A   4   F   MS
     STEWART, Nancy A   2   F   MS

#383 MEYER, Alexander   44   M   MS   Overseer
     MEYER, Massa?   25   F   MS
     MEYER, Phillip   16   M   MS   Laborer
     MEYER, Alexander   12   M   MS
     MEYER, July   10   F   MS
     MEYER, Harrison   6   M   MS
     MEYER, James   4   M   MS
     MEYER, Thomas   2   M   MS

#384 ALLEY, J. W.   44   M   GA   Wood Chopper
     ALLEY, Jane   39   F   ENGLAND   (BROWNJOHN, Jane)
     ALLEY, Emily   18   F   MS
     ALLEY, Eliza   15   F   MS
     ALLEY, Frederick   13   M   MS
     ALLEY, Andrew J   7   M   MS
     ALLEY, Mary   4   F   MS
     ALLEY, P. W.   1   M   MS

#385 GIBSON, Joseph   23   M   AL   Raftsman

#386 TANIER, C.   20   M   KY   Laborer

#387 SNIDER, J   27   M   PA   Laborer

```
#388  WESSELL, John            37   M   GERMANY  Merchant
      WESSELL, Mary K          41   F   GERMANY  (LEAR, Mary C)

#389  ROBINSON, Lewis M        43   M   NC   Grocery Keeper
      ROBINSON, Maria          38   F   GA
      ROBINSON, Mary           15   F   AL
      ROBINSON, Catherine      12   F   AL   in school
      ROBINSON, Cynthia E      10   F   AL   in school
      ROBINSON, Lucy Jane       4   F   MS
      ROBINSON, Helen B         3   F   MS

#390  WEIMS, John              36   M   SC   Planter
      WEIMS, Martha            38   F   GA
      WEIMS, John              11   M   MS
      WEIMS, Sarah M            9   F   MS
      WEIMS, William C          7   M   MS

#391  BRIDGE, Davis            23   M   MS   Planter
      BRIDGE, Mahala           30   F   AL
      BRIDGE, John              3   M   MS
      BRIDGE, William           1   F   MS

#392  SORRELLS, Henry          22   M   MS   Planter
      SORELLLS, Nancy          16   F   MS

#393  SORELLLS, Samuel         20   M   MS   Waggon Maker

#394  McDOWELL, A. J.          51   M   NC   Gin Wright
      McDOWELL, Harrison       38   F   LA
      McDOWELL, Dealia         14   F   MS
      McDOWELL, William T.M.   13   M   MS   in school
      McDOWELL, Ezelia          8   F   MS   in school
      McDOWELL, Sarah           5   M   MS
      McDOWELL, Harriet         2   F   MS

#395  GEORGE, Andrew           18   M   MS   Planter

#396  HERROD, Joseph           16   M   MS   Planter

#397  WHITE, Nancy             30   F   KY
      WHITE, Greenup           12   M   MS
      WHITE, Margaret           8   F   MS
      WHITE, Bartholemew        7   M   MS
      WHITE, Harriet            3   F   MS

#398  PLUNKETT, Benjamin       45   M   NC   (JORDON, Tabitha}
      PLUNKETT, Eveline        15   F   NC

#399  BOYD, John               30   M   MS   Planter      500
      BOYD, Elizabeth          22   F   MS   (BURNS, Sarah Elizabeth)
      BOYD, Martha              7   F   MS
      BOYD, Laura               3   F   MS
      BOYD, Charles            16   M   MS   in school   Student
```

```
#400 VAUGHAN, James W        47   M   NC   Planter
     VAUGHAN, Elizabeth      50   F   VA
     VAUGHAN, Elizabeth      25   F   VA
     VAUGHAN, Ann            22   F   VA
     VAUGHAN, Pamela         19   F   VA
     VAUGHAN, Joseph         17   M   VA   Laborer
     VAUGHAN, Maria          15   F   AL
     VAUGHAN, Sarah          12   F   MS
     VAUGHAN, Edwin           9   M   MS

#401 GUESS, Terrill          55   M   TN   Planter
     GUESS, Elizabeth        36   F   TN
     GUESS, Henry            16   M   MS   Laborer
     GUESS, John             14   M   MS
     GUESS, Mary             14   F   MS
     GUESS, George           12   M   MS
     GUESS, Nancy            10   F   MS
     GUESS, James             8   M   MS
     GUESS, Jemima            5   F   MS
     GUESS, Morgan            1   M   MS

#402 ELLIOTT, James H        26   M   MS                  400
     ELLIOTT, Emmy           28   F   NC   (MANNING, Emily)
     ELLIOTT, Lavinia         4   F   MS
     ELLIOTT, William         2   M   MS

#403 CANON, Susan            62   F   NC

#404 BRAGG, Sarah            35   F   MS   {ROBINSON, John W}
     JONES, John H           16   M   MS
     JONES, James M          10   M   MS
     BRAGG, Mary Jane         8   F   MS

#405 DILLON, John            55   M   KY   Blacksmith
     DILLON, Jane            45   F   KY
     DILLON, Sarah           14   F   KY   in school
     DILLON, Alania          11   F   KY   in school
     DILLON, Henry C          8   M   KY

#406 ROGILLIO, William       18   M   MS   Planter

#407 CUSACK, James W         41   M   SC
     CUSACK, Mary            34   F   VA   (FUQUA, Mary T)
     CUSACK, Cornelia        16   F   MS   in school
     CUSACK, Alice           15   F   MS   in school
     CUSACK, Irene           12   F   MS   in school

#408 CLARK, William L        26   M   VA   Overseer      400
```

```
#409  KOHLMANN, Henry          41    M    GERMANY    Merchant
      KOHLMANN, Mary           35    F    GERMANY
      KOHLMANN, Charles        11    M    GERMANY    in school
      KOHLMANN, Bettie          9    F    GERMANY    in school
      KOHLMANN, Ada             5    F    MS
      KOHLMANN, William         3    M    MS
      KOHLMANN, Jacob           1    M    MS

#410  BLACK, Samuel            25    M    GERMANY    Merchant

#411  STROMP, Jacob            27    M    GERMANY    Merchant

#412  JENNINGS, John J         25    M    SC    Merchant      200

#413  CLARK, Thomas G          39    M    NC    Merchant    2,000
      CLARK, Mary              30    F    MS
      BATTAILE, Frances W      20    M    VA    Clerk

#414  WALKER, Thompson         39    M    NC    Planter     1,000

#415  WALKER, Samuel           32    M    NC    Planter     1,000
      WALKER, Margaret         35    F    NC

#416  CHEATHAM, Morrison       31    M    VA    Carpenter  {PERKINS? Mary}

#417  BROWN, Beriah            30    M    MS    Planter
      BROWN, Frances           32    F    LA    (ERVIN, Frances)
      BROWN, Thomas             5    M    MS
      BROWN, Ophilia            4    F    MS
      BROWN, Rufus              2    M    MS

#418  GREER, Henry F           42    M    GA    Planter
      GREER, Elizabeth         25    F    AL
      GREER, James             19    M    MS    Overseer
      GREER, William           16    M    MS    in school
      GREER, Delia             12    F    MS    in school
      GREER, Ann F              9    F    MS    in school
      GREER. Jerimiah           7    M    MS
      GREER, Jonea              2    M    MS

#419  EDMONDS, Daniel F        34    M    OH    Tanner
      EDMONDS, Cynthia A       20    F    MS
      EDMONDS, James F          4    M    MS
      EDMONDS, Mary E        3/12    F    MS

#420  PYLES, Milton            49    M    SC    Lawyer 1,000 {WOMACK, E J}

#421  WHITCOMB, C. S.          36    M    NY    Planter     1,500
      WHITCOMB, Pamela         26    F    MS
      WHITCOMB, John H          6    M    MS    in school
      WHITCOMB, Jonas D         3    M    MS
      WHITCOMB, Sarah M         1    F    MS
```

```
#422 ROSS, Lewis G           34  M  TN  Grocery Keeper
     ROSS, Martha            11  F  MS
     ROSS, Alexander          9  M  MS  in school
     ROSS, Lewis G            7  M  MS  in school
     ROSS, Daniel H           4  M  MS  in school

#423 McKEE, Edward G         35  M  TN  Justice of the Peace
     McKEE, Maria            21  F  MS  (ARNOLD, Maria B)
     McKEE, Isabel E          5  F  MS
     McKEE, Edward C          3  M  MS

#424 GREEN, George           21  M  MS  Law Student

#425 GANBERRY, Marshall C    23  M  MS  Law Student

#426 WOOD, William W         45  M  KY  Physician   1,000
     WOOD, Mary P            28  F  MS

#427 STEVENS, Martha A       22  F  MS
     JOHNSON, Albert         17  M  MS  Clerk

#428 SOUTHARD, Joseph        25  M  VA  Stage Driver

#429 COLLUM, Eldred          20  M  GA  Blacksmith

#430 HOLT, Robert S          35  M  KY  Lawyer       1,000
     HOLT, Ann E             30  F  TN
     HOLT, Sarah E            6  F  MS
     HOLT, Joseph             4  M  MS
     HOLT, John W             2  M  MS

#431 MOSELY, Peter           75  M  VA  Planter      2,500
     MOSELY, Sarah           74  F  VA

#432 FRENCH, T. B.           20  M  IN  Stage Driver {PEARL, Alice}

#433 GIBBS, Henry H          30  M  OH  Tailor
     GIBBS, Sarah            23  F  NC  (ASHBY, Sarah Ann)
     GIBBS, Josephine         4  F  MS
     GIBBS, Minerva           2  F  MS

#434 LUSK, John              32  M  MS  Planter
     LUSK, Elizabeth         32  F  MS
     LUSK, Hiram              7  M  MS  in school
     LUSK, Francis            4  F  MS
     LUSK, James              6  M  MS

#435 LITTLE, N. H.           25  M  TN  Blacksmith
     PHIPPS, R.              18  M  TN  Blacksmith

#436 BECKOM, John S.         33  M  KY  Blacksmith
     BECKOM, Nancy           18  F  TN  Married this year
```

```
#437  DENSON, John B          25  M  KY  Merchant      500
      DENSON, Mary A          21  F  MS
      DENSON, William F        2  M  MS

#438  BROWN, Henry C          21  M  MS  Planter
      BROWN, Amanda           17  F  MS  married this year

#439  MOBLEY, Edward G        31  M  MS  Planter
      MOBLEY, Adeliza         24  F  LA
      MOBLEY, Jane             6  F  MS  in school
      MOBLEY, Eugena           4  F  MS
      MOBLEY, Gertrude         1  F  MS

#440  LUSE, Stephen           45  M  MS  Planter  5,200   (FORD, Frances}
      LUSE, Thaddeus          20  M  MS  Planter
      LUSE, Sally A           15  F  MS  in school
      LUSE, Henry             13  M  MS  in school
      LUSE, Olivia             4  F  MS
      LUSE, James N            2  M  MS

#441  RICHARDSON, George W    28  M  SC  Farmer
      RICHARDSON, Amelia C    22  F  AL  (WEIR, Amelia C)
      RICHARDSON, Sarah        2  F  MS
      RICHARDSON, Frances      1  F  MS

#442  CHERRY, J. B.           35  M  SC  Minister

#443  GARNER, Robert          17  M  MS  Clerk

#444  GRAY, J. P.             24  M  TN  Planter
      GRAY, Elizabeth         30  F  MS  (FRILEY, Elizabeth)
      GRAY, Sarah R            4  F  MS
      GRAY, David T?           2  M  MS

#445  WORMACK, John           40  M  GA  Merchant      500
      WORMACK, Sarah M        34  F  MS
      WORMACK, William Q      16  M  MS  Student in school
      WORMACK, John F          7  M  MS
      WORMACK, Sarah V         3  F  MS

#446  DEMART, Wilson Y        25  M  TN  Clerk

#447  GRUBBS, John A          20  M  TN  Planter

#448  GRESHAM, Williamson     48  M  GA  Planter     1,000
      GRESHAM, Mary           42  F  MS  (CRESWELL, Mary)
      GRESHAM, Rufus R        24  M  MS  Medical Student
      GRESHAM, Celestus       22  M  MS  Planter
      GRESHAM, Raspberry      18  M  MS  Student in school
      GRESHAM, Alvin G        11  M  MS  in school
      GRESHAM, Catherine      18  F  MS
      GRESHAM, Sarah A        15  F  MS  in school
      GRESHAM, Indiana         9  F  MS  in school
      GRESHAM, Minerva         1  F  MS
```

```
#449  MANNING, Henry E        32   M   NC   Merchant      500

#450  DICKSON, Joseph         45   M   MA   Blacksmith

#451  MANNING, Susan          55   F   NC

#452  FATURN,? Robert         63   M   VA   Planter       600
      FATURN,? Ann            65   F   KY

#453  ANDERSON, John W        28   M   LA   Planter
      ANDERSON, Mary P        26   F   VA
      ANDERSON, Lucretia       4   F   MS
      ANDERSON, William W      1   M   MS

#454  KENT, Robert            24   M   MS   Merchant
      KENT, Mary              18   F   MS   md this year (BOYKIN, Mary)

#455  CARR, Young             26   M   SC   Shoe maker
      CARR, Matilda C         25   F   MS   (CAUSEY or ZEAGLER, Matilda)
      GREEN, J.Q.A.           28   M   NY   Shoe maker

#456  MORRIS, Joseph F. M.    40   M   SC   Carpenter

#457  YOUNG, Robert A         19   M   SC   Clerk

#458  MANNING, Mary A         45   F   SC   500
      MANNING, Richard E      16   M   MS   Clerk        in school
      MANNING, Susan           8   F   MS   in school
      MANNING, Charles         4   M   MS

#459  DRENNING, Eliza         34   F   IRELAND        500
      DRENNING, Edward        11   M   IRELAND        in school
      DRENNING, Mary A         4   F   MS

#460  BOSTICK, Ferdinand      33   M   VA   Planter     1,000
      BOSTICK, Emily R        20   F   SC   (DEASON, Emily Catherine)
      BOSTICK, Martha M. P.    7   F   MS   in school

#461  YOUNG, Joseph A         43   M   SC   Blacksmith   700
      YOUNG, Augusta W        42   F   SC
      YOUNG, Catherine        15   F   MS
      YOUNG, Julia            13   F   MS   in school
      YOUNG, William          11   M   MS   in school
      YOUNG, Mary              9   F   MS   in school
      YOUNG, Virginia          7   F   MS   in school
      YOUNG, Thomas            5   M   MS   in school
      YOUNG, Ophelia           3   F   MS   in school

#462  DOUGHARTY, George W     29   M   MS   Lawyer
      DOUGHARTY, P. C.        23   F   SC   (KING, Prudence)
      DOUGHARTY, Mary          5   F   MS
      DOUGHARTY, Charles       3   M   MS
      DOUGHARTY, Alexander   6/12  M   MS
      CLARK, Josephine        14   F   MS   in school
```

```
#463  ROBERTS, Ransom          21  M  MS  Cabinet Maker
      HOWARD, M. M.            28  F  MS
      BUIE, Mary J            10  F  MS  in school

#464  SMITH, John             50  M  NC  Planter
      SMITH, Mary             50  F  MS  (FORT, Mary Smith)
      SMITH, John L           29  M  NC  Laborer
      ROBERTS, Ophelia        10  F  MS  in school {STIGLER, James}

#465  HALL, Willis            20  M  MS  Planter(RUSSELL, Catherine}

#466  GARNER, Sturdy F        42  M  SC  Planter      4,000
      GARNER, Sarah           27  F  MS
      GARNER, John            14  M  MS
      GARNER, William P       12  M  MS  in school
      GARNER, Milton S        10  M  MS  in school
      GARNER, Frances M        7  F  MS  in school
      GARNER, Charles W. Q.    3  M  MS
      GARNER, George W         1  M  MS

#467  KIRK, William           18  M  MS  Planter  (MORTON, Louisa}

#468  EDMONDS, Cyrus W        26  M  KY  Planter      1,500
      EDMONDS, Elizabeth      25  F  LA  (KIRK, Elizabeth)

#469  OWENS, William F        29  M  VA  Virginia (sic) (GARTLEY, Julia)

#470  GARRISON, Reliant       39  M  VA  Waggon Maker
      GARRISON, Rachel        27  F  KY  (BATES, Rachel)
      GARRISON, Caroline      13  F  MS  in school
      GARRISON, James          5  M  MS

#471  BATES, Robert L         16  M  MS  Laborer

#472  LOFTIN, R. B.           28  M  TN  Overseer  (BELL, Mary Ann)

#473  MANGUM, William H       41  M  MS  Deputy Sheriff
      MANGUM, Martha C        28  F  TN
      MANGUM, Catherine       10  F  MS  in school
      MANGUM, Louisa           8  F  MS  in school
      MANGUM, Frances          6  F  MS  in school
      MANGUM, William W        4  M  MS

#474  GANBERRY, William Y     28  M  MS  Physician    5,000
      GANBERRY, Helen B       26  F  KY
      GANBERRY, William E      4  M  MS
      GANBERRY, Marshall P     1  M  MS

#475  HATCH, Charles          30  M  IRELAND  Physician  1,300
      HATCH, Ann E            19  F  MS  (CULLEN, Ann E)
      CULLEN, Rebecca         50  F  VA
```

```
#476  HARRIS, Elizabeth           70   F   SC
      GANBERRY, Marcia J          21   F   MS
#477  HARRIS, Mary E              24   F   MS
      HARRIS, Ethelinda            6   F   MS

#478  CALDWELL, Thomas S          40   M   SC    Tavern Keeper
      CALDWELL, Julie G.          45   F   SC    800
      CALDWELL, Sarah              7   F   MS    in school

#479  COLLUM, Elbert              35   M   SC    Blacksmith
      COLLUM, Susan               30   F   AL
      COLLUM, John                12   M   AL
      COLLUM, Martin              10   M   AL
      COLLUM, Charles A            5   M   MS
      COLLUM, Mississippi          4   F   MS
      COLLUM, Ethelinda            1   F   MS
      BELEN, Morsin               15   M   AL
      BELEN, Mahala               13   F   AL

#480  BOND, Henry                 45   M   ENGLAND   Merchant   300
      BOND, Rebecca               23   F   AL
      BOND, Parnilia J          3/12   F   MS
      BOOTH, Martha               18   F   AL
      BOOTH, Miranda               6   F   AL   in school

#481  WILKINSON, Benjamin R       40   M   VA   Physician   2,000
      WILKINSON, Eliza C          30   F   Dist of Columbia (SMITH, Eliza)
      WILKINSON, Carey H           6   M   MS
      WILKINSON, Benjamin R        4   M   MS
      WILKINSON, Rosa              2   F   MS

#482  SIMMONS, Benjamin G         42   M   VA   Planter      500
      SIMMONS, Susan E            30   F   GA
      SIMMONS, Margaret S          7   F   MS
      SIMMONS, John N. B.          3   M   MS
      SIMMONS, Mary A              1   F   MS

#483  HALL, James F               45   M   VA   Planter    1,500
      HALL, Sarah                 45   F   SC

#484  BROWN, Alonzo L             25   M   MS   Planter    5,000
      BROWN, Alonorizine?         26   F   MS
      BROWN, Agnes C              19   F   SC
      EAMIGSON, Jesse B           12   M   MS

#485  PEASTER, James H            42   M   MS   Bricklayer   500
      PEASTER, Sarah              35   F   SC
      PEASTER, Samuel             12   M   MS   in school
      PEASTER, Lucinda             9   F   MS   in school
      PEASTER, Leonidas            7   M   MS   in school
```

```
#486  RATCLIFF, Henry L        30  M  MS  Planter     500
      RATCLIFF, Mary A         18  F  MS  married this year

#487  COLLINS, Joseph          33  M  MS  Planter     500
      COLLINS, Albina          25  F  VA
      COLLINS, James            5  M  MS  in school
      COLLINS, Mary             3  F  MS

#488  KIRK, Thomas J           22  M  MS  Planter     1,000 md this yr
      KIRK, Octavia H          20  F  TN  (MARSHALL, Octavia H)

#489  GRIMES, Benjamin         54  M  MD  Planter     500
      GRIMES, Mary             53  F  MS

#490  GRIMES, Theodore         22  M  MS  Planter  md this yr
      GRIMES, Elvira           20  F  MS  (MAYS, Frances E)

#491  COLLUM, Millingeville    30  M  SC  Overseer    1,000
      COLLUM, Mary J           24  F  GA
      COLLUM, Mary E            7  F  GA
      COLLUM, John L            6  M  MS
      COLLUM, William J         4  M  MS
      COLLUM, Millingeville     2  M  MS
      COLLUM, Jeffersonia E    15  F  GA

#492  COLLINS, Seaborn         54  M  GA  Planter     3,120
      COLLINS, Mary            52  F  GA  (MAY, Mary)
      COLLINS, Lucinda         18  F  MS
      COLLINS, Wiley           15  M  MS
      COLLINS, James           13  M  MS

#493  PRESTRIDGE, William A    25  M  MS  Planter md this yr
      PRESTRIDGE, Mary         19  F  MS  (COLLINS, Mary)

#494  COLLINS, Joshua G        30  M  MS  Planter
      COLLINS, Mary            20  F  MS

#495  NOLAN, James H           29  M  AL  Planter 1,500 md this yr
      NOLAN, Elizabeth         23  F  MS  (COLLINS, Elizabeth)
      NOLAN, Tilman             4  M  MS
      NOLAN, Maria L            2  F  MS

#496  PICKETT, William         46  M  SC  Planter     9,000
      PICKETT, Eliza           27  F  MS  (ANDERSON, Eliza)
      PICKETT, Mary E           9  F  MS  in school
      PICKETT, William          6  M  MS
      PICKETT, John             2  M  MS
      PICKETT, Susan            1  F  MS

#497  STEVENS, Lewis           53  M  TN  Planter     1,500
      STEVENS, Benjamin F      12  M  MS  in school
```

```
#498 DIXON, Perry              34   M   NC   Overseer (COLLINS, Lucinda)

#499 DONELSON, William M       29   M   TN   Planter      4,160
     DONELSON, Sarah           19   F   NC   married this year

#500 GRIFFIN, Henderson        25   M   MS   Overseer
     GRIFFIN, Sarah            19   F   AL

#501 BOWMAN, Claiborne         30   M   MS   Planter {HAYS, Elizabeth}
     BOWMAN, Robert            22   M   MS   Law Student
     BOWMAN, Virginia          32   F   MS
#502 O'REILLY, Sarah           27   F   MS   (BOWMAN, Sarah Riley)
     O'REILLY, Mary             6   F   MS
     O'REILLY, Kate             4   F   MS

#503 ROBERTS, Buttain P        32   M   LA   Overseer(ARMSTRONG, Frances M)

#504 KIRK, John W              24   M   MS   Overseer{TUCKER, Catherine}

#505 HEWETT, William           36   M   MS   Planter      500
     HEWETT, Margaret E        26   F   MS   (GOWEN, Margaret E)
     HEWETT, Johnathan         12   M   MS
     GOWAN, Joshua              7   M   MS
     HEWETT, Mary P          1/12   F   MS

#506 KUNKELL, Samuel K         38   M   PA   Well Digger(SPIERMAN, Elizabeth)

#507 CHRISTIAN, James          53   M   VA   Horse Trader

#508 FISHER, Robert            39   M   VA   Planter      500
     FISHER, Mary              25   F   MS   (RUSSELL, Mary W)
     FISHER, James A            2   M   MS

#509 FISHER, Elias             38   M   VA   Planter      500
     FISHER, Susanna V         16   F   MS   (HALL, Susannah V)

#510 BUIE, Milton              42   M   GA   Planter      500

#511 DIXON, C. M.              44   M   NC   Overseer     1,100

#512 HOLLIDAY, Nathan          45   M   GA   Overseer
     HOLLIDAY, Nancy           35   F   GA

#513 STEIN, Thomas C           34   M   MS   Overseer
     STEIN, Eliza A            32   F   LA   (LAMBERT, Eliza Ann)
     STEIN, Jefferson          10   M   MS   in school
     STEIN, Jane                8   F   MS
     STEIN, Elizabeth           6   F   MS
     STEIN, Margaret            4   F   MS
     STEIN, Thomas C, Jr.       1   M   MS
```

```
#514  LANGLY, Joseph J          37   M   NC   Overseer
      LANGLY, Martha            22   F   AL   (BUSBY? Martha)
      LANGLY, Margaret E         4   F   MS

#515  HENDRICK, John M          53   M   VA   Planter      1,500
      HENDRICK, Susan           47   F   NC   (BULL, Susan)
      HENDRICK, Charles W       22   M   MS   Planter
      HENDRICK, Sarah           11   F   MS   in school

#516  CHRISTOPHER, Washington   41   M   NC   Overseer
      CHRISTOPHER, Mary         42   F   NC
      CHRISTOPHER, Eliza A      13   F   NC
      CHRISTOPHER, Mary J       11   F   NC

#517  PICKETT, Micajah          38   M   LA   Planter     18,000
      PICKETT, Jane E           35   F   NC   (CLARK, Jane Eliza)

#519  KING, Livingston M P      21   M   MS   Planter      6,000
      KING, Harriet             19   F   MS

#520  FLEMING, Lewis D          41   M   VA   Overseer

#521  SMITH, Nathaniel T        38   M   NY   Physician    2,000
      SMITH, Francis A          38   F   TN   (DILLAHUNTY, Frances Ann)

#522  BULL, James C             39   M   GA   Planter 7,200 (KING, Lydia)
      BULL, Mary                15   F   MS
      BULL, David K             13   M   MS
      BULL, James H             10   M   MS

#523  BULL, Lovey               60   F   GA   (CAMPBELL, Lovey)

#524  KING, Burton A            28   M   MS   Overseer
      KING, Susan               25   F   MS   (ELLISON, Susan)
      KING, William              4   M   MS
      KING, Ann J                3   F   MS

#525  PICKETT, James M          30   M   AL   Planter
      PICKETT, Louisa           30   F   MS
      BULL, Mary J              12   F   MS
      BULL, Ann E               10   F   MS   in school
      BULL, James                9   M   MS
      PICKETT, Sarah             2   F   MS

#526  ZEIGLER, Matilda          19   F   MS
      ZEIGLER, James             4   M   MS

#527  WILLIAMS, William M       35   M   SC   Planter      1,000
      WILLIAMS, Elizabeth       26   F   MS   (SMITH?, Elizabeth B)
      WILLIAMS, Joseph N        14   M   MS
      WILLIAMS, W. Cicero       12   M   MS
      WILLIAMS, Christopher C   11   M   MS
      WILLIAMS, Susan D          9   F   MS
      WILLIAMS, Parham           4   M   MS
```

```
#528  KING, C. S.              24   M   AL   Overseer

#529  KEN, Alexander          30   M   NC   Overseer

#530  GEORGE, Robert          24   M   TN   Laborer (BOOTH, Martha S)

#531  SHARP, John M           55   M   NC   (RIDLEY, Sara Vincent)
      SHARP, Mary             51   F   TN   (MARTIN, Mary Allison)
      SHARP, Ann L            18   F   MS   in school
      SHARP, Elizabeth R      18   F   MS   in school

#532  COLLUM, Absolum         43   M   SC   Overseer
      COLLUM, Lucinda         41   F   SC
      COLLUM, John            18   M   GA
      COLLUM, William         17   M   GA
      COLLUM, Albert          14   M   GA   in school
      COLLUM, Caroline        11   F   GA   in school
      COLLUM, Edmond          10   M   GA   in school
      COLLUM, James            9   M   MS   in school
      COLLUM, Martin           4   M   MS
      COLLUM, Thomas           2   M   MS
      COLLUM, Leaborn       1/12   M   MS

#533  HENDERICKS, Daniel W    48   M   VA   Planter     6,900
      HENDERICKS, Mary        29   F   GA   (BULL, Mary)
      HENDERICKS, William     18   M   MS   Overseer
      HENDERICKS, John        16   M   MS   Laborer     in school
      HENDERICKS, Daniel       5   M   MS
      HENDERICKS, Sarah        3   F   MS
      HENDERICKS, Susan        3   F   MS

#534  CATO, Cyrus             18   M   MS   Overseer

#535  BRIGGS, John           42   M   MS   Planter     600

#536  RUCKER, John W         47   M   TN   Planter     2,500
      RUCKER, Maria M        42   F   TN
      RUCKER, William        19   M   TN   Student
      RUCKER, Sarah F        17   F   TN
      RUCKER, Eliza J        13   F   TN   in school
      RUCKER, Ann M           9   F   TN   in school
      RUCKER, Joanna          7   F   MS   in school
      RUCKER, Amanda          5   F   MS
      RUCKER, Catherine       3   F   MS
      RUCKER, Ellen           1   F   MS

#537  GORDON, James          27   M   MS   Planter     1,272
      GORDON, Martha         19   F   MS   (HALL, Martha)
      GORDON, Elizabeth       3   F   MS
      GORDON, Virginia     6/12   F   MS

#538  GORDON, John           48   M   GA   Planter     1,292
      GORDON, Nancy          76   F   GA
#539  RICKETTS, Temperance   35   F   MS
      RICKETTS, Adeline      12   F   MS   in school
      RICKETTS, James        10   M   MS
```

```
#540 GORDON, William        29  M  MS  Planter
     GORDON, Celia          24  F  MS
     GORDON, Robert          1  M  MS

#541 HUTSON, John W         32  M  NC  School Teacher

#542 COKER, Margaret        46  F  GA  (ELLISON, Mary Margaret)
     COKER, Charles         18  M  MS
     COKER, Jonathan        14  M  MS  in school
     COKER, Albert J        12  M  MS  in school
     COKER, Eliza           20  F  MS
     COKER, Margaret        10  F  MS  in school

#543 HENDERICKS, William W  45  M  VA  Planter
     HENDERICKS, Virginia L 31  F  MS  (KING, Virginia L)
     HENDERICKS, Charles L  12  M  MS  in school
     HENDERICKS, Martha P   10  F  MS  in school
     HENDERICKS, William     8  M  MS  in school
     HENDERICKS, Susan       6  F  MS
     HENDERICKS, James M     2  M  MS
     JONES, E.              20  M  MS

#544 BRISTER, John          44  M  SC  Planter
     BRISTER, Betsy         46  F  SC
     BRISTER, William       18  M  MS  Planter
     BRISTER, Susana        16  F  MS
     BRISTER, Rosana        13  F  MS  in school
     BRISTER, Samuel        14  M  MS  in school
     BRISTER, Elizabeth     12  F  MS  in school

#545 SMALLY, J. B.          30  M  KY  Horse Trainer

#546 JOHNSON, Frederick B   32  M  GA  Gun Wright
     JOHNSON, Temperance    21  F  MS
     JOHNSON, Thomas N       5  M  MS  in school
     JOHNSON, Eugenia        3  F  MS

#547 LAMB, Milton B         25  M  TN  Planter
     LAMB, Samuel H         12  M  TN

#548 CAMPBELL, James        65  M  NC  Planter   1,060
     CAMPBELL, Letitia      63  F  NC
     CAMPBELL, Sarah        34  F  NC

#549 WALLER, John C         36  M  VA  Planter   1,900
     WALLER, Casilla        21  F  MS  (LOTT, Casselia)
     WALLER, William         1  M  MS
     WALLER, Lafayette       1  M  MS

#550 CAMPBELL, Thomas       39  M  NC  Planter
     CAMPBELL, Mary         31  F  NC
     CAMPBELL, Catherine    10  F  MS
     CAMPBELL, William       9  M  MS
     CAMPBELL, Emeline       7  F  MS
     CAMPBELL, Sarah E       1  F  MS
```

```
#551 MOORE, Lewy              46  M  KY  Planter
     MOORE, Mary              35  F  TN
     MOORE, Lewis             19  M  MS  Laborer
     MOORE, Joseph G          16  M  MS  Laborer
     MOORE, Harrison          11  M  MS
     MOORE, James A            9  M  MS
     REDDISH, Elisha          12  M  AL

#552 JOHNSON, John            23  M  TN  Laborer

#553 BULL, Reuben             50  M  NC  Planter        10,000
     BULL, Mahala A           37  F  KY
     BULL, Nancy A            16  F  MS
     BULL, Susan J             7  F  MS
     BULL, John C              5  M  MS
     BULL, James H             2  M  MS
     KNIGHTEN, Joab           19  M  MS  Clerk

#554 BULL, Isaac L            22  M  MS  Laborer md this yr
     BULL, Sarah              19  F  MS  (NEEL, Sarah Jane?)

#555 BULL, William J          24  M  MS  Planter
     BULL, Sarah              17  F  MS
     BULL, Emily J. E.      4/12  F  MS
     BULL, Melinda C          18  F  AL
     BULL, Susan A             1  F  MS

#556 SCANTLING, William       35  M  IRELAND  Laborer

#557 YARBOROUGH, Micajah      35  M  MS
     YARBOROUGH, Minerva C    23  F  MS
     YARBOROUCH, Melissa       8  F  MS
     YARBOROUGH, James H       6  M  MS
     YARBOROUGH, Alfred        1  M  MS

#558 SPIARS, Polly           100  F  NC

#559 SAMPLE, Martha M. D. A.  20  F  LA  {GRIFFIN, James M}
     SAMPLE, Margaret J        1  F  MS
     SAMPLE, Isaac N          30  M  MS  Overseer

#560 BRISTER, Warrick         42  M  TN  Planter
     BRISTER, Lucinda         35  F  AL
     BRISTER, Warrick Jr.     10  M  MS  in school
     BRISTER, Lucinda          8  F  MS  in school
     BRISTER, John J           6  M  MS
     BRISTER, Henry F          2  M  MS

#561 AKERAGE, Jane            46  F  SC  (BRISTER, Jane)
     AKERAGE, John            18  M  AL
     AKERAGE, Indiana         17  F  AL
     AKERAGE, Samuel          16  M  AL  Laborer
     AKERAGE, Mary J          15  F  AL
     AKERAGE, Robert          12  M  AL
     AKERAGE, Paralee          9  F  AL
     AKERAGE, Cordelia         8  F  AL
```

```
#562 ESTIS, William A          23  M  AL  Laborer

#563 BLUMSON, George           24  M  AL  Laborer

#564 WARREN, Reuben            32  M  MS  Planter      620
     WARREN, Susan             27  F  AL  (ELLISON, Susannah)
     WARREN, Sarah E            7  F  MS  in school
     WARREN, Mary A             5  M  MS  in school
     WARREN, John S             3  M  MS
     WARREN, Moses              1  M  MS

#565 DANIELS, John C           24  M  GA  Planter      480
     DANIELS, Hester A         18  F  MS
     MARTIN, Isaac              2  M  MS

#566 BERRY, Edward             30  M  KY  Planter
     BERRY, Belinda            28  F  MS  (WARREN, Belinda)
     BERRY, John W              9  M  KY  in school
     BERRY, William H           6  M  MS
     BERRY, Richard G           3  M  MS

#567 DANIELS, David            45  M  GA  Planter      480
     DANIELS, Susan            19  F  GA
     DANIELS, Dozia            17  F  GA
     DANIELS, William          16  M  GA  Laborer
     DANIELS, Francis           5  F  MS
     DANIELS, Joseph            3  M  MS

#568 DIXON, R. D. S.           47  M  NC  Planter {RICKELLS, Adeline}

#569 HENDERSON, Duncan C       50  M  NC  Planter
     HENDERSON, Mary A         57  F  NC  (OGDEN, Mary Ann)
     HENDERSON, Lucy O         15  F  MS
     HENDERSON, Christopher    11  M  MS  in school
     HENDERSON, Elizabeth F     9  F  MS  in school
     HENDERSON, Daniel F        7  M  MS  in school
     HENDERSON, Joseph J        5  M  MS  in school
     OGDEN, George W           18  M  MS  in school      Student
     HENDERSON, Mary           56  F  NC
     McNIEL, William A. J.     24  M  GA  Overseer
     BISKHEIM?, Erasmus        28  M  NC  School Teacher

#570 ALSOP, Jesse              17  M  VA  Planter

#571 WATLINGTON, William F     36  M  VA  Overseer    1,500
     WATLINGTON, Elizabeth     22  F  AL  (WILMORE, Elizabeth)
     WATLINGTON, William        8  M  MS  in school
     WATLINGTON, Henry         21  M  MS

#572 WATLINGTON, Elizabeth     55  F  VA  (HALL, Elizabeth)
     WATLINGTON, Julius        20  M  VA  Laborer
     WATLINGTON, Keziah        15  F  VA  in school
     WATLINGTON, Francis       13  F  VA  in school
```

```
#573 BRISTER, Thompson, Jr.    27   M   MS   Planter        500
     BRISTER, Elizabeth        22   F   MS   (ELLISON, Elizabeth)
     BRISTER, William F         4   M   MS
     BRISTER, Thompson          2   M   MS
     BRISTER, Thompson         79   M   VA   Planter      2,000

#574 HAMPTON, Wesley          35   M   MS   Planter
     HAMPTON, Sally           29   F   GA
     HAMPTON, James           12   M   MS
     HAMPTON, William         10   M   MS
     HAMPTON, Susan            8   F   MS
     HAMPTON, Sarah            6   F   MS
     HAMPTON, Mahala           5   F   MS
     HAMPTON, Rhoda            2   F   MS

#575 KING, Allen             21   M   MS   Laborer
     KING, Lucinda           27   F   MS

#576 HUGHES, Catherine       35   F   TN
     HUGHES, Rhoda           13   F   MS
     HUGHES, Thomas           5   M   MS
     HUGHES, Nancy S          7   F   MS
     HUGHES, Ann              4   F   MS
     HUGHES, Tabitha         11   F   MS

#577 MEEK, James             32   M   TN   Planter      1,320
     MEEK, Harriet           20   F   GA   (BULL, Harriet)
     MEEK, Thomas             4   M   MS
     MEEK, Mary               2   F   MS
     MEEK, Anna               1   F   MS

#578 BRISTER, Samuel H       42   M   SC   Laborer
     BRISTER, Tenesse        40   F   AL
     BRISTER, Allez          18   F   MS
     BRISTER, Allen          16   M   MS   Laborer
     BRISTER, Tenesse        12   F   MS   in school
     BRISTER, Frances         5   M   MS   in school
     BRISTER, John            2   M   MS

#579 MAXEY, W. G. W.         40   M   VA   Planter
     MAXEY, Eliza            25   F   MS
     MAXEY, James            10   M   MS
     MAXEY, Martha            9   F   MS
     MAXEY, William           7   M   MS
     MAXEY, Celia             1   F   MS

#580 BRODNAX, Robert M       34   M   GA   Planter        300
     BRODNAX, Martha         30   F   AL
     BRODNAX, Cornelia        8   F   AL   in school
     BRODNAX, Rolent          3   M   MS   in school
     BRODNAX, John            3   M   MS
     BRODNAX, Amazon          1   F   MS

#581 NEWSOM, David           36   M   NC   Planter
     NEWSOM, Nancy           40   F   NC
```

```
#582 TERRILL, John           32  M  SC  Planter
     TERRILL, Francis        38  F  GA
     TERRILL, James F         6  M  MS  in school
     TERRILL, Mary E          4  F  MS  in school
     TERRILL, Martha          1  F  MS

#583 BEULL, Francis M        30  M  AL  Blacksmith
     BEULL, Sarah            18  F  MS
#584 BEULL, Elenor           50  F  NC
     BEULL, Joseph           11  M  MS

#585 HANNA, Joseph           23  M  PA  Blacksmith

#586 FATHEREE, B.B.          25  M  MS  Clerk
#587 WILLIAMS, John          41  M  NC  Carpenter
     WILLIAMS, Nancy A       38  F  GA
     WILLIAMS, Benjamin F    14  M  MS
     WILLIAMS, Samuel H      11  M  MS  in school
     WILLIAMS, Amanda M       8  F  MS  in school
     WILLIAMS, Martha J       5  F  MS  in school
     WILLIAMS, Frances A      2  F  MS

#588 BLAN, William           36  M  NC  500
     BLAN, Selina            23  F  MS
     BLAN, Nancy A            9  F  MS  in school
     BLAN, Lucy J             7  F  MS  in school
     BLAN, Louisa             4  F  MS
     BLAN, Jasper J           1  M  MS

#589 MOORE, Casandra         30  F  AL  (ELLISON, Cassie)
     MOORE, Martha           14  F  MS
     MOORE, Joseph            1  M  MS

#590 ELLISON, Lewis          30  M  AL  Planter    250
     ELLISON, Jane           25  F  AL  (BUSBY, Jane)
     ELLISON, Francis         6  F  MS
     ELLISON, Nancy           2  F  MS
     ELLISON, William         1  M  MS

#591 DANIEL, G. B.           25  M  SC  Planter
     DANIEL, Mary            18  F  MS
     DANIEL, Littleton        1  M  MS

#592 BUSBY, S. B.            45  M  NC  Planter
     BUSBY, James            37  M  AL
     BUSBY, Tenilla          16  F  MS
     BUSBY, Sarah            12  F  MS  in school
     BUSBY, Johnathan         9  M  MS  in school
     BUSBY, Emily             6  F  MS  in school
     BUSBY, Martha            7  F  MS  in school
     BUSBY, Marvin            2  M  MS
```

```
#593 ELLISON, Thomas P       40   M   TN   Planter
     ELLISON, Mary           35   F   AL   (MOORE, Mary)
     ELLISON, Belinda        17   F   MS
     ELLISON, Susan          11   F   MS   in school
     ELLISON, William        10   M   MS   in school
     ELLISON, Thomas          7   M   MS   in school
     ELLISON, Julia A         5   F   MS
     ELLISON, Mary            2   F   MS
     ELLISON, Caroline        1   F   MS

#594 GLICKAUF, Samuel        30   M   BOHEMIA          Merchant
     GLICKAUF, F.            22   F   BOHEMIA
     GLICKAUF, Betty          1   F   MS

#595 PUCKETT, Robert         23   M   VA   Planter
#596 COLE, Sterling          53   M   VA   Planter
     COLE, Rebecca           52   F   VA
     COLE, Rebecca R         22   F   VA
     COLE, Louisa M          19   F   VA
     COLE, George W          14   M   VA   in school
     COLE, Lafayette         12   M   VA   in school
     COLE, Charlotte E        9   F   VA   in school

#597 COOK, Sims P            24   M   SC   School Teacher
     COOK, Celia             20   F   MS   (KING, Celia)

#598 SMITH, William M        37   M   VA   Waggon Maker
     SMITH, Ann E            35   F   KY
     SMITH, Louisa           12   F   TN   in school
     SMITH, Martin           10   M   TN   in school
     SMITH, Elinora           5   F   MS   in school
     SMITH, Alphonso          3   M   MS

#599 LATHERS, John           53   M   OH   Gin Wright
     LATHERS, Catherine      52   F   TN

#600 ALSOP, Edward           27   M   VA   Gin Wright {FOULKS, Emeline}

#601 BRIGGS, Eugene          19   M   MS   Planter      3,000
     BRIGGS, Frederick       38   M   MS   Planter      3,000

#602 FINNICANE, George       35   M   IRELAND  Planter md this yr
     FINNICANE, Amanda       30   F   MS   (NOBLE, Amanda M)

#603 BOURG, Zenon            45   M   LA   Planter      500
     BOURG, Elizabeth        38   F   MS   (MATTHEWS, Elizabeth)
     BOURG, Edward           10   M   MS   in school
     BOURG, Eldridge          8   M   MS   in school
     BOURG, Lecra?            4   F   MS
```

```
#604  GERALD, George          62   M   SC   Planter        2,000
      GERALD, Elizabeth C      51   F   SC
      GERALD, Sarah A          20   F   MS
      GERALD, G. Bruce         16   M   MS

#605  PENNY, John W            45   M   SC   Overseer
      PENNY, Eliza             35   F   KY
      PENNY, Mary              15   F   MS
      PENNY, Rachel             7   F   MS
      PENNY, Elizabeth          4   F   MS
      PENNY, John A             2   M   MS

#606  GRADY, William E         38   M   GA   Trader
      GRADY, Mary              28   F   TN   (JONES, Mary)

#607  HANSEN, William          68   M   VA   Planter
      OLIVER, Octavia          35   F   VA

#608  ELLISON, Moses           47   M   GA   Planter    1,500 md this yr
      ELLISON, Martha          26   F   VA   (WALLINGTON, Martha)
      ELLISON, Thomas H        21   M   MS   Laborer
      ELLISON, Nancy           17   F   MS
      ELLISON, Claiborne       10   M   MS
      ELLISON, John W           6   M   MS
      ELLISON, Sarah         6/12   F   MS

#609  FORD, Thomas J           41   M   GA   Planter    1,200
      FORD, Peter H            21   M   AL   Overseer
      FORD, John W             19   M   AL   Student   in school
      FORD, Nancy              17   F   MS
      FORD, Thomas A           13   M   MS   in school
      FORD, Mary A             12   F   MS   in school
      FORD, Martha A            8   F   MS   in school
      FORD, Kendrick            3   M   MS
      WILSON, John             17   M   MS   in school   Student

#610  DAY, Robert              54   M   GA   Planter (MATHEWS, Nancy)
      DAY, William             26   M   MS   Planter
      DAY, Johnathan           23   M   MS   Planter
      DAY, Elizabeth           17   F   MS
      DAY, Robert Jr.          16   M   MS   in school   Student
      DAY, Allen               14   M   MS   in school
      DAY, Warren              12   M   MS   in school
      DAY, Nancy                9   F   MS   in school
      DAY, Frances              7   F   MS
      DAY, July                 5   F   MS
      DAY, Emma                 2   F   MS
      DAY, Nancy               45   F   GA   (DAY, Mathis)
```

```
#611 BLALOCK, William          47    M   KY   Planter        500
     BLALOCK, Sarah            45    F   TN
     BLALOCK, Mary A           25    F   MS
     BLALOCK, Milly            23    F   MS
     BLALOCK, Mahala           21    F   MS
     BLALOCK, John             20    M   MS   Laborer
     BLALOCK, Johnathan        17    M   MS   Laborer
     BLALOCK, Alfred           14    M   MS
     BLALOCK, Nancy            12    F   MS
     BLALOCK, Sarah A          10    F   MS
     BLALOCK, Frances E         7    F   MS
     BLALOCK, Catherine         1    F   MS

#612 PEPPER, Zedikiah          52    M   SC   Planter      2,000
     PEPPER, Sarah             52    F   NC   (BULL, Sarah)
     PEPPER, Zedikiah Jr.      24    M   MS   Planter
     PEPPER, Rachel            16    F   AL
     PEPPER, William           22    M   MS
     PEPPER, James             18    M   MS   Laborer
     PEPPER, Ambrose           16    M   MS   Student  in school
     PEPPER, John              14    M   MS   in school
     PEPPER, Bruce             12    M   MS   in school
     PEPPER, Jesse             10    M   MS   in school

#613 STERLING, Josiah          28    M   PA   Carriage Maker
     STERLING, Octavia         17    F   IN   (BRUNER, Octaviah R)
     STERLING, Isaac F        6/12   M   MS
     BRUNER, Patience          19    F   IN

#614 JOHNSON, James            22    M   MS   Laborer
     JOHNSON, Martha           19    F   MS
     JOHNSON, Margaret          1    F   MS

#615 JOHNSON, Samuel           38    M   NC   Overseer
     JOHNSON, Catherine        33    F   NC
     JOHNSON, Charles H         8    M   MS
     JOHNSON, George W          6    M   MS
     JOHNSON, John W            4    M   MS
     JOHNSON, Mary E          6/12    F   MS
     JOHNSON, Penelope         67    F   NC

#616 BELL, Joseph W            25    M   MS   Overseer

#617 MOORE, Mary               40    F   MS   4,000

#618 CLINTOCK, N. S. M.        29    M   TN   Overseer

#619 SCOTT, Lewis              19    M   MS   Planter

#620 SMITH, Wellington         23    M   VA   Overseer
     SMITH, Catherine          16    F   MS
```

```
#621  ETHRIDGE, Martha        37  F  GA
      ETHRIDGE, Elizabeth     20  F  MS
      ETHRIDGE, Mary          14  F  MS
      ETHRIDGE, Lecrvy        13  F  MS
      ETHRIDGE, Winifred       6  F  MS

#622  HANDLY, Elizabeth       35  F  AL  (STUBBLEFIELD, Elizabeth)
      HANDLY, Napoleon B      11  M  MS  in school
      HANDLY, Josephine       10  F  MS  in school
      HANDLY, Frances A        8  F  MS
      HANDLY, William          7  M  MS
      HANDLY, Ursula           5  F  MS

#623  PIERSON, William        25  M  VA  Overseer

#624  PIERSON, Joseph J       41  M  VA  Physician   1,000
      PIERSON, Louisiana      34  F  AL
      PIERSON, John J         16  M  AL  Student  in school

#625  STUBBLEFIELD, William   60  M  GA  Planter      4,200
      STUBBLEFIELD, Mary      40  F  SC  (SMITH, Mary Margaret)
      STUBBLEFIELD, Calvin    16  M  MS  Laborer
      STUBBLEFIELD, Simon P   14  M  MS
      STUBBLEFIELD, Amanda    12  F  MS
      STUBBLEFIELD, Jane       6  F  MS
      STUBBLEFIELD, Aurora     3  F  MS
      STUBBLEFIELD, Mary       1  F  MS

#626  PINKLESON, John         65  M  PA  Laborer

#627  FLETCHER, John P        24  M  TN  Overseer
      FLETCHER, Mary          24  F  AL
      FLETCHER, John           5  M  MS
      FLETCHER, William        3  M  MS

#628  WALLACE, Nicholas       38  M  TN  Planter      1,000
      WALLACE, Nancy          33  F  MS
      WALLACE, Phillip        17  M  MS  Laborer
      WALLACE, Richardson     15  M  MS
      WALLACE, Hiram F        12  M  MS
      WALLACE, Helen           8  F  MS
      WALLACE, Nancy           6  F  MS
      WALLACE, California      3  F  MS

#629  MOORE, Ezekiel          24  M  MS  Planter

#630  BENNETT, Charles W      25  M  NC  Planter      300
      BENNETT, Margaret       15  F  MS  (HEARD, Margaret A)
      POWELL, J. J.           24  M  NC  Overseer
```

```
#631 HEARD, Jesse F         53   M   GA   Planter      1,500
     HEARD, Sophia          41   F   GA   (MATTHEWS, Sophia)
     HEARD, Franklin        17   M   MS   Overseer
     HEARD, Wyatt           12   M   MS   in school
     HEARD, Keziah          10   M   MS   in school
     HEARD, Samuel H         4   M   MS   in school
     HEARD, Sarah L          2   F   MS

#632 DICKSON, Samuel Z      32   M   LA   Planter
     DICKSON, Lovey         29   F   MS   (PEPPER, Freelove)
     DICKSON, Laura         10   F   MS   in school
     DICKSON, Sarah          8   F   MS
     DICKSON, Susan          6   F   MS
     DICKSON, Edward         3   M   MS
     DICKSON, Jane           1   F   MS

#633 SMITH, Thomas          37   M   AL   Planter
     SMITH, Emeline         25   F   LA
     SMITH, James           10   M   MS
     SMITH, Leonidas         7   M   MS
     SMITH, Arnold           3   M   MS

#634 DICKSON, James         30   M   MS   Planter      250
     DICKSON, Elijah        26   M   MS   Planter   (WATLINGTON, Frances E)

#635 ETHRIDGE, Susan        44   F   SC   200
     ETHRIDGE, Reuben       24   M   AL   Planter
     ETHRIDGE, James        15   M   AL
     ETHRIDGE, Margaret     10   F   AL

#636 ANDERSON, John W       35   M   SC   Planter      1,000
     ANDERSON, Elizabeth    25   F   MS   Married this year
     ANDERSON, William      13   M   MS
     ANDERSON, Henretta     11   F   MS
     ANDERSON, Athela        9   F   MS
     ANDERSON, Sophronia     5   F   MS
     ANDERSON, Mary          3   F   MS

#637 PEPPER, Elisha         30   M   MS   Planter      1,000
     PEPPER, Rachel         26   F   LA   (WEST, Sarah Rachel)
     PEPPER, Franklin        5   M   MS
     PEPPER, William         3   M   MS

#638 PEPPER, E. B.          26   M   MS   Planter
     PEPPER, Elizabeth      23   F   AL   (KUHN, Elizabeth)
     PEPPER, John J          1   M   MS

#639 McCORMACK, John D      29   M   AL   Planter      500
     McCORMACK, Margaret    38   F   GA
     McCORMACK, Sarah L. J.   4   F   MS
```

```
#640 DEASON, Joseph L      21  M  KY  Planter  (ANDERSON, A)
     GRIFFIN, Marion       19  M  MS  Planter  (LAMBETH, Julia)

#641 McNEIL, Daniel N      22  M  GA  Planter
     McNEIL, Matthew       21  M  GA  Student     in school

#642 FOWELL, Isaac J       39  M  TN  Physician   500
     FOWELL, Mary          39  F  TN
     FOWELL, Eliza         18  F  IL
     FOWELL, Martha V      16  F  IL  in school
     FOWELL, Samuel C      12  M  IL  in school
     FOWELL, Helen         10  F  IL  in school
     FOWELL, Margaret       8  F  IL  in school
     FOWELL, P.             6  F  TN
     FOWELL, James          4  M  TN
     FOWELL, Isaac          2  M  MS
#643 CAPSHAW, William W    69  M  NC  Planter     350
     CAPSHAW, Mary         64  F  VA
     CAPSHAW, Windsor H     31  M  AL  Lawyer
     CAPSHAW, Eliza        29  F  AL
     CAPSHAW, James M      28  M  AL  Laborer
     CAPSHAW, Matilda      26  F  AL

#644 HUDSON, William K     53  M  VA  Planter
     HUDSON, Nancy         46  F  SC
     HUDSON, Letty         21  F  AL
     HUDSON, Jane          18  F  AL
     HUDSON, Elbert        16  M  AL  Laborer
     HUDSON, Judy          13  F  AL
     HUDSON, Washington    12  M  AL
     HUDSON, Henry          9  M  AL
     HUDSON, Francis        7  M  AL
     HUDSON, Sarah          7  M  AL
     HUDSON, Margaret       4  M  MS

#645 HALL, Joseph N        44  M  SC  Planter
     HALL, Harriet         41  F  SC
     HALL, Martha          22  F  SC

#646 BONNEY, Cynthia       19  F  SC  (HALL, Cynthia)
     BONNEY, Sarah J       10  F  TX  in school
     BONNEY, William        8  M  TX  in school
     BONNEY, Beatrice       5  F  MS
     BONNEY, Jane           3  F  MS

#647 WILLIAMS, John        35  M  VA  Planter

#648 BONNEY, Charles       25  M  ME  Planter
     BONNEY, Isabel         1  F  MS

#649 HASKINS, Henry        30  M  MS  Overseer
     HASKINS, Tabitha      15  F  MS  Married this year
```

```
#650  EXUM, Edward           36  M  SC  Planter
      EXUM, Mary             20  F  MS  (DAY, Mary Ann)
      EXUM, Kinchen           3  M  MS
      EXUM, Kinchen          30  M  SC  Planter        4,000

#651  PEASTER, Tapley H      36  M  SC  Overseer        200
      PEASTER, Delilah       28  F  MS
      PEASTER, Mary           9  F  MS
      PEASTER, Alfred         7  M  MS
      PEASTER, James          5  M  MS
      PEASTER, William        3  M  MS
      PEASTER, Jane           3  F  MS
      PEASTER, Elizabeth      1  F  MS

#652  PEASTER, Michael       74  M  SC  Planter
      PEASTER, Cynthia       72  F  SC
#653  KNIGHT, Elizabeth      23  F  SC
      KNIGHT, James L         5  M  TX
      HALL, Bart             17  M  MS  Laborer

#654  HARRISON, James A      35  M  VA  Overseer
      HARRISON, Susan        24  F  TN
      HARRISON, Mary F        2  F  MS

#655  BALL, Spencer          66  M  SC  Planter        2,500
      BALL, Matilda          52  F  SC
      BALL, Henry            17  M  SC  Laborer
      BALL, Blake R          14  M  MS
      BALL, Mary A. M.        9  F  MS

#656  LESSELL, John          44  M  SC  Wheel Wright
      LESSELL, Martha        43  F  GA
      LESSELL, Mary          15  F  GA
      LESSELL, Jennson       13  M  GA
      LESSELL, Harriet       11  F  GA
      LESSELL, John           9  M  GA
      LESSELL, Lenora         1  F  GA

#657  GREER, Marshall R      31  M  AL  Planter        1,300
      GREER, Jane D          21  F  MS  Married this year
      MILLER, Eveline V      12  F  MS
      MILLER, William D       5  M  MS
      MILLER, Mary F          3  F  MS
      MILLER, Henry C         8  M  MS

#658  MILLER, James M        25  M  MS  Planter
      MILLER, Delilah        16  F  AL

#659  WILBORN, W. Wyche      36  M  VA  Planter        2,500
      WILBORN, Elizabeth     29  F  VA
      WILBORN, James          2  M  MS
```

```
#659  BELL, John Z          52   M   SC   Planter
      BELL, Berthia         53   F   MS   (CASTLOW, B)
      BELL, Joseph          24   M   MS   Laborer
      BELL, Tabitha         22   F   MS
      BELL, Mary            20   F   MS
      BELL, Harriet         11   F   MS
      BELL, Jane            13   F   MS
      BELL, Alfred          10   M   MS

#660  COSTILOUGH, James     17   M   MS   Planter
      COSTILOUGH, Henry     15   M   MS

#661  MOBLY, Benjamin A.    40   M   TN   Gin Wright {WINSTED, Frances A}

#662  GRIFFIN, James M      27   M   MS   Planter      500
      GRIFFIN, Catherine    45   F   SC

#663  CHEW, Augustine       32   M   MS   Planter      7,500
      CHEW, Beverly G       28   M   MS   Planter      7,500

#664  CLARK, John B         42   M   SC   Planter (BLAND, Sarah A)
      CLARK, Lydia M        35   F   MS
      CLARK, Elvira L       12   F   MS   in school
      CLARK, George F       10   M   MS   in school
      CLARK, Augustus B      8   M   MS   in school
      CLARK, Alfred O        5   M   MS
      CLARK, Edward H     6/12   M   MS
      WATERS, Mary          16   F   MS   in school
      WATERS, Glycerian     14   F   MS   in school

#665  LUSE, Ann E           31   F   MS
      LUSE, Edwin            5   M   MS
      LUSE, Alice            3   F   MS
      LYSELL, Louisiana      6   F   GA

#666  WATERS, Adamson       41   M   MD   Planter
      WATERS, Mary          38   F   MS   (LUSE, Mary Berlinda)
      WATERS, Joseph        12   M   MS   in school
      WATERS, Susan          9   F   MS   in school
      WATERS, Laura          7   F   MS   in school
      WATERS, Alma           5   F   MS
      WATERS, John           2   M   MS

#667  ANDERSON, John W      35   M   TN   Overseer
      ANDERSON, Elizabeth   21   F   TN
      ANDERSON, Arabella    14   F   TN   in school
      ANDERSON, Margaret    12   F   TN   in school
      ANDERSON, Clinton     10   M   TN   in school
      ANDERSON, Franklin?    8   M   TN   in school
      ANDERSON, Larkin       6   M   TN   in school
      ANDERSON, Caledonia    4   F   MS
      ANDERSON, Elizabeth  6/12  F   MS

#668  SIMMONS, M. C.        68   M   NC   Carpenter
      YOUNG, Henry          19   M   MS   Laborer
```

```
#669 FORBES, William        38   M  SC      Planter        200
     FORBES, Anna           45   F  SC
     FORBES, James          10   M  MS
     FORBES, John            7   M  MS
     FORBES, Daniel          5   M  MS
     FORBES, Rosetta         3   F  MS
#670 NEIL, Matthew          19   M  MS      Laborer
     NEIL, Henry            15   M  MS

#671 LUSE, Calvin           35   M  MS      Planter        900
     LUSE, Clementina       25   F  MS
     LUSE, Nathan K          5   M  MS
     LUSE, Alexander         2   M  MS
     LUSE, Ann E          6/12   F  MS
     TRIBBLE, Ann           22   F  MS

#672 SWAYZE, Gabriel        60   M  MS      Planter      8,000
     SWAYZE, Mary           60   F  MS      (BRUNER, Mary Ormsby)
     SWAYZE, Hirum O        23   M  MS      Planter
     SWAYZE, J. A.          20   M  MS      Planter

#673 HOWELL, Mary           35   F  MS
     HOWELL, Joseph         15   M  MS
     HOWELL, Mary A         13   F  LA
     HOWELL, James M         9   M  MS
     HOWELL, Martha E        6   F  MS      in school
     HOWELL, Delilah         5   F  MS      in school
     HOWELL, John            3   M  MS

#674 MAY, Berry            63   M  GA      Planter      1,400
     MAY, L. B.            22   M  MS      Planter
     MAY, William         24   M  MS      Planter
     MAY, Thomas          15   M  MS      in school

#675 GRUBBS, William       62   M  VA      Planter {CANADAY, Elzabeth}
     GRUBBS, George        19   M  VA      Laborer
     GRUBBS, John          16   M  VA      Laborer

#676 O'BRIEN, Henry        65   M  IRELAND   Laborer

#677 YARBOROUGH, Thomas G  40   M  TN      Planter
     YARBOROUGH, Jane      42   F  MS
     YARBOROUGH, Lydia A   12   F  MS      in school
     YARBOROUGH, John       7   M  MS      in school
     YARBOROUGH, Jane       3   F  MS
     CAUSEY, Solomon       20   M  MS      Laborer {RAY, Martha M}
```

```
#678 WASKUM, James M        38    M   LA   Planter
     WASKUM, Eliza          38    F   MS   (GRIFFIN, Eliza)
     FORT, Robert H         20    M   MS   Planter
     FORT, James D          18    M   MS   Planter
     FORT, Martha J         16    M   MS
     FORT, Elias A          14    M   MS   in school
     FORT, Lecrecuis         8    M   MS   in school
     WASKUM, Thomas          6    M   MS   in school
     WASKUM, John            4    M   MS
     WASKUM, Griffin         2    M   MS
     WASKUM, Mary E       6/12    F   MS

#679 LOVE, Josephus         23    M   AL   Planter (COMPTON, Margaret E}
     LOVE, Falba            26    F   AL   (JOHNSON, James}
     HART, Meridith         26    M   MS   Overseer

#679 JAMES, Samuel L        33    M   MS   Planter {CALLIHAN, Ellen}
     JAMES, Thomas          10    M   MS   in school

#680 BROWN, James S         45    M   NC   Planter      150
     BROWN, Susan           38    F   SC
     BROWN, Mary            18    F   MS
     BROWN, Calvin          16    M   MS
     BROWN, Martha I        15    F   MS

#681 BONNEY, Thomas         22    M   GA   Raftsman

#682 ERWIN, Zadock          47    M   MS   Planter {ERWIN, Rachel}
     ERWIN, Leonard         16    M   MS   Laborer
     ERWIN, Margaret        14    F   MS
     ERWIN, Timoline        12    M   MS
     ERWIN, Reuben          10    M   MS
     ERWIN, Octavia          4    F   MS

#684 ERWIN, Claiborne       32    M   MS   Laborer (this name was out
                                             of order, was after #726)
#684 ERWIN, Mary            19    F   MS   (HARBIN, Mary A)
     ERWIN, John             1    M   MS

#685 HARBIN, John W         25    M   AL   Laborer
     HARBIN, Cornelius      18    F   LA   (ERWIN, Cornelia J)
     COTNAM, John           25    M   AL

#686 OGDEN, Henry           34    M   MS   Planter    3,000
     OGDEN, Harrison        14    M   MS   in school
     OGDEN, Elnora          11    F   MS   in school
     OGDEN, Wm. D            7    M   MS

#687 OGDEN, Benjamin        38    M   MS   Overseer
     OGDEN, Louisa          12    F   MS   in school

#688 HOLCOMB, Catherine     29    F   MS
     HOLCOMB, J. S.         11    M   MS
     HOLCOMB, M. A.         11    F   MS
     HOLCOMB, Olivia         7    F   MS
```

```
#689  SAUCER, John S              56    M   SC   Planter
      SAUCER, Letitia             61    F   SC
      SAUCER, Martha              20    F   SC
      SAUCER, Christopher         14    M   MS
      SAUCER, Wm                  12    M   MS
      SAUCER, Nancy               10    F   MS
      BRADSHAW, Alex.             23    M   MS   Laborer {SAUCER, Martha}

#690  O'QUINN, James              61    M   NC   Planter
      O'QUINN, Elizabeth          49    F   GA   (IRWIN, Elizabeth)
      O'QUINN, Martha             15    F   MS
      O'QUINN, Teresa             14    F   MS
      O'QUINN, David              11    M   MS
      O'QUINN, Z. E.               9    F   MS
      O'QUINN, Nancy               4    F   MS

#691  DEUTS, Margaret J           23    F   MS
      DEUTS, Elizabeth S           5    F   MS

#692  FISHER, William             26    M   AL   Laborer
      FISHER, Sarah E             25    F   MS   (O'QUINN, Sarah E)
      FISHER, James W              5    M   MS
      FISHER, John O'Q             1    M   MS

#693  WELLS, Soloman              39    M   MS   Planter
      WELLS, Adeline              22    F   MS   (FLETCHER, Adeline)
      WELLS, Ann                   7    F   MS
      WELLS, John                  5    M   MS
      WELLS, Medora                4    F   MS
      WELLS, Rebecca               1    F   MS

#694  FLETCHER, Catherine         45    F   KY
      FLETCHER, Thomas            18    M   MS   Laborer

#695  JEFFERS, Thomas             49    M   SC   Planter
      JEFFERS, Caroline           48    F   SC
      JEFFERS, Warren             20    M   SC   Laborer
      JEFFERS, Osborne             9    M   MS
      JEFFERS, Lee                 6    M   MS
      JEFFERS, Daniel              7    M   MS
      JEFFERS, John                4    M   MS
      JEFFERS, Jane                2    F   MS
      JEFFERS, Elizabeth          18    F   MS
      JEFFERS, Louisa             13    F   MS

#696  OGDEN, George               69    M   GA   Planter 3,000 {WALKER, Lucy}
#697  OGDEN, Theophilus           28    M   MS   Planter
      OGDEN, Mary J               25    F   MS   (SPIARS, Mary Ann)
      OGDEN, Elizabeth             5    F   MS
      OGDEN, Lucy W             6/12    F   MS
#698  McCARTY, Elizabeth          38    F   MS
      McCARTY, C. J. T.            2    M   MS
```

```
#699  WARE, James                34    M   KY   Planter      3,500
      WARE, Virginia C           20    F   VA
      WARE, Julian                7    M   MS
      WARE, Helen                 3    F   MS
      WARE, Mary               8/12    F   MS

#700  MURPHEE, John              46    M   MS   Planter      3,000
      MURPHEE, Elizabeth         37    F   MS   (GOODWIN, Elizabeth)
      GOODWIN, William           21    M   MS   Laborer

#701  SHACKELFORD, John          33    M   VA   Overseer     1,000

#702  JOHNSTON, Tilman J         53    M   VA   Overseer
      JOHNSTON, Nancy            74    F   VA

#703  HOLLOWAY, Sarah            24    F   VA
      HOLLOWAY, Mary              4    F   VA

#704  PRITCHARD, Theophilus P 38    M   MA   Planter     10,000

#705  CARRISEL?,William E        29    M   VA   Overseer

#706  GRACY, Joseph W            28    M   GA   Laborer
      GRACY, Mary J              27    F   AL
      GRACY, Martha L. J.         9    F   AL
      GRACY, William              5    M   MS
      GRACY, John W               4    M   MS

#707  GRACY, Palace              53    M   NC   Planter
      GRACY, Jane                46    F   SC
#708  GRACY, Mary J              20    F   MS
      GRACY, Martha A            14    F   AL
      HARRIS, Robert J           14    M   AL
      HARRIS, Nancy H            11    M   MS
      GRACY, Mary J              11    F   AL
      GRACY, William T            7    M   MS

#709  CARPENTER, Samuel          55    M   NY   Planter       320
      CARPENTER, Elizabeth       49    F   GA
#710  CARPENTER, Cyrus           23    M   MS   Laborer
      CARPENTER, Ann             18    F   MS
      CARPENTER, George           2    M   MS
      HADDICK, Drucilla          11    F   IL   in school

#711  SPENCER, William O         41    M   VA   Planter       400
      SPENCER, Alzira            32    F   MS
      SPENCER, Lycurgus           8    M   MS
      SPENCER, Sim F              6    M   MS
      SPENCER, Marshall G         3    M   MS
      SPENCER, Isaac              1    M   MS

#712  ROBERTS, Elizabeth         64    F   KY   1,200
      ROBERTS, Franklin P        26    M   MS
      ROBERTS, Sarah C           16    F   MS   (KNIGHTON, Sarah C)
      ROBERTS, Thomas G          24    M   MS   Planter
```

```
#713  BROWN, Wiley            54   M   NC   Planter      1,600
      BROWN, Rhoda            31   F   MS
      BROWN, Susanna          10   F   MS   in school
      BROWN, Temperance        8   F   MS   in school
      BROWN, Henry T           6   M   MS   in school

#714  HART, James             34   M   MS   Planter      1,200
      HART, Jane              33   F   MS   (SMITH, Jane)
      HART, Martha            10   F   MS   in school
      HART, Lucretia           6   F   MS   in school
      HART, Amanda             4   F   MS   in school
      HART, Mary L             2   F   MS
      ROBERTS, James          20   M   MS   Blacksmith

#715  HART, Daniel            31   M   MS   Planter       320
      HART, Eliza             28   F   MS   (ARMSTRONG, Eliza)
      HART, Thomas             3   M   MS
      HART, Flonzel            2   F   MS

#716  ARMSTRONG, Abner        18   M   MS   Laborer
      ARMSTRONG, Frances      16   F   MS

#717  HART, John              33   M   MS   Planter       960
      HART, Elizabeth         25   F   MS

#718  McEACHEN, Peter         48   M   SC   Planter      1,160
      McEACHEN, Lucretia      33   F   MS
      McCUTCHEN, Mary E       13   F   MS   in school
      McEACHEN, John A         4   M   MS
      GILL, William T         44   M   SC   Planter       800
      GILL, Amanda            33   F   GA
      GILL, Martha            15   F   MS   in school
      GILL, William           13   M   MS   in school
      GILL, John J             8   M   MS   in school
      GILL, Jackson            6   M   MS   in school
      GILL, Amy L              3   F   MS

#719  NORMAN, James A         27   M   MS   Laborer
      NORMAN, Elizabeth       25   F   AL   (JAMES?, Elizabeth)
      NORMAN, James F          3   M   MS
      NORMAN, Mary G         9/12   F   MS
      CROW? Mary              60   F   SC

#721  HADDICK, Dorsey M       35   M   TN   Planter
      HADDICK, Ann C          33   F   GA
      HADDICK, Louisa A       12   F   MS
      HADDICK, Burnwell S     10   M   MS
      HADDICK, Benjamin        8   M   MS
      HADDICK, Sarah C         4   F   MS
      WORTHY, Rebeckah        43   F   MS

#722  WORTHY, Benjamin F      10   M   MS
      WORTHY, Seaborn J. F.    6   M   MS
      DOUGLAS, Isaac E        23   M   MS
```

```
#723  EMFINGERS, William         34  M  SC  Planter        320
      EMFINGERS, Ivana           26  F  MS
      EMFINGERS, Sarah M. E.      9  F  MS  in school
      EMFINGERS, James M          6  M  MS  in school
      EMFINGERS, Martha A. M.     4  F  MS
      EMFINGERS, William L        2  M  MS

#724  HART, Christopher R        23  M  MS
      HART, M. V.                20  F  KY  (HARRISON, Virginia)
      HART, Marion                4  M  MS
      HART, Josephus J            2  M  MS

#725  ISBEY, Charles             37  M  GA  Planter      1,200
      ISBEY, Martha K            40  F  SC
      ISBEY, W. G. H. C.         18  M  MS  Laborer
      HADDICK, Tibitha J         13  F  TN

#726  JAMES, Peter               62  M  PA  Planter      3,200
      JAMES, Charlotte           54  F  MS  (SIDDON, Charlotte)
      JAMES, Peter O.            12  M  MS  in school
      JAMES, Benjamin F           8  M  MS  in school

#727  THOMAS, H. J.              37  M  TN  Planter (STEVENS, Rebecca)
      ANDERSON, James            32  M  SC  Negro Trader

#728  HUDSON, John               28  M  AL  Overseer
      HUDSON, Elizabeth          35  F  SC
      HUDSON, Melissa             6  F  MS
      HUDSON, James               2  M  MS
      HUDSON, Frances            13  F  MS
      BROWN, Sarah H             11  F  MS
      BROWN, Simon                8  M  MS
      BROWN, Elijah H             3  M  MS
      BROWN, Susan F              1  F  MS

#729  CRESWELL, Leonard          49  M  LA  Planter      1,200
      CRESWELL, Margaret         45  F  MS  (CLARK, Nancy Maranda)
      CRESWELL, James M          19  M  MS  Laborer
      CRESWELL, Rachel A         14  F  MS
      CRESWELL, Oscar H          10  M  MS
      CRESWELL, Salem             8  M  MS
      CRESWELL, Rayford           5  M  MS
      CRESWELL, Linford           3  M  MS

#730  CRESWELL, Miller           45  M  LA  900
      CRESWELL, Leonard          23  M  LA  300 (JOHNSTON, Rachel)
      CRESWELL, J. J.            21  M  LA  Laborer
      CRESWELL, Rachal           18  F  MS
```

```
#731  CAGE, Robert H           53   M   TN   Planter      10,200
      CAGE, Lucy T             40   F   TN
      CAGE, Albert H           17   M   MS   Student
      CAGE, Elizabeth H        14   F   MS
      CAGE, Catherine          12   F   MS
      CAGE, Minerva L           9   F   MS
      CAGE, Lucy T, Jr.         6   F   MS
      CAGE, Harry               4   M   MS
      CAGE, Jane H              2   F   MS
      WALKER, Lucretia M       24   F   VT

#732  LEA, Sarah E             26   F   TN   (HAYS, Sarah) (LEE, Calvin)
      LEA, Lucy                 6   F   MS

#733  MILLS, William           37   M   VA   Physician    7,000
      MILLS, Harriet B         27   F   PA
      MILLS, Henry C            4   M   MS
      MILLS, William J          1   M   MS

#734  HENSEN, Daniel? H        40   M   AL   Overseer     420
      HENSEN, Ann              18   F   MS
      HENSEN, Dorothy          18   F   MS
      HENSEN, Emma             16   F   MS
      HENSEN, John              7   F   MS   Laborer

#735  PAUL, John S             41   M   GA   Planter      15,000
      PAUL, Sarah J            22   F   AL
      PAUL, O. S.               2   M   MS

#736  YANDELL, William M       42   M   TN   Physician    15,000
      YANDELL, Ellnora         25   F   TN
      YANDELL, Wilson          17   M   TN   Overseer
      YANDELL, John S          10   M   TN   in school
      YANDELL, Susan J          4   F   MS
      YANDELL, Emma A           2   F   MS

#737  HENDERSON, Charles M     38   M   VA   Probate Clerk  2,000
      HENDERSON, Elizabeth F   25   F   KY   (RUSSELL, Elizabeth F)
      HENDERSON, Elizabeth K    5   F   MS
      HENDERSON, James W        3   M   MS
      HENDERSON, Charles M      1   M   MS
      HOUSEN, Margaret          9   F   MS

#738  HAGAN, David             27   M   MS   Planter   Married this year
      HAGAN, Sarah A           29   F   MS   (HOPE, Sarah Ann)
      HOPE, John                9   M   MS   in school
      HOPE, James               7   M   MS
      HOPE, Robert              3   M   MS
      HAGAN, Stephen           15   M   MS   in school
      HAGAN, John G            12   M   MS   in school
      HAGAN, Hiram             10   M   MS   in school
      HAGAN, Mary A             6   F   MS   in school
      ANDREWS, Joseph          49   M   PA   Planter      58,700
      GRAFF, John              25   M   FRANCE      Carpenter
```

```
#740  HILLMAN, Andrew L          36  M  VA  Carpenter

#741  ELLISON, Jospeh P          37  M  TN  Overseer (MOORE, Jane)
      ELLISON, Nancy             36  F  MS
      ELLISON, Joseph H           9  M  MS
      ELLISON, Susan              7  F  MS
      ELLISON, William            5  M  MS
      ELLISON, Joseph         10/12  M  MS

#742  PARNELL, Samuel            29  M  SC  Overseer

#743  CRUMP, George P            38  M  NC  Planter      5,255
      CRUMP, Phillip J           25  M  NC  Overseer

#744  PHILLIPS, Jane             60  F  SC  (A Wm md. BROWN, Jane)
      TERRY, Mary A              23  F  AL
      TERRY, Thomas B            14  M  AL

#745  GOWER, John H              30  M  TN  Overseer

#746  ROBERTS, George Q          42  M  NC  Planter
      ROBERTS, Mary A            25  F  NC
      ROBERTS, Carolina           6  F  MS
      ROBERTS, Mary A             4  F  MS
      ROBERTS, Georgiana          2  F  MS
      ROBERTS, Ellen              7  F  MS  1,800
      SCONYER, John              25  M  MS  Brick Maker

#747  BECKON, John S             32  M  KY  Overseer      1,000

#748  RASPBERRY, William G       45  M  GA  Planter      1,500
      RASPBERRY, Mary A          35  F  AL  (GIBSON,?Mary Ann)
      RASPBERRY, John T          12  M  MS  in school
      RASPBERRY, William G        8  M  MS
      RASPBERRY, Patience A       6  F  MS

#749  TIDWELL, Saunders          46  M  GA  Laborer (STINER, Sophia)
      TIDWELL, Wiley             15  M  AL  Laborer
      TIDWELL, William H          9  M  AL
      TIDWELL, M. A. E.           7  F  AL
      CLARK, J. J.               35  M  AL  Laborer
      GRAY, Phillip              30  M  GERMANY  Laborer
      ELLMORE, William           47  M  GA  Laborer (JOHNSON, Virginia)

#750  LAMKIN, Jerimiah           48  M  GA  Planter      3,000
      LAMKIN, Mary A             45  F  GA
      LAMKIN, Thomas G           24  M  GA
      LAMKIN, John C             18  M  GA  Clerk
      LAMKIN, Ronnilus?          16  M  GA  Laborer
      LAMKIN, M. A. E.           14  F  GA
      LAMKIN, M. I?              12  F  GA
      LAMKIN, T. F.               9  M  GA
      LAMKIN, H. C.               7  M  GA
      ROBINSON, Noah             19  M  NC  Laborer
      WOOLDRIDGE, Thomas         45  M  VA  Laborer
```

```
#751  LeLANDE, Joseph          25  M   CANADA   Laborer
      MIKIE, Patrick           35  M   IRELAND  Laborer

#752  LIVINGSTON, Samuel D     55  M   KY   Planter
      LIVINGSTON, P. A.        44  F   KY
      LIVINGSTON, Lucrin?      22  M   KY   Laborer
      LIVINGSTON, James        20  M   KY   Laborer
      LIVINGSTON, Samuel       17  M   MS   Laborer
      LIVINGSTON, William      14  M   KY
      LIVINGSTON, Henrietta    10  F   MS   in school
      LIVINGSTON, Ewing         6  M   MS

#753  WHITTAKER, Aaron N       48  M   MS   Overseer
      BURNS, Patrick           50  M   IRELAND  Ditcher

#754  HARRIS, William C        41  M   GA   Planter     13,000
      HARRIS, Elizabeth        31  F   SC

#755  HALL, Joseph             22  M   DE?  Overseer

#756  PEARCE, Stephen D.       40  M   ME   Raftsman

#757  HILL, William R          50  M   NC   Pontdoc?    2,000
      HILL, Nancy M            47  F   NC
      HILL, Joseph R           21  M   NC   Student     in school
      HILL, Ann E              17  F   NC   in school
      HILL, M. C.               8  F   MS
      HILL, Nancy              71  F   NC

#758  WRENN, C. S.             27  M   MS   Overseer
      GRIFFITH, Samuel         27  M   IN   Carpenter
      GRIFFITH, Hizikiah       25  M   IN   Carpenter
      HODGE, William           24  M   PA   Brick Maker

#759  GERMAN, William H        30  M   VA   Overseer    300
      GERMAN, Louisa           24  F   VA
      GERMAN, John F            8  M   MS   in school
      GERMAN, Catherine         6  F   MS
      GERMAN, George            4  M   MS
      GERMAN, Mary              3  F   MS

#760  LEVY, Samuel             41  M   VA   Wagon Maker
      LEVY, Eliza R            41  F   VA
      ALLGOOD, Richard         14  M   VA
      ALLGOOD, William         12  M   VA
      LEVY, John                5  M   VA

#761  LAMBETH, Susan H         27  F   VA   1,600 (HARRISON, Susan H)
      LAMBETH, Addison         21  M   VA   Planter
      LAMBETH, William         19  M   VA   in school
      LAMBETH, Fanny           13  F   VA   in school
      LAMBETH, Robert           8  M   VA
      LAMBETH, Horace           6  M   VA

#762  MEAD, Horace D           24  M   OH   Overseer (WILLIAMS, Elizabeth)
```

```
#763  HICKS, Daniel G        36    M   GA   Overseer
      HICKS, Sarah M         24    F   AL
      HICKS, Sarah A          8    F   MS
      HICKS, George W         2    M   MS

#764  HOUSTON, J. J.         33    M   TN   Overseer
      FINNEY, William        50    M   VA   Physician

#765  DOWNS, E. L.           28    M   MS

#766  WOOLFOLK, John H       34    M   KY   Planter      21,000

#767  WOOLFOLK, Dudley       34    M   KY   Planter       9,000
      WOOLFOLK, Sarah        26    F   KY

#768  ROOK, James W          33    M   TN   Overseer
      ROOK, S. A.            31    F   MS
      ROOK, E. A.             9    F   MS
      ROOK, Joseph            3    M   MS
      ROOK, Benj.             5    M   MS
      CAMPBELL, J. N.        18    M   MO   Planter      in school

#769  COVINGTON, Henry       20    M   VA   Raftsman

#770  HARRINGTON, John       30    M   NY   Raftsman

#771  BARROW, Millison       44    M   TN   Planter       6,200
      BARROW, S. J           30    F   TN
      BARROW, W. C.           8    M   MS
      BARROW, T. J.           6    M   MS
      BARROW, F. M.           3    M   MS

#772  McCUTCHEN, John H      35    M   AL   Overseer
      McCUTCHEN, L. E.       34    F   AL   (KING, Lucretia Edward)
      McCUTCHEN, T. N.       14    M   AL   in school
      McCUTCHEN, Wm. R.      10    M   AL   in school
      McCUTCHEN, Elizabeth    8    F   MS
      McCUTCHEN, James P      7    M   MS

#773  BRICKELL, Henry        46    M   SC   Planter      10,000
      BRICKELL, Betsey       29    F   TN
      BRICKELL, Mary         11    F   TN   in school
      BRICKELL, James         9    M   MS   in school
      BRICKELL, Lemenda       7    F   MS   in school

#774  SCOTT, W. P.           30    M   TN   Planter       5,000
      SCOTT, F. M.           22    F   AL   (BIBB, Fannie May)
      SCOTT, F. E.            2    M   MS

#775  WHITE, James J. B.     55    M   SC   Planter
      WHITE, Rebecca S       33    F   NC   49,000
      WHITE, B. F. L.         7    M   MS
      WHITE, L. B.            5    F   MS   in school
      WHITE, M. B.            4    F   MS   in school
      WHITE, H. R. W.         2    M   MS
      WHITE, J. J. B.       2/12   M   MS
```

#776 FAUST, Sarah C. W.   65 F SC   20,000

#777 ANDERSON, L. B.   40 M SC   Overseer

#778 BERKLEY, Jerry   35 M IRELAND   Ditcher
      MALONY, Andy   36 M IRELAND   Ditcher
      SRICRES? John   ? M IRELAND   Ditcher

#779 CARADINE, Henry F   42 M MS   (SMITH, Louisa)
      CARADINE, M. C.   32 F Dist. of Colombia   4,000
      CARADINE, James S   15 M MS   in school
      CARADINE, S. G.   12 F MS   in school
      CARADINE, W. S. G.   7 M MS   in school
      CARADINE, Beverly   3 M MS
      COLLINS, Louisiana   19 F MS
#780 GRIFFIN, Sarah G.   29 F MS   (HEWITT, Sarah Grayson)
      GRIFFIN, Sam'l S.   6 M MS   in school

#781 INGERSOLL, John   35 M PA   Planter   45,000

#782 THOMASSON, W. B.   40 M VA   Black Smith
      THOMASSON, Eliza   29 F GA
      THOMASSON, W. H.   8 M MS
      THOMASSON, Ulysses   7 M MS
      THOMASSON, Virginia   5 F MS
      THOMASSON, John   9/12 M MS
      BRANTLEY, Nancy   60 F VA

#783 BOYD, R. D.   42 M MS   Planter
      BOYD, N. A.   32 F GA
      BOYD, T. J   13 M MS   in school
      BOYD, F. E.   5 F MS
      BOYD, M. E.   3 F MS

#784 PHILLIPS, Haywood   29 M TN   Planter (HURST, Susan)
      PHILLIPS, Ther.   21 F MS   (HURST, Thermophlae)
      PHILLIPS, W. E.   5 M MS
      PHILLIPS, Wm   20 M MS   Laborer

#785 WATERMAN, Henry   40 M GERMANY   Laborer

#786 PHILLIPS, Benj.   36 M TN   Planter
      PHILLIPS, F. R.   22 F MS
      PHILLIPS, S. E.   4 M MS
      PHILLIPS, J. R. W.   2 M MS
      WILLIAMS, Wm   48 M VA   Laborer
      MYERS, John   18 M MD   Laborer (ARMSTRONG, Mary E)
      BROOCKS, Walter   36 M NC   Laborer   1,000
      STINSON, Robt.   40 M IRELAND   Laborer
      LAFFERTY, John   35 M IRELAND   Laborer

#787 PERRY, Emanuel   46 M OH   Laborer   1,000
      PERRY, Eliza   40 F PA

#788 PHILLIPS, Peter   22 M MS   Laborer (CLELAND, Irene)

```
#789 IGO, Daniel               42   M   PA   Raftsman

#790 RICHARDS, James P.        23   M   MS   Overseer (EVERETT, Jane)

#791 HAMER, Charles F          35   M   MS   Planter      20,000
     HAMER, E. M.              26   F   SC   (BRICKELL, Elizabeth M)
     HAMER, M. B.               5   M   MS
     HAMER, C. M.               3   F   MS
     HAMER, A. D.            6/12   F   MS
     BRICKELL, E. M.           77   F   SC   15,000
     CONGER, M. V.             21   M   MS   Planter

#792 BRICKELL, Wm A.           55   M   SC   Planter

#793 ABBEY, Richard            45   M   NY   Planter      16,000
     ABBEY, Julia              35   F   MS   (BATHIS, Julia)
     ABBEY, Julia              14   F   MS   in school

#794 MAY, Michajah             30   M   MS   Overseer
     MAY, Elizabeth            28   F   MS

#795 EVERETT, James            53   M   NC   Planter      800
     EVERETT, Judith           47   F   SC
     EVERETT, Eliza S          22   F   NC   in school
     EVERETT, James B          22   M   NC   Laborer
     EVERETT, Sarah E          18   F   NC
     EVERETT, Hardy W          16   M   NC   Laborer
     EVERETT, Henry F          14   M   NC   in school
     EVERETT, Riley M          11   M   TN   in school
     EVERETT, Rachel E          7   F   TN

#796 STEPHENS, Robert          66   M   VA   Planter      4,000
     STEPHENS, Rebecca         52   F   KY
     STEPHENS, Richard S       25   M   KY   Planter
     STEPHENS, Rebecca         18   F   KY
     STEPHENS, Thomas          16   M   KY   in school
     STEPHENS, Ann S           13   F   MS   in school
#797 HAYES, Elizabeth          28   F   KY   (STEPHENS, Elizabeth)
     HAYES, Rebecca H           7   F   MS

#798 RATCLIFF, Sam'l N         49   M   TN   Overseer
     RATCLIFF, Nancy           47   F   SC   (HAYES, Nancy)
     RATCLIFF, Sam'l H         14   M   MS   in school
     RATCLIFF, Calvin          12   M   MS   in school
     RATCLIFF, Nancy           10   F   MS   in school

#799 TWINER, John T            21   M   MS   Overseer (ROBINETT, Martha)

#800 GARDNER, Jesse            49   M   GA   Planter      4,000
     GARDNER, Mary E           28   F   MS   (PERRY, Mary)
```

```
#801 WINN, R. M.              44    M   VA   Tavern Keeper   2,600
     WINN, E. S.              32    F   VA
     KEYZER, A. R.            12    M   MS   in school
     WINN, C. V.               8    F   MS   in school
     WINN, J. B.               5    M   MS
     WINN, L.                  8    F   MS
     WINN, R. M. Jr.        6/12    M   MS
     GRAVES, A. B.            28    M   KY   Clerk
     ROYALL, J. M.            22    M   TN
     ROYALL, L. E.            18    F   TN   (ROYALL, Louisianna E)
     ROYALL, J. ?            13    F   TN   in school
     WINN, E. B.              29    F   TN
     WINN, K.                 69    F   VA
     MAYNARD, M. C.           17    F   TN
     DIXON, Geo. B.           42    M   VA   (CREECY, Carissandra)
     DABBS, J. W.             33    M   SC   Merchant
     CLARK, J. J.             22    M   TN   Tailor
     DEMENT, J. R.            23    M   KY   Brick Layer
     NUNNALLY, H. A.          27    M   AL   Merchant   300
     JENNINGS, R. T.          30    M   SC   Merchant
     MANN, C. T.              27    M   ME   Apothecary(Charles md HUGHES, M)
     POWELL, G. M.            25    M   KY   Clerk (Geo.M md BOURUS, Sophia)
     FOUCHEE, J. J.           30    M   MS   Saddler   5,000
     MATTINGLY, J. R.         27    M   KY   Saddler
     WILSON, Talbot           37    M   TN   Merchant
     CLEYMERE, A. J           25    M   SWITZERLAND   Music Teacher
     AVERY, M. G.            27?    M   OH   Tinner
     HOUSTON, H.              30    M   KY   Bar Keeper
     WALDO, C. M.             25    M   NJ   Tailor
     MOBLEY, M. R.            24    M   MS   Clerk  (THARP, Caroline E)
     RUPERT, P. J.            34    M   GERMANY  Merchant
     O'DONNELL, P.            34    M   IRELAND  Merchant   30,000
     CHAMBERS, B. F.          23    M   MD   Clerk
     EPPERSON, W. S.          21    M   TN   Clerk
     RUSSELL, J. T. Jr.       26    M   NJ   Clerk 1,500 (MARKHAM, Frances)
     COLLINS, A. J.           30    M   NC   Hack Driver 400
     BEAVER, J.               40    M   GERMANY       Pedlar
     CRIBBS, Abraham          37    M   OH   Stage Driver
     O'REILLY, J. E.          21    M   AL            6,000
     FLEMING, W. C.           27    M   VA   Carpenter   1,500
#802 JOHNSON, J. M.           26    M   AL   Livery Keeper
     JOHNSON, M. H            25    M   KY

#803 CALDWELL, J. V.          41    M   SC   Merchant   2,100
     CALDWELL, S. J.          30    F   VA   (FUQUA, Sarah J)
     CALDWELL, Bailey          7    M   MS   in school
     CALDWELL, M. A.           4    F   MS
     HEATH, John T            32    M   VA   Clerk

#804 DEVLIN, J. M.            38    M   SC   Merchant (HADEN, Mary Morten)
     DEVLIN, G. F.            22    F   ENG  (BARNETT, Georgianna F)
     DEVLIN, W. B.             2    M   MS
     BARRETT, Francis         45    F   ENGLAND
     DEVLIN, F.             6/12    M   MS
```

```
#805  POPE, P. B.            44  M  SC  Merchant    3,600
      POPE, S. G.            35  F  NC
      POPE, Irene            11  F  MS  in school
      POPE, Ophelia           9  F  MS  in school
      POPE, S. G.             6  F  MS
      POPE, W. C.             4  M  MS
      POPE, Emina             1  F  MS

#806  TAMBORNINE, D.         38  M  ITALY   Merchant
      CATES, J. S.           22  M  MS  Clerk

#807  RUNDELL, E. B.         32  M  NY  Clerk     2,000
      RUNDELL, H. J.         25  F  LA  (POTTS? Ellen J)
      POTTS, R. E.           11  M  MS
      POTTS, Z. W.            9  F  MS
      RUNDELL, E. A.          2  F  MS

#808  POWELL, B. F.          35  M  TN  Steam Boat Captain
      PARASOTT, Sherman      21  M  MS  Pilot
      HOGAN, W. H.           26  M  KY  Clerk (MILES, Mary Jane)
      LAMKIN, D. W.          20  M  GA  Clerk
      PEIRCE, Lewis          29  M  DE  Mate
      HAND, Stephen          25  M  NY  Watchman
      MITCHELL, Edward       25  M  IN  Engineerer
      GREEN, Martin          22  M  PA  Engineerer
      COCHRAN, Augustus      20  M  KY  Engineerer
      GOODRUM, W. M.         26  M  MS  Bar Keeper

#809  FUTRALL, R. A.         28  M  KY  Pilot
      FUTRALL, M. A.         24  F  MS  (McCOMBS, Mary D)

#810  AVERY, W. D.           29  M  OH  Tinner
      AVERY, J. J.            4  M  MS
      AVERY, Eliza            2  F  MS

#811  VINCENT, Francis       36  M  FRANCE          Merchant
      VINCENT, Virginia      20  F  FRANCE
      VEIRNN, Joseph          8  M  FRANCE          in school

#812  ROYSTER, Nathaniel     38  M  VA  Painter     800
      ROYSTER, E. J.         20  F  PA  (STILLY, Ellen J) 1,500
      STILLY, M.             45  F  PA
      HANNA, J. B.           30  M  IL  Bar Keeper

#813  LYNCH, A.              35  M  PA
      LINCH, Mary            20  F  ITALY
      LINCH, Jeanette         2  F  MS
```

```
#814 WINN, O.               42   M  VA   Carpenter  1,500
     WINN, E. B.            34   F  KY
     WINN, S. D.            10   M  AR   in school
     WINN, M. E.             8   F  TN   in school
     WINN, W. S.             2   M  MS
#815 LAND, William         30   M  IN   Pilot
     LAND, Susan           25   F  GA
     BAKER, Thomas         28   M  AL   Carpenter   500
     FERRELL, William      30   M  IRELAND Plasterer (DOWER, B)
     GARROTT, J. B.        25   M  NC   Overseer

#816 RAMMELSBERG, Hugo     23   M  PRUSIA     Barber

#817 WEDEKIND, C           34   M  GERMANY    Shoe Maker   350
     WEDEKIND, Mary        30   F  GERMANY (HUSMAN? Mary)
     SCHAFER, N.           43   M  GERMANY    Shoe Maker

#818 WESLING, John H       37   M  GERMANY    Merchant   2,500
     WESLING, Mary A       28   F  GERMANY
     WHELENBERG, Herman    13   M  GERMANY

#819 ROSSI, Charles        28   M  ITALY      Merchant   1,000

#820 LINK, J. J.           38   M  CANADA     Merchant   1,000
     LINK, Rachal          26   F  SC   (INGRAM, Rachel)
     LINK, John             8   M  MS   in school
     LINK, Elizabeth        4   F  TX
     LINK, Mary             1   F  TX
     MILLER, Caroline      14   F  AL   in school (HAMPTON, Wade)

#821 LINK, Noah D          36   M  CANADA  Merchant 15,000 (Louisa)
     LINK, M. E.           17   F  MS   (HOWARD, Mary E)
     LINK, Louisa           5   F  MS
     LINK, Amelia           3   F  MS
     LINK, Cha. S. C.       1   M  MS

#822 LANDER, Peter         35   M  PRUSSIA    Shoe Maker
     LANDER, M. A.         26   F  PA
     LANDER, M. J.          9   F  OH
     LANDER, C. F.          4   M  MS
     LANDER, John H         2   M  MS
     LANDER, M. H        2/12   M  MS
     QUIGLEY, Edward       50   M  PA         Shoe Maker
#823 STILLEY, J. H.        53   M  DE         Shoe Maker
     STILLEY, M. M.        48   F  PA
     SCANLAND, Michael     24   M  IRELAND    Shoe Maker
     O'CONNER, James       32   M  IRELAND    Shoe Maker
     O'ROURKER, David      25   M  IRELAND    Shoe Maker
     GREEN, James          40   M  IRELAND    Shoe Maker
     DUNN, Patrick         26   M  IRELAND    Shoe Maker
```

```
#824 HOBSON, N. W.           39  M  GA      Farmer        1,500
     HOBSON, M. B.           29  F  SC
     HOBSON, O. A.           11  M  AL      in school
     HOBSON, C. A.           10  F  AL      in school
     HOBSON, J. B.            8  M  MS      in school
     HOBSON, T. L.            6  M  MS      in school
     HOBSON, M. A.            5  F  MS      in school
     HOBSON, Ophelia E.       3  F  MS
     HOBSON, Harry            1  M  MS

#825 WRIGHT, William         52  M  VA      Clerk
     WRIGHT, M. C. S.        50  F  VA
     WRIGHT, Wm. Sl.         22  M  MO      Clerk
     WRIGHT, John M          18  M  MO      in school
     WRIGHT, M. A.           15  F  MO      in school
     WRIGHT, M. F.           13  F  MO      in school
     WRIGHT, A. S.           10  F  MO      in school
#826 KIDD, H. B.             32  M  KY      Physician     3,000
     KIDD, R. E.             27  F  VA      (WRIGHT, Rebecca E)
#827 LEWIS, J. C.            35  M  SC      Merchant     10,000
     LEWIS, Lucy C            9  F  MS      in school
     LEWIS, E. H.             7  F  MS      in school
     LEWIS, W. C.             4  M  MS
     LEWIS, M. A.             2  F  MS
     WILLIAMSON, R. R.       34  M  NC      Merchant
     ELLIS, N. W.            36  M  SC      Merchant
     ALLEN, J. M.            32  M  TN      Merchant
     RANDOLPH, L. W.         28  M  VA      Clerk
     COOK, Peter B.          22  M  SC      Student {DAVIS, Margaret}
     CASTIN, John F          24  M  MS      Clerk
     GHELL, Geo.             22  M  SC      Clerk

#828 LEAR, John              40  M  GERMANY  Merchant {DRENNING, Eliza}
     HAVERKAMP, J. H.        18  M  GERMANY       Clerk

#829 NELSMIRTH, Catherine    62  F  VA      House Keeper
     RICHARDSON, Catherine   26  F  MS      in school
     O'REILLY, Thomas        38  M  IRELAND       Ditcher
     COTTON, Thomas          19  M  MS      Laborer
     HINES, Riply            30  M  AL      Carpenter
     HINES, Thomas           19  M  MS      Carpenter
     RUNNELLS, Henry         12  M  IRELAND
     McCLOUD, G. A.          40  M  NY      Raftsman
     GRIFFITH, John          35  M  MS      (DERBIN, Catherine)

#830 ROCK, George            45  M  ITALY         Grocery Keeper

#831 FRAULEY, John           40  M  IRELAND       Merchant
     MILLER, F. E.           26  M  MS            Clerk

#832 MALONE, Thomas          47  M  IRELAND       Miller    8,000
     MALONE, Margarett       25  F  IRELAND  (KAYS, Margaret)
```

```
#833 GRIMME, Franz            37  M  GERMANY        Miller   4,600
     GRIMME, T. B.            37  M  GERMANY
     GRIMME, Mary            19  F  GERMANY
#834 HAGMAN, M. A.           40  F  GERMANY
     HAGMAN, T. B.            7  M  GERMANY

#835 MALONE, Michael         37  M  IRELAND        Clerk    1,000
     ROSEMEYER, Fred         37  M  GERMANY        Lawyer     650
     NICEMAN, Peter          37  M  GERMANY        Laborer
     KOHLMAN, Henry          43  M  GERMANY        Laborer
     WALKER, John            25  M  SC             Laborer
     McGRATH, Patrick        30  M  IRELAND        Laborer
     RIDEGAN, Edmund         22  M  IRELAND        Laborer
     DRISCOL, John           35  M  IRELAND        Laborer
     PATTERSON, Alexander    30  M  SCOTLAND       Laborer
     HONINGTON, Patrick      35  M  IRELAND        Laborer
     MAULDING, Wm.           25  M  KY             Laborer
     BUTLER, John            30  M  IRELAND        Laborer
     KENNEDY, Patrick        27  M  IRELAND        Laborer
     DONAVAN, James          30  M  IRELAND        Laborer

#836 SUMNER, Henry           38  M  GERMANY        Lawyer   2,000
     SUMNER, Mary J          25  F  GERMANY
     SUMNER, Franz            3  M  MS
     SUMNER, Mary             1  F  MS

#837 COLTON, John            30  M  IRELAND        Laborer    400
     COLTON, Orvin            7  M  IRELAND
     COLTON, Ann             12  F  IRELAND
#838 KELLY, Hugh             33  M  IRELAND        Laborer
     KELLY, Eliza            27  F  IRELAND
     KELLY, Ann               5  F  IN
     KELLY, Ellen             3  F  IN
     KELLY, Eliza             1  F  MS
     McKENNA, Ann            30  F  IRELAND (COLTON, John} above
     COLTON, Francis         36  M  IRELAND        Laborer

#839 HOLMES, Charles         38  M  NY  Merchant   15,000
     HOLMES, Julia C.        26  F  TN  (HICKS, Julia C)
     HOLMES, C. E.            5  M  MS
     HOLMES, G. H.            2  M  MS
     PENNY, James            38  M  NC  Clerk
     HOLMES, Horace          24  M  NY  Clerk
     HICKS, C. W.            24  M  TN  Merchant

#840 WALLIS, P. C.           36  M  MD  Steam Boat Capt. 2,000
     WALLIS, F. J.           28  F  MD
     WALLIS, V. E.           11  F  MS  in school
     WALLIS, A. L.            3  F  MS

#841 METZLER, Thomas         38  M  PA  Engineerer 500
     METZLER, M. A.          12  F  PA  in school
     METZLER, J. T.          10  M  AR  in school
```

```
#842  PAGE, J. A. W.           36   M   NC   Clerk          700
      PAGE, Elizabeth C        28   F   AL
      PAGE, Anderson            6   M   MS

#843  CORBIN, R. R.            49   M   VA   Physician    1,000
      CORBIN, M. K.            36   F   VA
      CORBIN, Charles F. W.     3   M   MS
      CORBIN, M. F. Perkins  6/12   M   MS
#844  PERKINS, A. S.           33   M   MA   Clerk        3,000
      PERKINS, F. M.           20   F   VA   (CORBIN, Frances M)
      PERKINS, M. V. F.      9/12   F   MS

#845  ANDERSON, John M         50   M   NC   Overseer       300
      ANDERSON, J. H. F.       11   M   MS   in school
      MARTIN, John             38   M   GERMANY      Shingle Maker
      WILLIAMS, James          25   M   MS   Laborer
      REED, J. M.              34   M   MA   Engineerer
      COLLIOTT, Joseph         38   M   TN   Laborer

#846  NILEY, John              39   M   GERMANY      Laborer
      NILEY, Mary              35   F   MS
      NILEY, Perry              8   M   MS   in school
      NILEY, Margaret           7   F   MS   in school
      NILEY, Alonzo          6/12   M   MS

#847  ANDERSON, G. G.          42   M   TN   Carpenter
      ANDERSON, B. S.          28   F   MS
      ANDERSON, V. K.           1   F   MS
      MARBLE, S. M.            23   M   MS   Painter
      MORGAN, J. M.            35   M   NY   Raftsman

#848  BRIDGES, J. T            45   M   TN
      BRIDGES, Margaret        28   F   AL
      BRIDGES, Catherine       13   F   MS   in school
      BRIDGES, R. J.            7   M   MS   in school
      PHILLIPS, Joseph          4   M   MS
      MERCHANT, William         4   M   MS

#849  BARNETT, James W.        37   M   VA   Physician   10,000
      BARNETT, M. T.           31   F   VA   (RANDOLPH, Mary T)
      BARNETT, B. N.           12   M   MS   in school
      BARNETT, Emma             9   F   MS   in school
      BARNETT, Lucy             7   F   MS   in school
      BARNETT, E. R.            4   M   MS
      BARNETT, Richard          2   M   MS

#850  LEAKE, Wm. J             35   M   VA   Physician    2,900
      LEAKE, M. L.             26   F   KY
      LEAKE, H. K.              3   M   MS
      KEIRN, W. L.             19   M   TN   Student

#851  BAXTER, Robert           27   M   TN   Laborer
      BAXTER, Mary             22   F   KY   (BARROW, Mary)
      BARROW, Wm.               6   M   MS
#852  FIELDS, David            30   M   TN   Raftsman
      FIELDS, Sarah            25   F   SC
```

```
#853  CARROLL, E. A.          28  F  AL
      CARROLL, M. F.           2  F  MS
      GILLMORE, Y. A.         40  M  GA   Raftsman  (SULLIVAN, Kezah)

#854  LAVENBERG, Levi         31  M  PRUSSIA          Merchant
      LAVENBERG, Amelia       21  F  GERMANY          Married this year
      MYERS, Elizabeth         2  F  LA
      LIVINGSTON, Philip      21  M  PRUSSIA          Pedler
      ROCHILD, Fanny          21  F  GERMANY
      LIVINGIN, Newman        19  M  PRUSSIA          Pedler
      BURLING, Julius         26  M  GERMANY          Pedler
      LIPMAN, Abraham         25  M  PRUSSIA          Pedler
      MORRIS, M.              26  M  PRUSSIA          Pedler
      LAVENBERG, Jacob        28  M  PRUSSIA          Merchant

#855  HORNE, J. B.            32  M  NC   Painter     600
      HORNE, S. J.            28  F  MS
      HORNE, M. E.            12  F  MS   in school
      HORNE, N. H             10  F  MS   in school
      HORNE, M. F.             7  F  MS
      HORNE, J. B.             5  M  MS
      HORNE, W. Q.             3  M  MS
      An Infant Child       6/12  M  MS   (Prob. James Barnett Horne)

#856  ROBERTS, C. D.          40  M  NC   Planter     6,000
      ROBERTS, M. J.          32  F  GA
      ROBERTS, Leroy           4  M  MS
      ROBERTS, Medora          2  F  MS

#857  SMITH, Henry            35  M  GERMANY          Drayman?    300
      SMITH, C. E.            24  F  GERMANY
      SMITH, H. H.             2  M  MS
      AIRESOLE, J. H.         50  M  GERMANY          Laborer

#858  GEUYER, Jules           33  M  GERMANY          Tobacconist
      GEUYER, J. M. A.        22  F  GERMANY
      GEUYER, H. R.            3  M  LA

#859  BRADFORD, Wm.           45  M  IRELAND          Merchant
      BURNES, Patrick         36  M  IRELAND          Cook

#860  SORRELLS, James         29  M  MS   Carpenter
      SORRELLS, Mila          28  F  MS   (MATHEWS, Emila)
      MATHEWS, Sam'l           5  M  MS
      SORRELLS, E. A.          6  F  MS
      SORRELLS, Allen         25  M  MS   Carpenter
#861  SORRELLS, A. C.         23  M  MS   Farmer
      SORRELLS, S. J.         19  F  MS
      SORRELLS, Henry Jr.      1  M  MS
      SORRELLS, Henry Sr.     21  M  MS   Laborer
      SORRELLS, Sam'l         19  M  MS   Laborer
```

```
#862 McELEVEE, John            65  M  SC        Merchant
     McELEVEE, Martha          60  F  NC
     McELEVEE, Elvy            30  F  SC        5,000
     PEARSALL, Charlotte       11  F  MS
     GIBB, Andrew              47  M  SCOTLAND        Merchant    200
     JEFFERY, John             40  M  SCOTLAND        Merchant

#863 MURRY, Thomas             32  M  IRELAND         Merchant
     CRAVENDOUGH, John         30  M  IRELAND         Baker
     CHENOWITH, Gabriel        38  M  KY              Shingle Maker
     FLOYD, M (smear)          25  M  NC              Laborer
     CURRY, Patrick            25  M  IRELAND         Laborer
     O'CONNER, James           37  M  IRELAND         Laborer
     HYATT, Richard            28  M  IRELAND         Farmer
     MURRAY, Wm.               55  M  IRELAND         Laborer

#864 BRASHEAR, A. B.           37  M  MD              Physician   700
     BRASHEAR, E. J.           19  F  MS    (SWISHER, Elizabeth J)
     BRASHEAR, C? C.            1  M  MS
     DIXON, Duncan              5  M  MS
     HARDIN, A. M.             35  M  KY              Merchant

#865 MITCHELL, S. V.           40  M  ME              Merchant
     MITCHELL, E. A.           32  F  TN
     EVANS, John H.            32  M  VA              Clerk      400
     RATCLIFF, J. N.           28  M  MS              Clerk      3,000

#866 BLUNK, Sam'l              48  M  IN              Laborer
     BLUNK, Eliza              22  F  MS
     BLUNK, J. E.               4  M  MS
     BLUNK, W. B.               8  M  MS    in school

#867 HOLLINGSWORTH, D. M.      24  M  GA    Cabinet Maker
     HOLLINGSWORTH, C.         21  F  LA    1,000 (BOWER, Caroline)
     HOLLINGSWORTH, Lewis       2  M  MS

#868 HOLLINGSWORTH, Elizabeth 60  F  NC    800 (NEWBERRY, Elizabeth)
     HOLLINGSWORTH, Isaac      22  M  GA    Merchant
     HOLLINGSWORTH, James      20  M  GA    Cabinet Maker
     HOLLINGSWORTH, Franklin   13  M  GA    in school
#869 PITMAN, Mary              20  F  GA
     BOWER, E. L.              24  M  LA    Merchant

#870 HAHN, George              45  M  MD    Carpenter   2,600
     HAHN, E. A.               30  F  OH    350
     HAHN, John                18  M  OH    Carpenter
     HAHN, Geo. E.             12  M  MS    in school
     HAHN, Otho J. R.           5  M  MS
     HAHN, A. E.               10  F  MS    in school
```

```
#871  PRIMM, C. H.           33   M   TN      Saddler      125
      PRIMM, A. R.           30   F   TN
      PRIMM, John B          13   M   TN      in school
      PRIMM, W. J.           11   F   TN      in school
      PRIMM, Mary A           9   F   TN      in school
      PRIMM, Lucy             7   F   TN
      WEDELL, John B.        20   M   TN      Saddler
      VANCLEVE, Thos. V.     18   M   TN      Saddler (CRESWELL, Rachel)

#872  GRIFFITH, Charles      35   M   ENGLAND         Gun Smith
      GRIFFITH, A. R.        33   F   VA
      GRIFFITH, Henry        13   M   VA      in school
      GRIFFITH, Ann           7   F   VA      in school
      GRIFFITH, Eliza         4   F   OH
      GRIFFITH, Joseph        2   M   MS

#873  CAYES, E. B.           32   M   KY      Tailor  1,000 (JOHNSON, Eliza)
      CAYCE, Lydia           24   F   TN      (HANNA, Lydia)
      CAYCE, Linda?           4   F   MS
      HANNA, Noreissa        45   F   TN
      HANNA, Corinne          4   F   MS

#874  NILES, J. W. J.        36   M   CT      Banker       16,000
      NILES, E. A.           35   F   MS
      NILES, S. L. G.        10   M   TX      in school

#875  SMITH, Alex            38   M   NC      Cashier      2,500
      SMITH, F. M. E.        22   F   MS      (GOOSEY, Frances M. E)
      BOYLEY, B. A.          12   F   TN      in school

#876  PICKETT, R. K.         42   M   SC      Merchant     10,00
      PICKETT, S. C.         38   F   MS      (JENKINS, Sarah C)
      PICKETT, Wm            13   M   MS      in school
      PICKETT, Georgeana     11   F   MS      in school
      PICKETT, Mary           9   F   MS      in school
      PICKETT, J. M.          7   M   MS      in school

#877  HYATT, L. L.           36   M   RI      Merchant
      HYATT, R. P.           23   F   MS
      HYATT, Ann              4   F   MS
      HYATT, F. M.            1   M   MS

#878  WILSON, T. J.          30   M   MD      Merchant     8,000
      WILSON, A. C.          24   F   MS      (MARTIN,? Adeline C?)
      WILSON, L. L. S.       65   F   MD
      KENNEDY, M. O. C.      43   M   IRELAND         Merchant4,000
      KENNEDY, A. M.          7   F   MS
      KENNEDY, Claire         5   F   MS
```

```
#879  HAGMAN, John           40    M   GERMANY            Tailor    5,000
      HAGMAN, Thekla         29    F   GERMANY     (CLOK, Thakla)
      HAGMAN, Theresa         4    F   MS
      HAGMAN, Charles        29    M   GERMANY            Laborer
      SCHOULTER, J. H.       26    M   GERMANY            Laborer
      BRISTIL, Thomas        34    M   GERMANY            Laborer
      HENSINGER, Joseph      35    M   GERMANY            Laborer
      CARY, Thomas           40    M   IRELAND            Laborer
      HAUMAKIN, Thomas       25    M   IRELAND

#880  NICHOLS, William       74    M   ENGLAND            Architec?  8,000
      NICHOLS, Lydia         44    F   NC

#881  JONES, G. W.           30    M   GA   Printer        500
      JONES, Melvina         26    F   GA
      JONES, M. E.            8    F   GA   in school
      JONES, E. M.            3    F   MS
      JONES, Leake            1    M   MS

#882  KIMBALL, Susan         30    F   MS   House Keeper    960?
      KIMBALL, S. R.          9    F   MS   in school

#776  MASSEY, S. T.                M   (These two names were out of
      JAMES, D. A.                 M    order and only had this info)

#883  CRANE, W. C.           34    M   VA   Minister Bapt.400
      CRANE, C. J.           21    F   VA
      CRANE, W. C.            4    M   MS
      CRANE, A. D.            2    F   MS

#884  BURRUS, James R        37    M   TN   Lawyer      7,000
      BURRUS, L. P.          20    F   GA   (WALKER, Laurentina Ophelia)
      BURRUS, W. P.           3    M   MS
      BURRUS, E. E.       11/12    F   MS

#885  WALKER, D.             30    M   LA   Editor Dimveras?  400
      WALKER, J. A.          28    F   NY   Teacher
      WALKER, E. W.           6    F   MS   in school
      WALKER, R. S.           3    M   MS

#886  STEVENS, James A       41    M   PA   Printer     2,400
      STEVENS, C. A.         30    F   MD
      STEVENS, A. P.         16    M   MS   Clerk
      STEVENS, C. E.         10    M   MS   in school
      STEVENS, Theodore       4    M   MS   in school
      STEVENS, S. F.          2    F   MS
      THORN, Albert C.       25    M   LA   Painter (BRUNER, Patience)
      RODGERS, G. W.         16    M   LA   Painter

#887  REIMAN, Morris         25    M   RUSSIA            Merchant
      REIMAN, Lency          22    F   RUSSIA
      HOULBERG, F.           21    M   GERMANY
```

```
#888  BLUNDELL, James          32   M   ENGLAND        Drugist1,800
      BLUNDELL, D. E.          24   F   KY    (GRAVES, D. F.)
      BLUNDELL, G. P.           4   M   MS
      BLUNDELL, V. A.           2   F   MS

#889  THOMPSON, R. N.          40   M   SC    Drugist     1,200
      THOMPSON, E. W.          30   F   TN    (DIBRELL, Elizabeth Watson)
      PEASE, John B            10   M   TN    in school {EVANS, Emma}
      DIBRALL, Virginia         8   F   TN    in school

#890  WEST, James R            65   M   MS    Farmer      3,000
      WEST, E. D.              46   F   CT    (Elizabeth D)
      WEST, T. S.              10   F   MS    in school
      WEST, L. D.               8   F   MS    in school
      FORBES, W. A.             8   M   MS    in school

#891  BARKSDALE, F.            32   M   TN    Merchant    8,600
      BARKSDALE, J.            25   F   MS    (PARRISOT, Josephine)
      BARKSDALE, Emily          2   F   MS
      PARASOT, Amandus         16   M   MS    in school

#892  SHROPSHIRE, John E.      36   M   KY    Merchant    1,500
      SHROPSHIRE, M. J.        34   F   KY    (WITHERS, Martha J)
      SHROPSHIRE, A. M.        16   F   MO    in school
      SHROPSHIRE, M. V.        14   F   MO    in school
      SHROPSHIRE, M. H.        12   F   MO    in school
      SHROPSHIRE, S. C.        10   F   MO    in school
      SHROPSHIRE, Emily         6   F   MS    in school
      SHROPSHIRE, James         1   M   MS
      WALLACE, Charles          4   M   MS

#893  MARKS, Isaac             22   M   PRUSSIA        Merchant
      MARKS, Susan Ann         19   F   MS    Married this year
      SCHULTZ, Henry           21   M   AUSTRIA        Clerk

#894  HARRISON, Hiram          34   M   PA    Merchant    8,000
      HARRISON, M. A.          21   F   NY    (BAKER, Margaret Ann)
      HARRISON, Lilla        6/12   F   MS
      BARRETT, W. J.                M          (was left blank)
      CLARK, D. S.             25   M   PA    Clerk

#895  RICHARDS, J. R.          51   M   MA    3,500 {KEMPTON, Eliza}
      RICHARDS, S. P.          18   F   VA
      RICHARDS, B. G.           2   M   MS
      KEMPTON, Mary            16   F   MD    Teacher      200
      KEMPTON, John            13   M   MS    in school
      KEMPTON, Wm.             11   M   MS    in school
      KEMPTON, Geo. C.         10   M   MS    in school
      KEMPTON, Sam'l D.         6   M   MS

#896  BARKSDALE, E.            25   M   TN    Editor
      BARKSDALE, A. J.         22   F   TN
      BARKSDALE, C. H.          6   M   MS

#897  BOWMAN, Edward           25   M   MS    Lawyer      2,500
      BOWMAN, Lydia A          20   F   MO    (DORSEY, Lydia)
```

```
#898 NYE, N. G.              43   M   TN   Lawyer      10,000
     NYE, L. A.              40   F   NC   (PERRY, L. A.) 5,000
     NYE, D. J.              19   M   TN   in school
     NYE, W. H. H.           10   M   MS   in school
     NYE, S. E.              28   M   TN   Lawyer       3,000

#899 MICHIE, John J          40   M   VA   Lawyer 12,000 (GERALD, Elnora)

#900 EVANS, Richard          35   M   VA   Overseer

#901 BLACKMAN, C. J.         37   M   TN   Tavern Keeper
     WYMAN, Wm.                   M        (was left blank)
     TERBERVILLE, M. J.      42   M   VA   Carpenter    100
     WINCAUGH,                    M        (was left blank)
     GILLESPIE, D. A.        35   M   LA   (smeared)    750

#902 GIBBS, Q. D.            35   M   TN   Lawyer      20,000
     GIBBS, S. A.            31   F   KY   (DORSEY, Sarah)
     GIBBS, W. D.            11   M   MS
     GIBBS, L. A.             7   F   TN
     GIBBS, G. A.             6   M   MS
     GIBBS, W. S.             4   M   MS
     GIBBS, Barnett        6/12   M   MS

#903 LAMKIN, William F       27   M   GA   Clerk

#904 JOHNSON, Abel B.        27   M   KY   Brick Layer
     JOHNSON, Martha         21   F   OH
     JOHNSON, Marcellus       1   M   MS

#905 JACKSON, James          48   M   NC   Farmer
     JACKSON, Charity B      47   F   NC
     JACKSON, James W        13   M   NC   in school
     JACKSON, Elizabeth      10   F   NC   in school
     JACKSON, Chelly M        9   F   NC   in school
     JACKSON, E.              8   F   NC

#906 HARRISON, Sam'l         25   M   OH   Bar Keeper

#907 HAYMAN, Henry           38   M   KY   Merchant (HALL,?Mary A?)
     HAYMAN, John            12   M   MS   in school

#908 McCLEARY, J. A.         31   M   ATLANTIC OCEAN    Gin Wright

#909 MILLER, Joseph          24   M   VA   Grocery Keeper
     BRANNON, Edward         41   M   OH   Carpenter
     MARSHALL, Henry         43   M   NH   Carpenter
     BROOMFIELD, John S.     20   M   MS   Clerk

#910 THARP, James            33   M   OH   Merchant
     THARP, Mary P           30   F   OH
     THARP, Emma              5   F   MS   in school
     THARP, Adelade           4   F   OH
     THARP, James W       1 1/2   M   MS
     THARP, one infant     6/12   F   MS
     BAKER, M. P.            27   M   VA   Saddler
```

```
#911 WHITE, Greenup           53   M   KY
     WHITE, Margaret          60   F   VA   800
     HANNA, John               7   M   MS
     WHITE, B. G. S.           6   M   TX
     WHITE, Wm. V             19   M   TN   Brick Mayson

#912 McFARLAND, John          30   M   IRELAND        Merchant  3,000

#913 WILSON, R. B.            35   M   PA   Brick Mason 3,000 {Sarah E}
     WILSON, David            25   M   PA   Plasterer
     KIRMAN, Mary             40   F   PA
     KIRMAN, Chs. D.           7   M   OH
#914 WILSON, John C.          29   M   PA   Livery-Keeper 1,000
     WILSON, Martha J.        17   F   MS   (PHILLIPS, Martha Jerusha)

#915 DORMAN, D. A.            31   M   MA   Physician
     DORMAN, ? J.             22   F   GA
     DORMAN, Sarah E.          3   F   MS
     DORMAN, Cora J.           1   F   MS

#916 BELL, James H.           24   M   AL   Probate Clerk
     BELL, M. E.              20   F   MS   (JOHNSON, Mary Elizabeth)
     BELL, L. C.           2 1/2   F   MS
     BELL, Jane                1   F   MS
     BELL, J. P.              52   F   VA
     BELL, W. H.              22   M   AL

#917 FUGUA, John W.           38   M   VA   Sheriff  {LEWIS, Mary T}
     FUGUA, Sarah             30   F   MD   (JACKSON, Sarah C)
     FUGUA, Sam'l L.          12   M   MS   in school
     FUGUA, Eliza H        10 1/2   F   MS   in school
     FUGUA, Sarah D.           9   F   MS   in school
     FUGUA, Mary J             7   F   MS   in school
     FUGUA, Louisa G.          5   F   MS   in school
     FUGUA, Albert M.          4   M   MS
     FUGUA, John W.            2   M   MS
     FUGUA, Hibernia J.        1   F   MS
     JACKSON, Henrietta S.    11   F   MS   in school
     JACKSON, Edward A.        9   M   MS   in school

#918 BARRETT, Wm. J.          23   M   ENGLISH CHANNEL Clerk

#919 HENDERSON, A. W.         26   M   MD   Clerk

#920 HICKS, C. W.             23   M   TN   Merchant

#921 MAIER, Moses             21   M   BAVARIA        Clerk

#922 WILSON, John I.          39   M   MD   Merchant   20,000
     WILSON, Pauline          22   F   TN   (PERRY, Pauline)
     WILSON, John F.          11   M   MS   in school
     WILSON, Robt. C.          9   M   MS   in school
     WILSON, Pauline A.        4   F   MS
     WILSON, Nat. N.        6/12   M   MS
```

```
#923  JOHNSTON, James          42   M   NC   Miller
      JOHNSTON, Mary Ann       35   F   OH   3,000
      JOHNSTON, Jane E.        13   F   IN
      JOHNSTON, Louisa         11   F   IN
      JOHNSTON, Wm.            19   M   IN   Engineener
      JOHNSTON, Thos. J.       17   M   IN   Student       in school

#924  HUNTER, John A.          48   M   NC   Clerk  (WILKINSON?, Nancy)
      HUNTER, Elizabeth        42   F   NC
      HUNTER, Aramesia         15   F   NC   in school
      HUNTER, E. R.            13   F   MS   in school
      HUNTER, Isaac H. J?      21   M   NC   Clerk

#925  MOORE, J. W.             24   M   NY   Brickmason

#926  JENKINS, M. A.           38   M   MS   County Treasure
      JENKINS, R. O.           32   F   KY   (Rosalie O)
      JENKINS, E. C.           14   F   MS   in school
      JENKINS, Geo. C.         12   M   MS   in school
      JENKINS, Mary E.         10   F   MS   in school
      JENKINS, Carter           8   M   MS   in school
      JENKINS, Sarah            6   F   MS
      JENKINS, Frank            4   M   MS
      JENKINS, Augustus         2   M

#927  STAMM, Henry             38   M   PA   Carpenter    3,000
      STAMM, Eliza             38   F   MS
      STAMM, Henry             11   M   MS
      ROBINSON, Thomas         36   M   GA   Carpenter

#928  HIGH, John               35   M   PA   Butcher   (LONG, Mary)
      HIGH, M. E.              12   F   MS   in school
      HIGH, Lelia L.            5   F   MS   in school

#929  SHANDS, A. C.            29   M   VA   Brickmason

#930  HANNA, John C.           36   M   TN   Overseer

#931  EASDON, John B.          28   M   SCOTLAND       Carpenter
      EASDON, Margarett        21   F   PA   (STILLEY, Margaretta)
      EASDON, Walker            3   M   MS

#932  WRIGHT, S. S.            29   M   VA   Lawyer
      WRIGHT, J. M.            20   F   VA
      WRIGHT, Mary S.           3   F   MS
      WRIGHT, S. S.          1/12   M   MS

#932  BIRNHAM, George          36   M   LOWER CANADA    Carpenter
      BIRNHAM, Sophia          34   F   KY
      HARRIS, Geo.             13   M   LA   in school
      HARRIS, Sam'l            11   M   MS   in school
      HARRIS, Alma              7   F   MS   in school
      HARRIS, Clara             5   F   MS   in school
```

```
#933 PUGH, Wm. E.             41  M  NC  Lawyer      7,400
     PUGH, Martha E.          20  F  TN  (MITCHELL, Martha E.)
     PUGH, Wm. D.              3  M  MS
     PUGH, Henry G.            1  M  MS

#934 WARREN, John            72  M  NC  Planter {VAUGHAN, Priscilla)

#935 COONEY, John            25  M  IRELAND      Laborer
     COONEY, Bridget         25  F  IRELAND  (RYAN, Bridget)

#936 YOUNG, John C.          34  M  OH  Carpenter   1,500
     YOUNG, M. A.            34  M  NJ
     YOUNG, Anderson J.      12  M  OH  in school
     YOUNG, Isaac            10  M  OH  in school
     YOUNG, Laura             8  F  OH  in school

#937 BROWN, T. A.            26  M  IN  Tinner

#938 THORNTON, Albert        27  M  LA  Painter

#939 CLEARY, John            34  M  NY  Bar Keeper

#940 WILSON, Sam'l H.        38  M  PA  Watchmaker  1,800
     WILSON, Mary F          20  F  TN  (WHITMAN, Mary Frances)
     WILSON, Henry S          3  M  MS
#941 WHITMAN, Sophia         50  F  OH  (TILLAYE, Sophia)
     WHITMAN, Nostrand       17  M  TN  Watch Maker
     WHITMAN, Charles        13  M  MS  in school
     WHITMAN, Ulysis          5  M  MS
     WHITMAN, Mary            3  F  AR

#942 PUGH, N. T.             23  M  NC  Justice of Peace

#943 BENTON, Emuel?          21  M  MS

#944 MILLER, Thos. P.        26  M  MS  Clerk

#945 LAWRENCE, J. H.         38  M  MD  Lawyer
     LAWRENCE, V. D.         25  F  MS  (Virginia D)
     LAWRENCE, Upton K        9  M  MS  in school
     LAWRENCE, W. L.          5  M  MS

#946 DRISKOLL, John          31  M  IRELAND      Laborer

#947 MALONY, And.            30  M  IRELAND      Laborer

#948 LIGHT, James A.         35  M  OH  Minister
     LIGHT, Maria T.         31  F  KY

#949 QUACKENBOSS, F. W.      43  M  NY  Lawyer
     QUACKENBOSS, Mary P.    28  F  LA  (MELLEN, Mary)
     QUACKENBOSS, Emma        9  F  MS  in school
     QUACKENBOSS, Eliza C.    7  F  MS  in school
     QUACKENBOSS, J. A. Q.    3  F  MS
     QUACKENBOSS, H. M.    1/12  M  MS
```

```
#950  WILKINSON, G. B.          31  M  VA       Lawyer
      WILKINSON, Cornelia       20  F  MS       (PERKINS, Cornelia)

#951  FLEMING, Wm.              28  M  VA       Carpenter
      FLEMING, Caroline         20  F  GERMANY

#952  TYLER, Henry C.           22  M  MA       Jeweler? {CUSACK, Cornelia}

#953  GARING, Augustus          46  M  GERMANY           Butcher
      GARING, Francis?          42  F  GERMANY
      GARING, Harriet           20  F  GERMANY
      GARING, Barbary           15  F  LA
      GARING, Eliza             13  F  MS
      GARING, Joseph             6  M  MS

#954  TRANER, Terence           35  M  IRELAND           Brickmason
      TRANER, Anna M.           32  F  IRELAND  (SIBLEY, Mrs. Mariah Ann)
      KAYS, Mary M.             13  F  NY       in school

#955  McQUISTTON, M. P.         35  M  PA       Lawyer
      McQUISTTON, Amanda        34  F  MS       (REDDING, Amanda)
      REDDING, Eliz.            13  F  MS       in school
      REDDING, James            11  M  MS       in school
      REDDING, Mary              9  F  MS       in school
      REDDING, John              6  M  MS       in school

#956  STRANE, E. F.             31  M  SC
      STRANE, M. S.             22  F  TN
      STRANE, M. S.              6  F  AR

#957  PARKER, James             29  M  CT       Raftsman {HALL, Sarah}
      BLEVINS, G. B.            28  M  IN       Raftsman {COON, Nancy Ann}

#958  REYNONS, John             50  M  IRELAND           Laborer
      REYNONS, Henry            12  M  IRELAND
      REYNONS, John              8  M  IRELAND
      REYNONS, Michael           5  M  IRELAND

#959  LUCKEY, Wm.               23  M  AL       Clerk

#960  LEWIS, Mordica            47  M  TN       Laborer      3,000
      LEWIS, Margaret           36  F  VA
      LEWIS, Volney C.           6  M  MS
      LEWIS, Horace              4  M  MS

#961  GRAFTON, John B.          35  M  MS       Livery Keeper {CASHELL, Maria E}
      GRAFTON, Letitia L.        8  F  MS       in school
      GRAFTON, Laura             6  F  MS       in school

#962  WILKINSON, Edward C       46  M  VA       Lawyer       15,000
      WILKINSON, Eliza C        30  F  KY
      SLAUGHTER, Nat. G.        20  M  KY       Clerk
```

```
#963  KEYS, R. E.                36  M  OH  City Marshall
      KEYS, Eliz. M.             32  F  KY  2,000  (MARKHAM, Elizabeth M)
      MARKHAM, Frances M.        16  F  MS
      HENDERSON, Rebecca W.      55  F  VA

#964  PERRY, Nat.                37  M  TN  Planter
      PERRY, A. L.               21  F  TN  (NELSON, A. Louisa)
      PERRY, Sarah                6  F  MS
      PERRY, Elizabeth            4  M  MS
      PERRY, John                 3  M  MS
      PERRY, Nat. N.              1  M  MS

#965  EDWARDS, W. C.             28  M  OH  Carpenter
      EDWARDS, Catherine         21  F  OH
      EDWARDS, Catherine F.       4  F  OH

#966  BENTON, Malvina S.         40  F  KY
      GOODMAN, Laura J           19  F  MS

#967  THORN, Eliz.               25  F  MS
      THORN, John                 4  M  MS
      THORN, Estha                7  F  MS

#968  JONES, Peter               40  M  VA
      JONES, Thos.               42  M  VA
      SHAW, E. D.                55  F  VA

#969  PURVIS, John J             45  M  TN  Planter      4,000
      PURVIS, Eliza. E.          40  F  AL  (KING, Eliza E)
      PURVIS, John R.             1  M  MS
      PURVIS, Dorothy             5  F  MS
      PURVIS, Purlina L.          3  F  MS
      KING, Sarah B.             23  F  AL
```

```
#970 MANSFIELD, S.               24    M   MS     Physician [Sylvester]
     MANSFIELD, S.               18    F   GA     (SPENCER, Saphronia N)
     MANSFIELD, Wm.            2/12    M   MS
     MANSFIELD, S. J.           15    F   MS     {HALL, Dixon}
     RODGERS, S. M. R.          13    M   TN
     GARDNER, Jesse Jr.         18    M   MS
     GARDNER, Mary J.           16    F   MS     (BURNS, Mary Jane)
     CONVEY, George W.          35    M   OH     Carpenter
     STRODE, M. C.              25    M   OH     Blacksmith
     BARNES, Gib.               35    M   MS     Clerk
     BARNES, Frances            22    F   TN     (KEEBLES, Frances H.)
     SLADE, Ed.                  6    M   MS
     HOLLINGSWORTH, James F.    21    M   GA     Cabinet Maker
     GRUBBS, Wm. S.             26    M   TN     Grocery Keeper  7,000
     WARRICK, Robert            26    M   IRELAND      Printer
     PARMER, B. H.              16    M   MS           Printer
     PENDER, Gabriel                  M   NC
     PENDER, Nancy                    F   NC     (FRILEY, Nancy)
     STROUP, Baruch             29    M   GERMANY      Merchant   300
     STROUP, Soloman            20    M   GERMANY      Merchant
     HUGHES, J. J.              40    M   MS   Planter   55,000
     ADAMS, Edmund S.           34    M   MS   Planter
     LANGAN, (smeared)          40    M   IRELAND      Planter   20,000
     LANGAN, P. H?              37    F   VA           4,000
     O'FERRELL, John            12    M   NY
```

ARMSTRONG, George	. . . .	28
ARMSTRONG, John	. . . .	28
ARMSTRONG, Lucinda	. . . .	28
ARMSTRONG, Mary	. . . .	28
ARMSTRONG, Mary E	. . . .	77
ARMSTRONG, Sibley	. . . .	28
ARMSTRONG, Thomas	. . . .	28
ARMSTRONG, William	. . . . . .	28
ARNOLD, Maria B	. . . .	45
ARNOLD, Mary	. . . .	38
ASHBY, Sarah Ann	. . . .	45
AVERY, Eliza	. . . .	80
AVERY, J. J	. . . .	80
AVERY, M. G	. . . .	79
AVERY, W. D	. . . .	80
BAILEY, John W. C.	. . . .	39
BAILEY, Maria T	. . . .	39
BAILEY, Martha E	. . . .	39
BAILEY, Mary J	. . . .	39
BAILEY, Missouri	. . . .	39
BAILEY, Pleasant B	. . . . . .	39
BAILEY, Thomas K	. . . .	39
BAIN, Elinor	. . . .	36
BAIN, Mary	. . . .	36
BAIN, Robertson	. . . .	36
BAIN, Walter	. . . .	36
BAINS, Cyntha	. . . .	1
BAINS, Moses	. . . .	1
BAKER, Benjamin	. . . .	6
BAKER, Lutilda	. . . .	3
BAKER, M. P	. . . .	90
BAKER, Margaret Ann	. . . . . .	89
BAKER, Thomas	. . . .	81
BALFOUR, Mary J	. . . .	36
BALL, Blake R	. . . .	65
BALL, Henry	. . . .	65
BALL, Mary A. M	. . . .	65
BALL, Matilda	. . . .	65
BALL, Spencer	. . . .	65
BALLANCE, Caroline	. . . . . .	28
BALLANCE, Charle W	. . . . . .	28
BALLANCE, Eliza	. . . .	28
BALLANCE, James	. . . .	28
BALLANCE, Mary A	. . . .	28
BALLARD, Andrew J	. . . . . .	7
BALLARD, John	. . . .	7
BALLARD, Sarah R	. . . .	7
BANKS, Winston	. . . .	25
BARDGES, Henry	. . . .	20
BARFIELD, Andrew	. . . .	27
BARFIELD, George	. . . .	27
BARFIELD, John	. . . .	32
BARFIELD, Louisanna	. . . . . .	32
BARFIELD, Mary	. . . .	27
BARFIELD, Mercy	. . . .	32
BARFIELD, Mercy S	. . . .	32

BARFIELD, Nancy	. . . .	27
BARFIELD, Nathan L	. . . . .	32
BARFIELD, Rebecca	. . . . . .	32
BARFIELD, Simeon	. . . . . .	27
BARFIELD, Susan	. . . .	27
BARFIELD, Thomas C	. . . . .	32
BARKSDALE, A. J	. . . .	89
BARKSDALE, C. H	. . . .	89
BARKSDALE, E	. . . .	89
BARKSDALE, Emily	. . . . . .	89
BARKSDALE, F	. . . .	89
BARKSDALE, Fountain L	. . . .	17
BARKSDALE, Harrison	. . . . .	17
BARKSDALE, J	. . . .	89
BARKSDALE, Laura	. . . . . .	17
BARKSDALE, Lycurgus	. . . . .	17
BARKSDALE, Samuel L	. . . . .	17
BARKSDALE, William	. . . . .	17
BARNES, Frances	. . . .	96
BARNES, Gib	. . . .	96
BARNETT, B. N	. . . .	84
BARNETT, E. R	. . . .	84
BARNETT, Emma	. . . .	84
BARNETT, Georgianna F	. . . .	79
BARNETT, James W	. . . . . .	84
BARNETT, Lucy	. . . .	84
BARNETT, M. T	. . . .	84
BARNETT, Richard	. . . . . .	84
BARRETT, Francis	. . . . . .	79
BARRETT, W. J	. . . .	89
BARRETT, Wm. J	. . . .	91
BARROW, F. M	. . . .	76
BARROW, Mary	. . . .	84
BARROW, Millison	. . . . . .	76
BARROW, Nancy	. . . .	21
BARROW, S. J	. . . .	76
BARROW, Samuel	. . . .	21
BARROW, T? J	. . . .	76
BARROW, W. C	. . . .	76
BARROW, Wm	. . . .	84
BARTON, Daniel J	. . . .	8
BASS, Alfred	. . . .	20
BATES, Rachel	. . . .	48
BATES, Robert L	. . . .	48
BATHIS, Julia	. . . .	78
BATTAILE, Charles	. . . . . .	40
BATTAILE, Edmonia	. . . . . .	40
BATTAILE, Frances W	. . . . .	44
BATTAILE, Mary	. . . .	40
BATTAILE, William	. . . . . .	40
BAXTER, Mary	. . . .	84
BAXTER, Robert	. . . .	84
BEALE, Margaret T	. . . . . .	26
BEALE, Maria T	. . . .	26
BEALE, William C	. . . . . .	26
BEAUMIN, James W	. . . . . .	7

BEAVER, J	79	BERRY, Martha J	35
BECKOM, John S.	45	BERRY, Richard G	56
BECKOM, Nancy	45	BERRY, Samuel	35
BECKON, John S	74	BERRY, Susana	35
BELCHER OR PEARCE, Amanda	19	BERRY, Thomas A	35
BELEN, Mahala	49	BERRY, William H	56
BELEN, Morsin	49	BERRY, Young	35
BELL, Alfred	66	BEULL, Elenor	58
BELL, Asa	27	BEULL, Francis M	58
BELL, Berthia	66	BEULL, Joseph	58
BELL, Cornelius	27	BEULL, Sarah	58
BELL, David M	27	BIBB, Fannie May	76
BELL, Eliza	27	BILES, James	5
BELL, Elizabeth	27	BIRNHAM, George	92
BELL, Endora	27	BIRNHAM, Sophia	92
BELL, Harriet	66	BISKHEIM?, Erasmus	56
BELL, J. P	91	BLACK, Samuel	44
BELL, James H	91	BLACKMAN, Bettie	36
BELL, James R	36	BLACKMAN, C. J	90
BELL, Jane	27, 66, 91	BLACKMAN, Henry G	36
BELL, John Z	66	BLACKMAN, Isabel	36
BELL, Joseph	66	BLACKMAN, Mary J	36
BELL, Joseph W	61	BLACKMAN, Susan	36
BELL, L. C	91	BLALOCK, Alfred	61
BELL, Lucius G	6	BLALOCK, Catherine	61
BELL, M. E	91	BLALOCK, Frances E	61
BELL, Mary	66	BLALOCK, John	61
BELL, Mary Ann	48	BLALOCK, Johnathan	61
BELL, Mary R	36	BLALOCK, Mahala	61
BELL, Rachel	27	BLALOCK, Mary A	61
BELL, Rayford	36	BLALOCK, Milly	61
BELL, Robert	27	BLALOCK, Nancy	61
BELL, Tabitha	66	BLALOCK, Sarah	61
BELL, W. H	91	BLALOCK, Sarah A	61
BELLOW, Elisha	5	BLALOCK, William	61
BENNETT, Charles W	62	BLAN, Jasper J	58
BENNETT, Margaret	62	BLAN, Louisa	58
BENTLEY, Elizabeth	28	BLAN, Lucy J	58
BENTLEY, John S	29	BLAN, Nancy A	58
BENTLEY, Julia J	29	BLAN, Selina	58
BENTLEY, Nancy	29	BLAN, William	58
BENTLEY, Samuel A	29	BLAND, Sarah A	66
BENTLEY, William J	29	BLANKS, Elizabeth	13
BENTON, Emuel?	93	BLANKS, James	13
BENTON, Malvina S	95	BLANKS, John	13
BERKLEY, Jerry	77	BLANKS, Mary J	13
BERRY, Belinda	56	BLANKS, Richard	13
BERRY, Edward	56	BLEVINS, G. B	94
BERRY, Effie A	35	BLUMSON, George	56
BERRY, Elizabeth	35	BLUNDELL, D. E	89
BERRY, Israel	35	BLUNDELL, G. P	89
BERRY, James C	24	BLUNDELL, James	89
BERRY, John W	56	BLUNDELL, V. A	89
BERRY, Joseph C	35	BLUNK, Eliza	86
BERRY, Julia R	35	BLUNK, J. E	86
BERRY, Margaret E	24	BLUNK, Sam'l	86

BLUNK, W. B	86	BOYD, Thomas J	24
BOND, Henry	49	BOYKIN, Mary	47
BOND, Parnilia J	49	BOYLEY, B. A	87
BOND, Rebecca	49	BRADFORD, Wm	85
BONNEY, Beatrice	64	BRADFORD?, Mary	33
BONNEY, Caleb D	8	BRADSHAW, Alex	69
BONNEY, Charles	64	BRADSHAW, James N	11
BONNEY, Cynthia	64	BRADSHAW, Letetia	4
BONNEY, Edward	9	BRADSHAW, Sarah	4
BONNEY, Isabel	64	BRAGG, Mary Jane	43
BONNEY, Jane	64	BRAGG, Sarah	43
BONNEY, Laura E	9	BRANNEN, Harrison	4
BONNEY, Moses H	9	BRANNEN, Joseph	4
BONNEY, Sarah	9	BRANNON, Edward	90
BONNEY, Sarah J	64	BRANTLEY, Nancy	77
BONNEY, Thomas	68	BRASHEAR, A. B	86
BONNEY, William	64	BRASHEAR, C? C	86
BOOTH, Martha	49	BRASHEAR, E. J	86
BOOTH, Martha S	53	BRAZEALE, Davis	8
BOOTH, Miranda	49	BRAZEALE, Elliott F	8
BOSTICK, Emily R	47	BRAZEALE, Niaha?	8
BOSTICK, Ferdinand	47	BRICKELL, Betsey	76
BOSTICK, Martha M. P	47	BRICKELL, E. M	78
BOSWELL, Thomas R	20	BRICKELL, Elizabeth M	78
BOURG, Edward	59	BRICKELL, Henry	76
BOURG, Eldridge	59	BRICKELL, James	76
BOURG, Elizabeth	59	BRICKELL, Lemenda	76
BOURG, Lecra?	59	BRICKELL, Mary	76
BOURG, Zenon	59	BRICKELL, Wm A.	78
BOURUS, Sophia	79	BRIDGE, Davis	42
BOVARD, Mary J. F	21	BRIDGE, John	42
BOWER, Caroline	86	BRIDGE, Mahala	42
BOWER, E. L	86	BRIDGE, William	42
BOWMAN, Claiborne	51	BRIDGES, Catherine	84
BOWMAN, Edward	89	BRIDGES, J. T	84
BOWMAN, Lydia A	89	BRIDGES, Margaret	84
BOWMAN, Margaret	23	BRIDGES, R. J	84
BOWMAN, Robert	51	BRIDGFORTH, Amanda C	23
BOWMAN, Sarah Riley	51	BRIDGFORTH, Eliza A	23
BOWMAN, Virginia	51	BRIDGFORTH, James C	23
BOYD, Charles	42	BRIDGFORTH, Maria	23
BOYD, Elizabeth	42	BRIDGFORTH, Martha	23
BOYD, F. E	77	BRIDGFORTH, Mary A	23
BOYD, Frances E	24	BRIDGFORTH, Robert F	23
BOYD, John	42	BRIDGFORTH, Robert M	23
BOYD, Laura	42	BRIDGFORTH, William M	23
BOYD, M. E	77	BRIGGS, Eugene	59
BOYD, M. E.	24	BRIGGS, Frederick	59
BOYD, Martha	42	BRIGGS, John	53
BOYD, N. A	77	BRIGMAN, Elizabeth	13
BOYD, Nancy A	24	BRIGMAN, James W	18
BOYD, R. D	77	BRIGMAN, Thomas	13
BOYD, Richard	30	BRISTER, Allen	57
BOYD, Robert D	24	BRISTER, Allez	57
BOYD, Sinah A	21	BRISTER, Betsy	54
BOYD, T. J	77	BRISTER, Elizabeth	54, 57

BRISTER, Frances 57	BROWN, Mary 68
BRISTER, Henry F 55	BROWN, Miles I 27
BRISTER, Jane 55	BROWN, Ophilia 44
BRISTER, John 54, 57	BROWN, Rhoda 71
BRISTER, John J 55	BROWN, Rufus 44
BRISTER, Lucinda 55	BROWN, Sarah H 72
BRISTER, Rosana 54	BROWN, Sarah K 31
BRISTER, Samuel 54	BROWN, Simeon F 38
BRISTER, Samuel H 57	BROWN, Simon 72
BRISTER, Susana 54	BROWN, Susan 27, 68
BRISTER, Tenesse 57	BROWN, Susan F 72
BRISTER, Thompson 57	BROWN, Susanna 71
BRISTER, Thompson, Jr 57	BROWN, T. A 93
BRISTER, Warrick 55	BROWN, Temperance 71
BRISTER, Warrick Jr 55	BROWN, Thomas 44
BRISTER, William 54	BROWN, Wiley 71
BRISTER, William F 57	BROWN?, Melissa 40
BRISTIL, Thomas 88	BROWNJOHN, Jane 41
BRODNAX, Amazon 57	BRUCE, Catharine 39
BRODNAX, Cornelia 57	BRUCE, Thomas J 39
BRODNAX, John 57	BRUMFIELD, Charles 33
BRODNAX, Martha 57	BRUMFIELD, George W 33
BRODNAX, Robert M 57	BRUMFIELD, Harriet 33
BRODNAX, Rolent 57	BRUMFIELD, Jesse 33
BROOCKS, Elizabeth 28	BRUMFIELD, Lucy 33
BROOCKS, James A 28	BRUMFIELD, Oscar 33
BROOCKS, James P 28	BRUMFIELD, Thomas A 33
BROOCKS, Joab F 28	BRUNER, Mary Ormsby 67
BROOCKS, Martha A 28	BRUNER, Octaviah R 61
BROOCKS, Walter 77	BRUNER, Patience 61, 88
BROOKS, Charles H S. 39	BUCKHANAN, Daniel 29
BROOKS, Elizabeth 39	BUCKHANAN, David 29
BROOKS, Hugh 39	BUCKHANAN, Nancy 29
BROOKS, Mary 39	BUCKHANAN, Sarah 29
BROOKS, Thomas 39	BUCKHANAN, Thomas 29
BROOMFIELD, John S 90	BUCKHANAN, William 29
BROWN, Abner 31	BUCKLEY, Eleanor 18
BROWN, Agnes C 49	BUFORD, Eliza Ann 11
BROWN, Alonorizine? 49	BUIE, Mary J 48
BROWN, Alonzo L 49	BUIE, Milton 51
BROWN, Amanda 46	BULL, Ann E 52
BROWN, Bandon 31	BULL, David K 52
BROWN, Beriah 44	BULL, Emily J. E 55
BROWN, Buksaule 31	BULL, Harriet 57
BROWN, Calvin 68	BULL, Isaac L 55
BROWN, Charles 27	BULL, James 52
BROWN, Clasus? A 38	BULL, James C 52
BROWN, Elijah H 72	BULL, James H 52, 55
BROWN, Frances 27, 44	BULL, John C 55
BROWN, Henry C 46	BULL, Lovey 52
BROWN, Henry T 71	BULL, Mahala A 55
BROWN, James S 68	BULL, Mary 52, 53
BROWN, Jane 74	BULL, Mary J 52
BROWN, John 34	BULL, Melinda C 55
BROWN, Katura 31	BULL, Nancy A 55
BROWN, Martha I 68	BULL, Reuben 55

BULL, Sarah	55, 61	CALDWELL, Thomas S	49
BULL, Susan	52	CALLIHAM, George W	10
BULL, Susan A	55	CALLIHAM, Harriet	10
BULL, Susan J	55	CALLIHAM, Robert	10
BULL, William J	55	CALLIHAN, Ellen	68
BUNCH, William	17	CALVIT, Jane	29
BURK, Amelia	32	CALVITT, Ada	2
BURKHEAD, J. C.	31	CALVITT, Alexander	16
BURLING, Julius	85	CALVITT, Charles	2
BURNES, Patrick	85	CALVITT, Elizabeth	2, 16
BURNS, Martha Ann	30	CALVITT, Frances J	7
BURNS, Mary Jane	96	CALVITT, George	7
BURNS, Mary L	34	CALVITT, John	2
BURNS, Patrick	75	CALVITT, Joseph	15
BURNS, Sarah Elizabeth	42	CALVITT, Martha A	2
BURRUS, Addison	21	CALVITT, Mary	2, 7
BURRUS, E. E	88	CALVITT, Priscilla	7
BURRUS, Enos H	21	CALVITT, Samuel	7
BURRUS, James	21	CALVITT, Thomas	7
BURRUS, James R	88	CAMPBELL, Angeline	20
BURRUS, L. P	88	CAMPBELL, Augustus	20
BURRUS, Lucy M	21	CAMPBELL, Catherine	54
BURRUS, Mary A	21	CAMPBELL, Emeline	54
BURRUS, Rebecca I	21	CAMPBELL, Emily	20
BURRUS, W. P	88	CAMPBELL, J. N	76
BURRUS, William A	21	CAMPBELL, James	54
BUSBY, Emily	58	CAMPBELL, Letitia	54
BUSBY, James	58	CAMPBELL, Lovey	52
BUSBY, Jane	58	CAMPBELL, Mary	54
BUSBY, Johnathan	58	CAMPBELL, Sarah	54
BUSBY, Martha	58	CAMPBELL, Sarah E	54
BUSBY, Marvin	58	CAMPBELL, Thomas	54
BUSBY, S. B.	58	CAMPBELL, William	54
BUSBY, Sarah	58	CANADAY, Elzabeth	67
BUSBY, Tenilla	58	CANON, Susan	43
BUSBY? Martha	52	CAPSHAW, Eliza	64
BUTLER, John	83	CAPSHAW, James M	64
BUTLER, Mary	14	CAPSHAW, Mary	64
BUTTON, William S	17	CAPSHAW, Matilda	64
BYNUM, Ann S	9	CAPSHAW, William W	64
CABANISS, Martha	23	CAPSHAW, Windsor H	64
CAGE, Albert H	73	CARADINE, Beverly	77
CAGE, Catherine	73	CARADINE, Henry F	77
CAGE, Elizabeth H	73	CARADINE, James S	77
CAGE, Harry	73	CARADINE, M. C	77
CAGE, Jane H	73	CARADINE, S. G	77
CAGE, Lucy T	73	CARADINE, W. S. G	77
CAGE, Lucy T, Jr	73	CARMAN, Delanson	8
CAGE, Minerva L	73	CARMAN, Missouri	8
CAGE, Robert H	73	CARMAN, Richard	8
CALDWELL, Bailey	79	CARMAN, Valentine P	12
CALDWELL, J. V	79	CARNES?, Jane	24
CALDWELL, Julie G.	49	CARPENTER, Ann	70
CALDWELL, M. A	79	CARPENTER, Cyrus	70
CALDWELL, S. J	79	CARPENTER, Elizabeth	70
CALDWELL, Sarah	49	CARPENTER, George	70

CARPENTER, Robert S	8	CHEATHAM, William	16
CARPENTER, Samuel	70	CHENOWITH, Gabriel	86
CARR, Matilda C	47	CHERRY, J. B.	46
CARR, Young	47	CHEW, Augustine	66
CARRADINE?, Margaret	31	CHEW, Beverly G	66
CARRAWAY, John	32	CHEW, Robert E	20
CARRISEL?,William E	70	CHEW, Thomas R	20
CARROLL, E. A	85	CHEW, William S	20
CARROLL, M. F	85	CHEW?, Sarah R	16
CARRUTH, Eveline	17	CHILDRESS, Samuel	9
CARRUTH, Jane	17	CHILDRESS, William G	9
CARRUTH, Samuel O	17	CHRISTIAN, James	51
CARRUTH, Thomas	17	CHRISTOPHER, Eliza A	52
CARSON, Alfred T	21	CHRISTOPHER, Mary	52
CARSON, Charles	21	CHRISTOPHER, Mary J	52
CARSON, George	13	CHRISTOPHER, Washington	52
CARSON, Jasper	16	CLARK, Alfred O	66
CARSON, John	30	CLARK, Augustus B	66
CARSON, John Jr.	16	CLARK, Charles H	35
CARSON, Laura	21	CLARK, Council	9
CARSON, Lavitius	16	CLARK, D. S	89
CARSON, Margaret J	13	CLARK, David	3
CARSON, Mary E	16	CLARK, Delany	3
CARSON, Robert	21	CLARK, Edward H	66
CARY, Thomas	88	CLARK, Elijah J	35
CASHELL, Maria E	94	CLARK, Elizabeth	10
CASON, Jane	24	CLARK, Ellen	28
CASON, Jane E	24	CLARK, Elvira L	66
CASON, John A	24	CLARK, George F	66
CASON, Pennington	24	CLARK, J. J	79
CASSELS, Hester A	3	CLARK, J. J.	74
CASTIN, John F	82	CLARK, Jane	10
CASTLOW, B	66	CLARK, Jane Eliza	52
CATES, J. S	80	CLARK, Jethro	9
CATO, Cyrus	53	CLARK, Jethro B	3
CAUSEY or ZEAGLER, Matilda	47	CLARK, John	3
CAUSEY, Celeste	36	CLARK, John B	66
CAUSEY, Charles	36	CLARK, Josephine	47
CAUSEY, Cornelius	36	CLARK, Lydia M	66
CAUSEY, Jesse	36	CLARK, Mary	44
CAUSEY, Solomon	67	CLARK, Mary Elizabeth	
CAUSEY, William	36	Eleanor	28
CAYCE, Linda?	87	CLARK, Mary M	10
CAYCE, Lydia	87	CLARK, Nancy J	10
CAYES, E. B	87	CLARK, Nancy Maranda	72
CESSNA, Elizabeth Ann	17	CLARK, Reuben	9, 10
CHAMBERS, B. F	79	CLARK, Sally	9
CHAMBERS, Catherine	27	CLARK, Susannah	3
CHAMBERS, E. B.	27	CLARK, Thomas G	44
CHAMBERS, H. F.	27	CLARK, Travis R	35
CHAMBERS, M. A.	15	CLARK, William	10
CHAMBERS, M.A	6	CLARK, William L	43
CHAMBERS, Mary E	27	CLEARY, John	93
CHAMBERS, Solomon G	27	CLELAND, Irene	77
CHANDLER, J. H	30	CLEYMERE, A. J	79
CHEATHAM, Morrison	44	CLINTOCK, N. S. M	61

CLOK, Thakla 88	COLTON, Francis 83
COCHRAN, Augustus 80	COLTON, John 83
COKER, Albert J 54	COLTON, Orvin 83
COKER, Charles 54	COMPTON, Henry 26
COKER, Eliza 54	COMPTON, John 26
COKER, Jonathan 54	COMPTON, Mabrella 26
COKER, Margaret 54	COMPTON, Margaret 68
COLE, Charlotte E 59	CONGER, M. V 78
COLE, George W 59	CONNELLY, Nancy 41
COLE, Lafayette 59	CONVEY, George W 96
COLE, Louisa M 59	COODY, Archibald 10
COLE, Rebecca 59	COODY, Archibald, Jr. 10
COLE, Rebecca R 59	COODY, Eliza 10
COLE, Sterling 59	COODY, Eliza J 3
COLLINS, A. J 79	COODY, Emily 10
COLLINS, Adolphus 34	COODY, Henry C 7
COLLINS, Albina 50	COODY, Joseph A 10
COLLINS, Elizabeth 50	COODY, Lydia 7
COLLINS, James 50	COODY, Mary Jane 11
COLLINS, Joseph 50	COODY, Penninah 11
COLLINS, Joshua G 50	COODY, Robert 7
COLLINS, Lemuel P 34	COODY, Silas W 10
COLLINS, Louisiana 77	COODY, Warren 2, 3
COLLINS, Lucinda 50, 51	COODY, Zephemiah 3
COLLINS, Mary 50	COOK, Amanda 17
COLLINS, Phoebe J 34	COOK, Celia 59
COLLINS, Samuel 34	COOK, Culbertson 17
COLLINS, Seaborn 50	COOK, Elizabeth A 17
COLLINS, Sewell F 34	COOK, John W 17
COLLINS, Wiley 50	COOK, Margaret 17
COLLIOTT, Joseph 84	COOK, Milton W 17
COLLUM, Absolum 53	COOK, Nathan P 17
COLLUM, Albert 53	COOK, Peter B 82
COLLUM, Caroline 53	COOK, Rebecca Ann 10
COLLUM, Charles A 49	COOK, Sims P 59
COLLUM, Edmond 53	COOK, Thomas B 17
COLLUM, Elbert 49	COON, Nancy Ann 94
COLLUM, Eldred 45	COONEY, Bridget 93
COLLUM, Ethelinda 49	COONEY, John 93
COLLUM, James 53	COOPER, Benjamin 29
COLLUM, Jeffersonia E 50	COOPER, Edward W 21
COLLUM, John 49, 53	COOPER, Eveline 29
COLLUM, John L 50	COOPER, Jonathan 21
COLLUM, Leaborn 53	COOPER, Margaret J 13
COLLUM, Lucinda 53	COOPER, Martha E 21
COLLUM, Lucretia A 2	COOPER, Mary 29
COLLUM, Martin 49, 53	COOPER, Mary A 29
COLLUM, Mary E 50	COOPER, Sarah 1
COLLUM, Mary J 50	COOPER, Soloman B 29
COLLUM, Millingeville 50	COOPER, William H.H. 29
COLLUM, Mississippi 49	CORBIN, Charles F. W 84
COLLUM, Susan 49	CORBIN, Frances M 84
COLLUM, Thomas 53	CORBIN, M. F. Perkins 84
COLLUM, William 53	CORBIN, M. K 84
COLLUM, William J 50	CORBIN, R. R. 84
COLTON, Ann 83	COSTILOUGH, Henry 66

COSTILOUGH, James	66	CUNNINGHAM, William	24
COTNAM, John	68	CURRY, Patrick	86
COTTER?, Caroline	36	CUSACK, Alice	43
COTTINGIN, Annie	40	CUSACK, Cornelia	43, 94
COTTON, Thomas	82	CUSACK, Irene	43
COUSINS, Mary Ann	22	CUSACK, James W	43
COVINGTON, Henry	76	CUSACK, Mary	43
COWAN, Hugh	1	DABBS, J. W.	79
COWAN, Matilda O	1	DANIEL, G. B.	58
COWAN, Rebecca	1	DANIEL, Littleton	58
COWAN, Sarah	1	DANIEL, Mary	58
COWAN, Sarah J	1	DANIELS, David	56
COX, Clarissa R	31	DANIELS, Dozia	56
COX, David	31	DANIELS, Francis	56
COX, Elvira	25	DANIELS, Hester A	56
COX, George A	25	DANIELS, John C	56
COX, Hampton	31	DANIELS, Joseph	56
COX, Josephine	31	DANIELS, Susan	56
COX, Mary E	31	DANIELS, William	56
COX, Sarah A	25	DAVIS, Elizabeth O	34
COX, Virginia E	25	DAVIS, Eugenia R	34
COX, William	31	DAVIS, Franklin	34
CRAIG, David	5	DAVIS, Letitia	22
CRAIG, John	5	DAVIS, Margaret	34, 82
CRANE, A. D	88	DAVIS, Martha J	8
CRANE, W. C	88	DAVIS, Mary	37
CRAVENDOUGH, John	86	DAVIS, Mary E	34
CREECY, Carissandra	79	DAVIS, Nancy	9
CRESWELL, J. J	72	DAVIS, Robert V	34
CRESWELL, James M	72	DAVIS, William H	34
CRESWELL, Leonard	72	DAY, Allen	60
CRESWELL, Linford	72	DAY, Elizabeth	60
CRESWELL, Margaret	72	DAY, Emma	60
CRESWELL, Mary	46	DAY, Frances	60
CRESWELL, Miller	72	DAY, Johnathan	60
CRESWELL, Oscar H	72	DAY, July	60
CRESWELL, Rachal	72	DAY, Mary Ann	65
CRESWELL, Rachel	87	DAY, Mathis	60
CRESWELL, Rachel A	72	DAY, Nancy	60
CRESWELL, Rayford	72	DAY, Robert	60
CRESWELL, Salem	72	DAY, Robert Jr	60
CRIBBS, Abraham	79	DAY, Warren	60
CRIPPEN, Jane	41	DAY, William	60
CROW? Mary	71	DEASON, Emily Catherine	47
CRUMP, George P	74	DEASON, Joseph L	64
CRUMP, Phillip J	74	DEMART, Wilson Y	46
CULLEN, Ann E	48	DEMENT, J. R	79
CULLEN, Rebecca	48	DENNIS, John M	28
CUNNINGHAM, Caroline	24	DENSON, Henrietta	26
CUNNINGHAM, Catherine	24	DENSON, John B	46
CUNNINGHAM, Charles	24	DENSON, Mary A	46
CUNNINGHAM, Eliza	24	DENSON, William F	46
CUNNINGHAM, Elizabeth	24	DENTON, Frances	15
CUNNINGHAM, Mary	24	DENTON, Mary Neel	15
CUNNINGHAM, Mary A	24	DENTON, Solomon	15
CUNNINGHAM, Moses B	24	DENTON, Solomon G	15

DERBIN, Catherine	82	DORMAN, Sarah E	91
DESMOND, Council	12	DORSEY, Elizabeth Ann	6
DEUTS, Elizabeth S	69	DORSEY, Ellen D	6
DEUTS, Margaret J	69	DORSEY, Lydia	89
DEVLIN, F	79	DORSEY, Sarah	90
DEVLIN, G. F	79	DOUGHARTY, Alexander	47
DEVLIN, J. M	79	DOUGHARTY, Charles	13, 47
DEVLIN, W. B	79	DOUGHARTY, George W	47
DIBRALL, Virginia	89	DOUGHARTY, Mary	47
DIBRELL, Elizabeth Watson	89	DOUGHARTY, P. C.	47
DICKSON, Ann R	10	DOUGHARTY, Sarah A	13
DICKSON, Arabella O	10	DOUGLAS, Henry	6
DICKSON, Edward	63	DOUGLAS, Isaac E	71
DICKSON, Elijah	63	DOWER, B	81
DICKSON, James	63	DOWNS, E. L.	76
DICKSON, Jane	63	DRENNING, Edward	47
DICKSON, John L	10	DRENNING, Eliza	47, 82
DICKSON, Joseph	47	DRENNING, Mary A	47
DICKSON, Laura	63	DREWRY, Frances H	14
DICKSON, Lovey	63	DRISCOL, John	83
DICKSON, Marian L	10	DRISKOLL, John	93
DICKSON, Samuel Z	63	DUFFEY, Elizabeth E	3
DICKSON, Sarah	63	DUNN, Averey? G	37
DICKSON, Susan	63	DUNN, Celeste	35
DILLAHUNTY, Frances Ann	52	DUNN, Celeste A	37
DILLEY, Abraham T	4	DUNN, Charles	36
DILLEY, Benjamin R	4	DUNN, David	37
DILLEY, Eugene P	4	DUNN, David J	37
DILLEY, Joseph A	4	DUNN, John B	37
DILLEY, Lemenda H	4	DUNN, Lavinia G	37
DILLEY, Lucy A	4	DUNN, Patrick	81
DILLEY, Robert W	4	DUNN, Rebecca M	37, 39
DILLEY, Samuel	4	DUNN, Richard L	37
DILLEY, Samuel U	4	DUNN, William	37
DILLEY, Sarah C	4	DYER, Absolom	27
DILLON, Alania	43	DYER, Elizabeth	27
DILLON, Henry C	43	DYER, Francis B	27
DILLON, Jane	43	DYER, Harriet E	27
DILLON, John	43	DYER, Leana	15
DILLON, Sarah	43	DYER, Mary Jane	15
DIXON, Benujah?	32	EAMIGSON, Jesse B	49
DIXON, C. M.	51	EASDON, John B	92
DIXON, Duncan	86	EASDON, Margarett	92
DIXON, Geo. B	79	EASDON, Walker	92
DIXON, Mary	32	ECHOLS, William A	24
DIXON, Perry	51	EDGAR, Angeline	20
DIXON, R. D. S.	56	EDGAR, Laura	21
DONAVAN, James	83	EDGAR, Martha E	21
DONELSON, Sarah	51	EDMONDS, Cynthia A	44
DONELSON, William M	51	EDMONDS, Cyrus W	48
DOOLING, Clarissa	24	EDMONDS, Daniel F	44
DOOLING, Susan	24	EDMONDS, Elizabeth	48
DOOLING, Thomas J	24	EDMONDS, James F	44
DORMAN, ? J	91	EDMONDS, Mary E	44
DORMAN, Cora J	91	EDMONDSON, America	15
DORMAN, D. A	91	EDMONDSON, Angeline B	12

EDMONDSON, Danscilla S 15	ELLISON, Thomas P 59
EDMONDSON, John J 15	ELLISON, William . . 58, 59, 74
EDMONDSON, John S 15	ELLMORE, William 74
EDMONDSON, Mary 15	EMFINGERS, Ivana 72
EDMONDSON, Mary F 12	EMFINGERS, James M 72
EDMONDSON, Mississippi 15	EMFINGERS, Martha A. M . . . 72
EDMONDSON, Samuel S 12	EMFINGERS, Sarah M. E 72
EDMONDSON, Sarah E 15	EMFINGERS, William 72
EDMONDSON, Union 30	EMFINGERS, William L 72
EDMONDSON, William C 15	EPPERSON, W. S 79
EDMONDSON, William P 12	ERVIN, Frances 44
EDMONDSON, William S 12	ERVIN, M. J. 12
EDMONDSON, Zachery 30	ERWIN, Archibald 2
EDMUNDSON, Atlantic 7	ERWIN, Claiborne 68
EDMUNDSON, George 7	ERWIN, Cornelia J 68
EDMUNDSON, James W 7	ERWIN, Daniel 2
EDMUNDSON, Josephus 7	ERWIN, David 2
EDMUNDSON, Louisa 7	ERWIN, David C 2, 8
EDMUNDSON, Mary 7	ERWIN, Elizabeth 5
EDMUNDSON, Sarah 7	ERWIN, Emily 38
EDMUNDSON, William 7	ERWIN, Frances 5
EDWARDS, Catherine 95	ERWIN, Henry F 2
EDWARDS, Catherine F 95	ERWIN, Hugh C 5
EDWARDS, W. C 95	ERWIN, John 68
EISHAM, Margaret 1	ERWIN, Leonard 68
Eliza. 10	ERWIN, Margaret 2, 68
Elizabeth D 89	ERWIN, Margaret A 2
ELLIOTT, Emmy 43	ERWIN, Mary 5, 68
ELLIOTT, James H 43	ERWIN, Octavia 68
ELLIOTT, Lavinia 43	ERWIN, Rachel 68
ELLIOTT, William 43	ERWIN, Reuben 68
ELLIS, N. W 82	ERWIN, Timoline 68
ELLISON, Belinda 59	ERWIN, William C 2
ELLISON, Caroline 59	ERWIN, William W 5
ELLISON, Cassie 58	ERWIN, Zadock 68
ELLISON, Claiborne 60	ESTIS, William A 56
ELLISON, Elizabeth 15, 57	ETHRIDGE, Elizabeth 62
ELLISON, Francis 58	ETHRIDGE, James 63
ELLISON, James 24	ETHRIDGE, Lecrvy 62
ELLISON, Jane 58	ETHRIDGE, Margaret 63
ELLISON, John W 60	ETHRIDGE, Martha 62
ELLISON, Joseph 74	ETHRIDGE, Mary 62
ELLISON, Joseph H 74	ETHRIDGE, Reuben 63
ELLISON, Jospeh P 74	ETHRIDGE, Susan 63
ELLISON, Julia A 59	ETHRIDGE, Winifred 62
ELLISON, Lewis 58	EUESTES, Jacob 31
ELLISON, Martha 60	EVANS, Emma 89
ELLISON, Mary 59	EVANS, John H 86
ELLISON, Mary Margaret 54	EVANS, Richard 90
ELLISON, Moses 60	EVERETT, Agnes 14
ELLISON, Nancy 58, 60, 74	EVERETT, Agnes C 22
ELLISON, Sarah 60	EVERETT, Benjamin 14
ELLISON, Susan 52, 59, 74	EVERETT, Eliza 14
ELLISON, Susannah 56	EVERETT, Eliza S 78
ELLISON, Thomas 59	EVERETT, Hardy W 78
ELLISON, Thomas H 60	EVERETT, Henry C 14

EVERETT, Henry F	. . . .	78
EVERETT, Henry H	. . . .	22
EVERETT, James	 14,	78
EVERETT, James B	. . . .	78
EVERETT, Jane	 22,	78
EVERETT, John	. . . .	14
EVERETT, John Jr.	. . . .	14
EVERETT, Judith	. . . .	78
EVERETT, Lavina	. . . .	14
EVERETT, Lucy J	. . . .	22
EVERETT, Mary E	. . . .	22
EVERETT, Rachel E	. . . . . .	78
EVERETT, Rebecca A	. . . . . .	22
EVERETT, Riley M	. . . .	78
EVERETT, Sarah E	. . . .	78
EVERETT, Thomas	. . . .	22
EVERETT, Thomas Jr	. . . . . .	22
EVERETT, William D	. . . . . .	22
EWING, Ann	. . . .	9
EWING, Ann B	. . . .	9
EWING, Benjamin B	. . . .	9
EWING, Martin W	. . . .	9
EWING, Robert W	. . . .	9
EXUM, Edward	. . . .	65
EXUM, Kinchen	. . . .	65
EXUM, Mary	. . . .	65
FARLEY, James	. . . .	21
FARLEY, John J	. . . .	21
FARLEY, Mary F	. . . .	21
FARLEY, William	. . . .	21
FATHEREE, B.B.	. . . .	58
FATURN,? Ann	. . . .	47
FATURN,? Robert	. . . .	47
FAUST, Sarah C. W	. . . .	77
FENHOOD, Catherine	. . . . . .	11
FERGUSON, Alexander	. . . . . .	33
FERGUSON, Andrew J	. . . . . .	33
FERGUSON, Emeline	. . . . . .	33
FERRELL, William	. . . .	81
FERRIS, Amanda	. . . .	33
FERRIS, Caroline A	. . . . . .	35
FERRIS, Colombus	. . . .	33
FERRIS, Dozia	. . . .	35
FERRIS, George F	. . . .	35
FERRIS, Josiah H	. . . .	35
FERRIS, Martha F	. . . .	35
FERRIS, Sarah E	. . . .	35
FERRIS, Susan S	. . . .	35
FERRIS, William D	. . . .	33
FIELDS, David	. . . .	84
FIELDS, Sarah	. . . .	84
FINNEY, William	. . . .	76
FINNICANE, Amanda	. . . . . .	59
FINNICANE, George	. . . . . .	59
FINNUCANE, Dawson W	. . . . . .	6
FISHER, Amanda D	. . . .	41

FISHER, Andrew J	. . . . . .	41
FISHER, Elias	. . . .	51
FISHER, Ellen M. A.	. . . . .	41
FISHER, Francis E	. . . . . .	41
FISHER, Holley	. . . .	41
FISHER, James A	. . . .	51
FISHER, James W	. . . .	69
FISHER, John	. . . .	41
FISHER, John O'Q	. . . .	69
FISHER, Mary	. . . .	51
FISHER, Robert	. . . .	51
FISHER, Sarah E	. . . .	69
FISHER, Susanna V	. . . . . .	51
FISHER, William	. . . .	69
FLEMING, Caroline	. . . . . .	94
FLEMING, Lewis D	. . . . . .	52
FLEMING, W. C	. . . .	79
FLEMING, Wm	. . . .	94
FLETCHER, Adeline	. . . . . .	69
FLETCHER, Catherine	. . . . .	69
FLETCHER, John	. . . .	62
FLETCHER, John P	. . . . . .	62
FLETCHER, Mary	. . . .	62
FLETCHER, Rebecca	. . . . . .	5
FLETCHER, Thomas	. . . . . .	69
FLETCHER, William	. . . . . .	62
FLOWER, Sarah	. . . .	8
FLOWERS, Benjamin L	. . . . .	33
FLOYD, M	. . . .	86
FORBES, Anna	. . . .	67
FORBES, Daniel	. . . .	67
FORBES, James	. . . .	67
FORBES, John	. . . .	67
FORBES, Rosetta	. . . .	67
FORBES, W. A	. . . .	89
FORBES, William	. . . .	67
FORD, Frances	. . . .	46
FORD, John W	. . . .	60
FORD, Kendrick	. . . .	60
FORD, Martha A	. . . .	60
FORD, Mary A	. . . .	60
FORD, Nancy	. . . .	60
FORD, Peter H	. . . .	60
FORD, Thomas A	. . . .	60
FORD, Thomas J	. . . .	60
FORDEN, Richard	. . . .	27
FORDEN, William	. . . .	27
FORT, Elias A	. . . .	68
FORT, James D	. . . .	68
FORT, Lecrecuis	. . . .	68
FORT, Martha J	. . . .	68
FORT, Mary Smith	. . . . . .	48
FORT, Robert H	. . . .	68
FOSTER, A.Y.	. . . .	6
FOSTER, Archer H	. . . . . .	4
FOSTER, Archibald H	. . . . .	12

FOSTER, Chana	6	FRUZIER, Sarah A	32
FOSTER, Isaac J	12	FUGATE, Emeline R	25
FOSTER, J H	12	FUGATE, Middleton	25
FOSTER, Lucy	38	FUGATE, Vincent H	25
FOSTER, Lucy M	12	FUGUA, Albert M	91
FOSTER, Margaret E	12	FUGUA, Eliza H	91
FOSTER, Martha	6, 12	FUGUA, Hibernia J	91
FOSTER, Mary A	12	FUGUA, John W	91
FOSTER, Rebecca	12	FUGUA, Louisa G	91
FOSTER, Samuel M	12	FUGUA, Mary J	91
FOSTER, Thomas O	12	FUGUA, Sam'l L	91
FOUCHEE, J. J	79	FUGUA, Sarah	91
FOULKS, Emeline	59	FUGUA, Sarah D	91
FOULKS, Emiline	32	FUQUA, Mary T	43
FOULKS, Milissa	32	FUQUA, Sarah J	79
FOULKS, Rebecca	32	FUTRALL, M. A	80
FOULKS, Tapley	32	FUTRALL, R. A	80
FOULKS, Thomas	32	GALE, Inez F	7
FOULKS, William	32	GALE, James B	7
FOWELL, Eliza	64	GALE, Mary F	7
FOWELL, Helen	64	GALLOWAY, J	11
FOWELL, Isaac	64	GALTNEY, Albert	28
FOWELL, Isaac J	64	GALTNEY, Clarissa	28
FOWELL, James	64	GALTNEY, Indiana	28
FOWELL, Margaret	64	GALTNEY, J. J.	28
FOWELL, Martha V	64	GALTNEY, Martha	28
FOWELL, Mary	64	GALTNEY, Olivia	28
FOWELL, P.	64	GALTNEY, Thomas	28
FOWELL, Samuel C	64	GALTNEY, Victoria	28
FOX, Daniel N	8	GANBERRY, Helen B	48
FRAULEY, John	82	GANBERRY, Marcia J	49
FRENCH, T. B.	45	GANBERRY, Marshall C	45
FRIEDLANDER, Henry	16	GANBERRY, Marshall P	48
FRIEDLANDER, Lear	16	GANBERRY, William E	48
FRIEDLANDER, Nancy	16	GANBERRY, William Y	48
FRIEDLANDER, Samuel	16	GANDY, Elliot	26
FRIEDLANDER, Sarah	16	GANDY, Harriet	26
FRILEY, David	31	GANDY, John H	26
FRILEY, Elizabeth	46	GANDY, William E	26
FRILEY, Emily	31	GARDNER, Elizabeth	15, 30
FRILEY, James	31	GARDNER, Jesse	78
FRILEY, John L	31	GARDNER, Jesse Jr	96
FRILEY, Joseph	31	GARDNER, Lewis	15
FRILEY, Louisa F	31	GARDNER, Martha E	15
FRILEY, Martin M	31	GARDNER, Mary A	15
FRILEY, Nancy	96	GARDNER, Mary E	78
FRILEY, Sarah	31	GARDNER, Mary J	96
FRILEY, Tabitha C	31	GARDNER, Sarah J	15
FRILEY, Venitia	31	GARDNER, Seaborn	15
FRILEY, William	31	GARDNER, William J	15
FRISBY, Clarissa	28	GARING, Augustus	94
FRUZIER, Julia	32	GARING, Barbary	94
FRUZIER, Mary	32	GARING, Eliza	94
FRUZIER, Robert	32	GARING, Francis?	94
FRUZIER, Robert P	32	GARING, Harriet	94
FRUZIER, Sarah	32	GARING, Joseph	94

GARNER, Charles W. Q.	48	GIBBS, Henry H	45
GARNER, Frances M	48	GIBBS, Josephine	45
GARNER, George W	48	GIBBS, L. A	90
GARNER, John	48	GIBBS, Minerva	45
GARNER, Milton S	48	GIBBS, Q. D	90
GARNER, Robert	46	GIBBS, S. A	90
GARNER, Sarah	48	GIBBS, Sarah	45
GARNER, Sturdy F	48	GIBBS, W. D	90
GARNER, William P	48	GIBBS, W. S	90
GARNOTT?, John B	36	GIBSON, Joseph	41
GARRISON, Caroline	48	GIBSON,?Mary Ann	74
GARRISON, James	48	GILBERT, Maria A	3
GARRISON, Rachel	48	GILL, Amanda	71
GARRISON, Reliant	48	GILL, Amy L	71
GARROTT, J. B	81	GILL, Elizabeth	30
GARTLEY, Julia	48	GILL, Frances S	30
GARTLY, Elizabeth O	34	GILL, Harrison	41
GARTLY, Julia	34	GILL, Jackson	71
GARTLY, Margaret	34	GILL, Jeremiah A	30
GARTLY, William	34	GILL, Jeremiah N	30
GARTLY, William F	34	GILL, John J	71
GARY, Benjamin C	37	GILL, John R	30
GARY, Eliza	37	GILL, Lydia	41
GARY, Josephine	37	GILL, Magnus R	30
GARY, Malinda A	37	GILL, Margaret A	30
GARY, Mary	37	GILL, Martha	71
GARY, Mary A	37	GILL, Martha F	30
GARY, Robert	37	GILL, Mary J	30
GEORGE, Andrew	42	GILL, Susanna	41
GEORGE, Robert	53	GILL, William	71
GERALD, Elizabeth C	60	GILL, William J	41
GERALD, Elnora	90	GILL, William T	71
GERALD, G. Bruce	60	GILLESPIE, D. A	90
GERALD, George	60	GILLIAN, Eliza L	26
GERALD, Sarah A	60	GILLIAN, Endora	26
GERMAN, Catherine	75	GILLIAN, Leslie	26
GERMAN, George	75	GILLIAN, Susan E	26
GERMAN, John F	75	GILLMORE, Y. A	85
GERMAN, Louisa	75	GLASSBURN, Lavinia	37
GERMAN, Mary	75	GLICKAUF, Betty	59
GERMAN, William H	75	GLICKAUF, F	59
GERRARD, Abner F	38	GLICKAUF, Samuel	59
GERRARD, Benjamin A	38	GLOVER, Daniel	5
GERRARD, Elizabeth	38	GOODMAN, Laura J	95
GERRARD, Jesse	38	GOODRUM, W. M	80
GERRARD, Lydia C	38	GOODWIN, Elizabeth	70
GERRARD, Robert G	38	GOODWIN, William	70
GERRARD, Tabitha	38	GOOSEY, Frances M. E	87
GERRARD, William	38	GORDON, Celia	54
GEUYER, H. R	85	GORDON, Elizabeth	53
GEUYER, J. M. A	85	GORDON, James	53
GEUYER, Jules	85	GORDON, John	53
GHELL, Geo.	82	GORDON, Martha	53
GIBB, Andrew	86	GORDON, Nancy	53
GIBBS, Barnett	90	GORDON, Robert	54
GIBBS, G. A	90	GORDON, Virginia	53

GORDON, William 54	GRESHAM, Rufus R 46
GOWAN, Joshua 51	GRESHAM, Sarah A 46
GOWEN, Margaret E 51	GRESHAM, Williamson 46
GOWER, John H 74	GRIFFIN, B. Harvey 22
GRACY, Jane 70	GRIFFIN, Catherine 66
GRACY, John W 70	GRIFFIN, Eliza 68
GRACY, Joseph W 70	GRIFFIN, Henderson 51
GRACY, Martha A 70	GRIFFIN, James M 55, 66
GRACY, Martha L. J 70	GRIFFIN, Marion 64
GRACY, Mary J 70	GRIFFIN, Sam'l S 77
GRACY, Palace 70	GRIFFIN, Sarah 51
GRACY, William 70	GRIFFIN, Sarah G 77
GRACY, William T 70	GRIFFITH, A. R 87
GRADY, Mary 60	GRIFFITH, Ann 87
GRADY, William E 60	GRIFFITH, Charles 87
GRAFF, John 73	GRIFFITH, Eliza 87
GRAFTON, John B 94	GRIFFITH, Henry 87
GRAFTON, Laura 94	GRIFFITH, Hizikiah 75
GRAFTON, Letitia L 94	GRIFFITH, John 82
GRAVES, A. B. 79	GRIFFITH, Joseph 87
GRAVES, D. F 89	GRIFFITH, Samuel 75
GRAY, Elizabeth 46	GRIMES, Benjamin 50
GRAY, David T? 46	GRIMES, Elvira 50
GRAY, J. P 46	GRIMES, Mary 50
GRAY, Phillip 74	GRIMES, Theodore 50
GRAY, Sarah R 46	GRIMME, Franz 83
GRAYSON, Frances A 33	GRIMME, Mary 83
GRAYSON, Francis T 16	GRIMME, T. B 83
GRAYSON, Mary 33	GRISHAM, Martin V B 3
GRAYSON, Mary J 33	GRIZZAND, Mary A 13
GRAYSON, Robert C 33	GRUBBS, George 67
GRAYSON, Sarah R 16	GRUBBS, John 67
GRAYSON, Thomas T 16	GRUBBS, John A 46
GREEN, Eliza 18	GRUBBS, William 67
GREEN, George 45	GRUBBS, Wm. S 96
GREEN, J.Q.A. 47	GUESS, Elizabeth 43
GREEN, James 81	GUESS, George 43
GREEN, John F 21	GUESS, Henry 43
GREEN, Martin 80	GUESS, James 43
GREER. Jerimiah 44	GUESS, Jemima 43
GREER, Ann F 44	GUESS, John 43
GREER, Delia 44	GUESS, Mary 43
GREER, Elizabeth 44	GUESS, Morgan 43
GREER, Henry F 44	GUESS, Nancy 43
GREER, James 44	GUESS, Terrill 43
GREER, Jane D 65	GUICE, Alexander 32
GREER, Jonea 44	GUICE, Amanda C 33
GREER, Marshall R 65	GUICE, Augusta 32
GREER, William 44	GUICE, Ephraim 32
GRESHAM, Alvin G 46	GUINN, Charles E 3
GRESHAM, Catherine 46	GUINN, Morris M 3
GRESHAM, Celestus 46	GUTHREY, Andrew 39
GRESHAM, Indiana 46	GUTHREY, Eliza 39
GRESHAM, Mary 46	GWINN, Elizabeth L 3
GRESHAM, Minerva 46	HADDICK, Allen 23
GRESHAM, Raspberry 46	HADDICK, Ann C 71

HADDICK, Benjamin	. . . .	71
HADDICK, Burnwell S	. . . . . .	71
HADDICK, Dorsey M	. . . . . .	71
HADDICK, Drucilla	. . . . . .	70
HADDICK, Eliza A	. . . .	23
HADDICK, Louisa A	. . . . . .	71
HADDICK, Sarah C	 23,	71
HADDICK, Sophia	. . . .	23
HADDICK, Tibitha J	. . . . . .	72
HADEN, Mary Morten	. . . . . .	79
HAGAN, David	. . . .	73
HAGAN, Elizabeth	. . . .	16
HAGAN, Eugenia	. . . .	16
HAGAN, George S	. . . .	16
HAGAN, Henry	. . . .	16
HAGAN, Hiram	. . . .	73
HAGAN, James	. . . .	16
HAGAN, John G	. . . .	73
HAGAN, Martha	. . . .	29
HAGAN, Mary A	. . . .	73
HAGAN, Mary E	. . . .	16
HAGAN, Sarah A	 16,	73
HAGAN, Stephen	. . . .	73
HAGAN, William H	. . . .	16
HAGAN, Wm. B	. . . .	26
HAGMAN, Charles	. . . .	88
HAGMAN, John	. . . .	88
HAGMAN, M. A	. . . .	83
HAGMAN, T. B	. . . .	83
HAGMAN, Thekla	. . . .	88
HAGMAN, Theresa	. . . .	88
HAHN, A. E	. . . .	86
HAHN, E. A	. . . .	86
HAHN, Geo. E	. . . .	86
HAHN, George	. . . .	86
HAHN, John	. . . .	86
HAHN, Otho J. R	. . . .	86
HAINING, Eliza	. . . .	10
HALE, Elenor	. . . .	40
HALEY, William	. . . .	34
HALL, Archibald C	. . . . . .	11
HALL, Bart	. . . .	65
HALL, Cynthia	. . . .	64
HALL, Dixon	. . . .	96
HALL, Elizabeth	 15,	56
HALL, Elvira	. . . .	11
HALL, Harriet	. . . .	64
HALL, James F	. . . .	49
HALL, Joseph	. . . .	75
HALL, Joseph N	. . . .	64
HALL, Laurena Matilda	. . . . .	9
HALL, Laurina M	. . . .	11
HALL, Martha	 53,	64
HALL, Mary B	. . . .	11
HALL, Octavia E	. . . .	11
HALL, Samuel S	. . . .	11

HALL, Sarah	 49,	94
HALL, Susannah V	. . . . . .	51
HALL, Tempe	. . . .	15
HALL, William	. . . .	9
HALL, Willis	. . . .	48
HALL, ?Mary A	. . . .	90
HALL, Indiana Catharine	. . .	8
HAMBERLIN	. . . .	3
HAMBERLIN, Ann	. . . .	11
HAMBERLIN, Anne M	. . . . . .	5
HAMBERLIN, Catherine	. . . .	4
HAMBERLIN, Catherine S	. . . .	4
HAMBERLIN, Elvira	. . . . . .	4
HAMBERLIN, Frances	. . . . .	11
HAMBERLIN, Isaac	. . . . . .	4
HAMBERLIN, James	. . . . . .	11
HAMBERLIN, James D	. . . . .	11
HAMBERLIN, John A	. . . . . .	11
HAMBERLIN, John W	. . . . . .	5
HAMBERLIN, Mary J	. . . . . .	11
HAMBERLIN, Mary Jane	. . . . .	2
HAMBERLIN, Mississippi	. . .	10
HAMBERLIN, Missouri	. . . . .	8
HAMBERLIN, Monroe	. . . . . .	4
HAMBERLIN, Moses	. . . . . .	11
HAMBERLIN, Rachel	. . . . . .	2
HAMBERLIN, Roland M	. . . . .	11
HAMBERLIN, Sarah	. . . . . .	4
HAMBERLIN, Stephen L	. . . . .	11
HAMBERLIN, Thomas	. . . . . .	4
HAMBERLIN, William	. . . . .	10
HAMBERLIN, William A	. . . . .	12
HAMER, A. D	. . . .	78
HAMER, C. M	. . . .	78
HAMER, Charles F	. . . . . .	78
HAMER, E. M.	. . . .	78
HAMER, M. B	. . . .	78
HAMILTON, Mary B	. . . . . .	11
HAMPTON, James	. . . .	57
HAMPTON, Mahala	. . . .	57
HAMPTON, Rhoda	. . . .	57
HAMPTON, Sally	. . . .	57
HAMPTON, Sarah	. . . .	57
HAMPTON, Susan	. . . .	57
HAMPTON, Wade	. . . .	81
HAMPTON, Wesley	. . . .	57
HAMPTON, William	. . . . . .	57
HANCOCK, George M	. . . . . .	40
HANCOCK, John H	. . . .	40
HAND, Stephen	. . . .	80
HANDLY, Elizabeth	. . . . . .	62
HANDLY, Frances A	. . . . . .	62
HANDLY, Josephine	. . . . . .	62
HANDLY, Napoleon B	. . . . .	62
HANDLY, Ursula	. . . .	62
HANDLY, William	. . . .	62

HANNA, Corinne	87	HART, Georgana	11
HANNA, J. B	80	HART, Harrison H	11
HANNA, John	91	HART, James	11, 71
HANNA, John C	92	HART, Jane	71
HANNA, Joseph	58	HART, John	9, 71
HANNA, Lydia	87	HART, Josephus J	72
HANNA, Noreissa	87	HART, Louisa G	9
HANSEN, William	60	HART, Lucretia	71
HARBIN, Cornelius	68	HART, M. V.	72
HARBIN, John W	68	HART, Marion	72
HARBIN, Mary A	68	HART, Martha	71
HARDIN, A. M.	86	HART, Mary A	11
HARDWICK, Jeff	13	HART, Mary L	71
HARMON, Hezekiah	33	HART, Meridith	68
HARMON, Rebecca	33	HART, Minerva	9
HARRINGTON, John	76	HART, Mississippi	9
HARRIS, Alma	92	HART, Sabra	9
HARRIS, Clara	92	HART, Susan E	11
HARRIS, Elizabeth	49, 75	HART, Thomas	71
HARRIS, Ethelinda	49	HASKINS, Henry	64
HARRIS, Geo	92	HASKINS, Tabitha	64
HARRIS, Henrietta	26	HATCH, Ann E	48
HARRIS, Jonathan M	2	HATCH, Charles	48
HARRIS, Joseph F	2	HAUMAKIN, Thomas	88
HARRIS, Mary E	49	HAVERKAMP, J. H	82
HARRIS, Nancy H	70	HAYES, Elizabeth	78
HARRIS, Robert J	70	HAYES, Nancy	78
HARRIS, Sam'l	92	HAYES, Rebecca H	78
HARRIS, Susannah	5	HAYMAN, Henry	90
HARRIS, Thomas	26	HAYMAN, John	90
HARRIS, William C	75	HAYS, Elizabeth	51
HARRISON, Hiram	89	HAYS, Sarah	73
HARRISON, James A	65	HEARD, Franklin	63
HARRISON, Lilla	89	HEARD, Jesse F	63
HARRISON, M. A	89	HEARD, Keziah	63
HARRISON, Mary F	65	HEARD, Margaret A	62
HARRISON, Sam'l	90	HEARD, Samuel H	63
HARRISON, Susan	65	HEARD, Sarah L	63
HARRISON, Susan H	75	HEARD, Sophia	63
HARRISON, Virginia	72	HEARD, W. Farkney	36
HARROLD, Amanda	5	HEARD, Wyatt	63
HARROLD, James	5	HEATH, John T	79
HARROLD, John	12	HELM, Fanny B	33
HARROLD, Lydia	12	HELM, Lucretia B	33
HARROLD, Mary	12	HELM, Lucretia C	33
HARROLD, William	5	HELM, Samuel	33
HARROLD, William S	12	HELM, William J	33
HART, Amanda	71	HELM, William W	33
HART, Christopher R	72	HENDERICKS, Charles L	54
HART, Daniel	71	HENDERICKS, Daniel	53
HART, Delilah	11	HENDERICKS, Daniel W	53
HART, Eliza	71	HENDERICKS, James M	54
HART, Eliza A	11	HENDERICKS, John	53
HART, Eliza J	11	HENDERICKS, Martha P	54
HART, Elizabeth	71	HENDERICKS, Mary	53
HART, Flonzel	71	HENDERICKS, Sarah	53

HENDERICKS, Susan	53, 54
HENDERICKS, Virginia L	54
HENDERICKS, William	53, 54
HENDERICKS, William W	54
HENDERSON, A. W	91
HENDERSON, Charles M	73
HENDERSON, Christopher	56
HENDERSON, Daniel F	56
HENDERSON, Duncan C	56
HENDERSON, Elizabeth F	56, 73
HENDERSON, Elizabeth K	73
HENDERSON, James W	73
HENDERSON, Joseph J	56
HENDERSON, Lucy O	56
HENDERSON, Mary	56
HENDERSON, Mary A	56
HENDERSON, Rebecca W	95
HENDRICK, Charles W	52
HENDRICK, John M	52
HENDRICK, Sarah	52
HENDRICK, Susan	52
HENDRICKS, Emeline R	25
HENDRICKS, Mary J	40
HENRY, Dixon	33
HENRY, Eleanor	33
HENRY, Franklin B	33
HENRY, Harriet C	33
HENRY, James M	33
HENRY, Jefferson D	33
HENRY, Mary L	33
HENRY, Milton L	33
HENSEN, Ann	73
HENSEN, Daniel? H	73
HENSEN, Dorothy	73
HENSEN, Emma	73
HENSEN, John	73
HENSINGER, Joseph	88
HERRIN, Catherine M. J	39
HERRIN, Charles	4
HERRIN, Edward	4
HERRIN, Isaac	4
HERRIN, John	4
HERRIN, John W	4
HERRIN, Mary	4
HERRIN, Rhoda	4
HERRIN, Robert	4
HERRIN, Saline	4
HERRIN, Stephen	4
HERRIN, William	4
HERROD, Herry H	26
HERROD, Holley	41
HERROD, John	26
HERROD, Joseph	26, 42
HERROD, Labora	26
HEWETT, Johnathan	51
HEWETT, Margaret E	51

HEWETT, Mary P	51
HEWETT, William	51
HEWITT, Sarah Grayson	77
HEWTON, Sarah R?	3
HICKS, C. W	83, 91
HICKS, Daniel G	76
HICKS, George W	76
HICKS, Julia C	83
HICKS, Sarah A	76
HICKS, Sarah M	76
HIGH, John	92
HIGH, Lelia L	92
HIGH, M. E	92
HILDERBRAND, David	2
HILDERBRAND, Joseph	2
HILDERBRAND, Louisa S	2
HILDERBRAND, Mary F	2
HILDERBRAND, Philip	2
HILDERBRAND, Rachel	2
HILDERBRAND, Rachel A	2
HILDERBRAND, Thomas	2
HILL, Ann E	75
HILL, Cynthia A	19
HILL, Joseph R	75
HILL, M. C	75
HILL, Nancy	75
HILL, Nancy M	75
HILL, William R	75
HILLMAN, Andrew L	74
HINES, Riply	82
HINES, Thomas	82
HIRSH, Samuel	6
HOBSON, C. A	82
HOBSON, Harry	82
HOBSON, J. B	82
HOBSON, M. A	82
HOBSON, M. B	82
HOBSON, N. W	82
HOBSON, O. A	82
HOBSON, Ophelia E	82
HOBSON, T. L	82
HODGE, William	75
HODGES, Jesse	6
HODGES, John H	7
HOGAN, Mary	29
HOGAN, W. H	80
HOLCOMB, Catherine	68
HOLCOMB, J. S	68
HOLCOMB, M. A	68
HOLCOMB, Olivia	68
HOLLIDAY, Charlotte	32
HOLLIDAY, Dixon	32
HOLLIDAY, Nancy	51
HOLLIDAY, Nathan	51
HOLLIMAN, Abner S	10
HOLLIMAN, Elijah D	10

HOLLIMAN, Fielding C	10	HOOTER, Mary	4
HOLLIMAN, Mary A	10	HOOTER, Massie	1
HOLLIMAN, Pamelia	10	HOOTER, Michael	4
HOLLIMAN, Pamelia H	10	HOOTER, Michael Jr.	4
HOLLIMAN, R A	10	HOOTER, Minerva A	13
HOLLIMAN, Thomas L	10	HOOTER, Nancy	13
HOLLIMAN, Thomas R	10	HOOTER, Sarah A	4
HOLLINGSWORTH, C	86	HOOTER, Sarah E	1
HOLLINGSWORTH, D. M	86	HOOTER, Sarah S	2
HOLLINGSWORTH, Elizabeth	86	HOOTER, William L	13
HOLLINGSWORTH, Franklin	86	HOPE, James	73
HOLLINGSWORTH, Isaac	86	HOPE, John	73
HOLLINGSWORTH, James	86	HOPE, Robert	73
HOLLINGSWORTH, James F	96	HOPE, Sarah Ann	73
HOLLINGSWORTH, Lewis	86	HORNE, J. B	85
HOLLOMAN, William Emery	9	HORNE, M. E	85
HOLLOWAY, Mary	70	HORNE, M. F	85
HOLLOWAY, Sarah	70	HORNE, N. H	85
HOLMES, Adrian D	20	HORNE, S. J	85
HOLMES, Benjamin R	20	HORNE, W. Q	85
HOLMES, C. E	83	HORNE, An Infant Child	85
HOLMES, Charles	83	HOULBERG, F	88
HOLMES, G. H	83	HOUSEN, Margaret	73
HOLMES, Horace	83	HOUSTON, H.	79
HOLMES, John P	20	HOUSTON, J. J.	76
HOLMES, Julia C	83	HOWARD, M. M.	48
HOLMES, Laura	20	HOWARD, Maria Louise	13
HOLMES, Louisa	20	HOWARD, Mary A. G	3
HOLT, Ann E	45	HOWARD, Mary E	81
HOLT, John W	45	HOWARD, Phebe	13
HOLT, Joseph	45	HOWELL, Delilah	67
HOLT, Robert S	45	HOWELL, James M	67
HOLT, Sarah E	45	HOWELL, John	67
HONINGTON, Patrick	83	HOWELL, Joseph	67
HOOKER, Easter A	37	HOWELL, Martha E	67
HOOKER, Elizabeth	37	HOWELL, Mary	67
HOOKER, Jackson	37	HOWELL, Mary A	67
HOOKER, John	37	HOWELL, Robert W	38
HOOKER, Jutha E	37	HUDSON, Elbert	64
HOOKER, Melissa A	37	HUDSON, Elizabeth	72
HOOKER, Robin	37	HUDSON, Frances	72
HOOKER, Samuel	37	HUDSON, Francis	64
HOOKER, Samuel N	37	HUDSON, Henry	64
HOOKER, Sarah	37	HUDSON, James	72
HOOKER, Tabitha	37	HUDSON, Jane	64
HOOTER, Anne	5	HUDSON, John	72
HOOTER, Cyntha J	1	HUDSON, Judy	64
HOOTER, James	13	HUDSON, Letty	64
HOOTER, James A	13	HUDSON, Margaret	64
HOOTER, James N.	1	HUDSON, Melissa	72
HOOTER, John L	13	HUDSON, Nancy	64
HOOTER, John S	4	HUDSON, Sarah	64
HOOTER, John W	13	HUDSON, Washington	64
HOOTER, L. J	13	HUDSON, William K	64
HOOTER, Margaret	4	HUDUALL, William W	20
HOOTER, Maria L	13	HUFFMAN, Caroline	31

HUFFMAN, Elizabeth	31	JACKSON, Edward A	91
HUFFMAN, John	31	JACKSON, Elizabeth	90
HUFFMAN, Margaret	31	JACKSON, Flemming	29
HUFFMAN, Mary	31	JACKSON, Henrietta S	91
HUGHES, Ann	57	JACKSON, Henry C	14
HUGHES, Catherine	57	JACKSON, James	90
HUGHES, J. J.	96	JACKSON, James W	90
HUGHES, M	79	JACKSON, Jane	19
HUGHES, Nancy S	57	JACKSON, Jesse H	19
HUGHES, Rhoda	57	JACKSON, Margaret E	24
HUGHES, Tabitha	57	JACKSON, Martha	19
HUGHES, Thomas	57	JACKSON, Martha E	14
HUGHS, Margaret	26	JACKSON, Mary	14
HUNT, Cenia	5	JACKSON, Mary A	29
HUNT, Thomas	5	JACKSON, Matthew	29
HUNT, Thomas J	5	JACKSON, Sarah C	91
HUNTER, Aramesia	92	JACKSON, Upton	29
HUNTER, E. R	92	JACKSON, William C	14
HUNTER, Elizabeth	92	JAGGERS, Lucinda A	5
HUNTER, H. W.	28	JAGGERS, Martha E	5
HUNTER, Isaac H. J?	92	JAMES, Benjamin F	72
HUNTER, John A	92	JAMES, Charlotte	72
HURST, Judith Nutt	16	JAMES, D. A	88
HURST, Susan	77	JAMES, Peter	72
HURST, Thermophlae	77	JAMES, Peter O.	72
HUSMAN? Mary	81	JAMES, Samuel L	68
HUTSON, John W	54	JAMES, Thomas	68
HYATT, Ann	87	JAMES?, Elizabeth	71
HYATT, F. M	87	JARRET, Lavina	38
HYATT, L. L	87	JEFFERS, Caroline	69
HYATT, R. P	87	JEFFERS, Daniel	69
HYATT, Richard	86	JEFFERS, Elizabeth	69
IGO, Daniel	78	JEFFERS, Jane	69
INGERSOLL, John	77	JEFFERS, John	69
INGRAM, Hannah	17	JEFFERS, Lee	69
INGRAM, Moses	17	JEFFERS, Louisa	69
INGRAM, Nathaniel	17	JEFFERS, Osborne	69
INGRAM, Rachel	81	JEFFERS, Thomas	69
INGRAM, Richard	17	JEFFERS, Warren	69
INGRAM, Susanna	17	JEFFERSON, Elizabeth	24
IRWIN, Elizabeth	69	JEFFERY, John	86
IRWIN, Elizabeth?	3	JENKINS, Augustus	92
IRWIN, Julia Helen	11	JENKINS, Caroline	18
ISBEY, Charles	72	JENKINS, Carter	92
ISBEY, Martha K	72	JENKINS, E. C	92
ISBEY, W. G. H. C.	72	JENKINS, Edward	18
ISENHOOD, Martha	13	JENKINS, Elijah	18
ISENHOOD, William	11	JENKINS, Emma	18
ISONHOOD, Frances	11	JENKINS, Frank	92
IVOY, Nancy	35	JENKINS, Geo. C	92
JACKSON, Ailsey	29	JENKINS, George	18
JACKSON, Cavill	14	JENKINS, Henry	18
JACKSON, Charity B	90	JENKINS, John	18
JACKSON, Chelly M	90	JENKINS, M. A	92
JACKSON, Druscilla	19	JENKINS, Maria	18
JACKSON, E	90	JENKINS, Mary	18

JENKINS, Mary E	92	JOHNSTON, James	92
JENKINS, R. O	92	JOHNSTON, Jane E	92
JENKINS, Sarah	92	JOHNSTON, Louisa	92
JENKINS, Sarah C	87	JOHNSTON, M.S.A.	30
JENNINGS, John J	44	JOHNSTON, Mary	30
JENNINGS, R. T	79	JOHNSTON, Mary Ann	92
JOHNS, Ellen	13	JOHNSTON, Nancy	70
JOHNS, George W	13	JOHNSTON, Rachel	72
JOHNS, Sarah	13	JOHNSTON, Thos. J	92
JOHNS, William	13	JOHNSTON, Tilman J	70
JOHNS, William O	13	JOHNSTON, Walter L	30
JOHNSON, Abel B	90	JOHNSTON, William B	28
JOHNSON, Abner	32	JOHNSTON, Wm	92
JOHNSON, Albert	45	JONES, Daniel	40
JOHNSON, Ann E	31	JONES, E.	54
JOHNSON, Benjamin F	33	JONES, E. M	88
JOHNSON, Caleb	32	JONES, Eliza	40
JOHNSON, Catherine	61	JONES, G. W	88
JOHNSON, Charles H	61	JONES, James M	43
JOHNSON, Eliza	87	JONES, John H	43
JOHNSON, Elizabeth	31	JONES, Leake	88
JOHNSON, Eugenia	54	JONES, M. E	88
JOHNSON, Frances	25, 31	JONES, Mary	60
JOHNSON, Frederick B	54	JONES, Melvina	88
JOHNSON, George W	61	JONES, Peter	95
JOHNSON, Hiram	31	JONES, Samuel W	40
JOHNSON, J. M	79	JONES, Thos	95
JOHNSON, James	31, 32, 61, 68	JORDON, Tabitha	42
JOHNSON, Jehu	31	JUDKINS, John F	14
JOHNSON, John	31, 34, 55	JUDKINS, Martha J	14
JOHNSON, John W	61	KAYES, Michael	39
JOHNSON, Lafayette	25	KAYS, Margaret	82
JOHNSON, Laura	31	KAYS, Martha J	39
JOHNSON, Loranne	34	KAYS, Mary A	39
JOHNSON, Louisa	34	KAYS, Mary M	94
JOHNSON, M. H	79	KAYS, O Daniel	39
JOHNSON, Marcellus	90	KAYS, Patrick H	39
JOHNSON, Margaret	61	KEEBLES, Frances H	96
JOHNSON, Martha	61, 90	KEIRN, W. L	84
JOHNSON, Mary	32	KEITH, Katury	31
JOHNSON, Mary E	61	KELLY, Ann	83
JOHNSON, Mary Elizabeth	91	KELLY, Eliza	83
JOHNSON, Miles	31	KELLY, Ellen	83
JOHNSON, Miranda	32	KELLY, Hugh	83
JOHNSON, Nancy	31	KEMPTON, Eliza	89
JOHNSON, Oliver	32	KEMPTON, Geo. C	89
JOHNSON, Penelope	61	KEMPTON, John	89
JOHNSON, Robert E	34	KEMPTON, Mary	89
JOHNSON, Samuel	61	KEMPTON, Sam'l D	89
JOHNSON, Sarah	32	KEMPTON, Wm	89
JOHNSON, Sarah A	35	KEN, Alexander	53
JOHNSON, Temperance	54	KENNEDY, A. M	87
JOHNSON, Thomas	32	KENNEDY, Claire	87
JOHNSON, Thomas N	54	KENNEDY, M. O. C	87
JOHNSON, Virginia	74	KENNEDY, Patrick	83
JOHNSON, William	32	KENT, Mary	47

KENT, Robert	47	KOHLMANN, Ada	44
KEYS, Eliz. M	95	KOHLMANN, Bettie	44
KEYS, R. E	95	KOHLMANN, Charles	44
KEYZER, A. R.	79	KOHLMANN, Henry	44
KIDD, H. B	82	KOHLMANN, Jacob	44
KIDD, R. E	82	KOHLMANN, Mary	44
KIERNON, Frank	34	KOHLMANN, William	44
KIMBALL, S. R	88	KUHN, Elizabeth	63
KIMBALL, Susan	88	KUNKELL, Samuel K	51
KING, Aaron	22	LAFFERTY, John	77
KING, Allen	57	LAMB, Milton B	54
KING, Ann	22	LAMB, Samuel H	54
KING, Ann J	52	LAMBERT, Eliza Ann	51
KING, Burton A	52	LAMBETH, Addison	75
KING, C. S.	53	LAMBETH, Fanny	75
KING, Catherine	3	LAMBETH, Horace	75
KING, Celia	59	LAMBETH, Julia	64
KING, Douglas S	22	LAMBETH, Robert	75
KING, Elias	22	LAMBETH, Susan H	75
KING, Eliza E	95	LAMBETH, William	75
KING, Frances E	22	LAMKIN, D. W	80
KING, Harriet	52	LAMKIN, H. C	74
KING, James D	22	LAMKIN, Jerimiah	74
KING, John D	22	LAMKIN, John C	74
KING, John H	22	LAMKIN, M. A. E.	74
KING, Letitia	22	LAMKIN, M. I	74
KING, Livingston M P	52	LAMKIN, Mary A	74
KING, Lucinda	57	LAMKIN, Ronnilus?	74
KING, Lucretia Edward	76	LAMKIN, T. F.	74
KING, Lydia	52	LAMKIN, Thomas	40
KING, Maria	22	LAMKIN, Thomas G	74
KING, Maria E	22	LAMKIN, William F	90
KING, Martha L	30	LAND, Susan	81
KING, Mary L	12	LAND, William	81
KING, Ocatvia	21	LANDER, C. F	81
KING, Prudence	47	LANDER, John H	81
KING, Sarah B	95	LANDER, M. A	81
KING, Susan	52	LANDER, M. H	81
KING, Thomas S	22	LANDER, M. J	81
KING, Virginia L	54	LANDER, Peter	81
KING, William	52	LANGAN,	96
KING, William L	22	LANGAN, P. H?	96
KING, William P	22	LANGFORD, Mary C	41
KIRK, Elizabeth	48	LANGLY, Joseph J	52
KIRK, John W	51	LANGLY, Margaret E	52
KIRK, Octavia H	50	LANGLY, Martha	52
KIRK, Thomas J	50	LASSITER, Avery A	28
KIRK, William	48	LASSITER, Brown	28
KIRMAN, Chs. D	91	LASSITER, George A	28
KIRMAN, Mary	91	LASSITER, James F	28
KNIGHT, Elizabeth	65	LASSITER, Walter	28
KNIGHT, Harriet	33	LASSITER, Wesley M	28
KNIGHT, James L	65	LATHERS, Catherine	59
KNIGHTEN, Joab	55	LATHERS, John	59
KNIGHTON, Sarah C	70	LAUGHORN, Elias M	28
KOHLMAN, Henry	83	LAVENBERG, Amelia	85

LAVENBERG, Jacob	85	LEWIS, Margaret	94
LAVENBERG, Levi	85	LEWIS, Mary	33
LAVENDER, Elizabeth	9	LEWIS, Mary T	91
LAVENDER, Ferdinand W	9	LEWIS, Mordica	94
LAVENDER, Henry C	9	LEWIS, Thomas C	17
LAVENDER, Jerome P	9	LEWIS, Volney C	94
LAVENDER, Joseph P	9	LEWIS, W. C	82
LAVENDER, Saber	9	LIGHT, James A	93
LAWRENCE, J. H	93	LIGHT, Maria T	93
LAWRENCE, Upton K	93	LILLYBRIDGE, Susan	4
LAWRENCE, V. D	93	LINCH, Jeanette	80
LAWRENCE, W. L	93	LINCH, Mary	80
LEA, Lucy	73	LINK, Amelia	81
LEA, Sarah E	73	LINK, Cha. S. C	81
LEAKE, H. K	84	LINK, Elizabeth	81
LEAKE, M. L	84	LINK, J. J	81
LEAKE, Wm. J	84	LINK, John	81
LEAR, John	82	LINK, Louisa	81
LEAR, Mary C	42	LINK, M. E	81
LEE, Calvin	73	LINK, Mary	81
LeLANDE, Joseph	75	LINK, Noah D	81
LEMMONS, Andrew M	25	LINK, Rachal	81
LEMMONS, Caroline	25	LIPMAN, Abraham	85
LEMMONS, Cornelius	25	LITTLE, N. H.	45
LEMMONS, Daniel	26	LIVINGIN, Newman	85
LEMMONS, David	25	LIVINGSTON, Ewing	75
LEMMONS, James	25	LIVINGSTON, Henrietta	75
LEMMONS, Jane	26	LIVINGSTON, James	75
LEMMONS, John	25	LIVINGSTON, Lucrin?	75
LEMMONS, Levi	26	LIVINGSTON, P. A.	75
LEMMONS, Malcomb	25, 26	LIVINGSTON, Philip	85
LEMMONS, Margaret	25	LIVINGSTON, Samuel	75
LEMMONS, Martha	26	LIVINGSTON, Samuel D	75
LEMMONS, Mary	26	LIVINGSTON, William	75
LEMMONS, Nancy	26	LOFTIN, R. B.	48
LEMMONS, Sarah	25	LONG, A. V.	30
LEMMONS, William	25	LONG, Charles	30
LESSELL, Harriet	65	LONG, Elizabeth	30
LESSELL, Jennson	65	LONG, Jesse G	30
LESSELL, John	65	LONG, Malvina	30
LESSELL, Lenora	65	LONG, Martha L	30
LESSELL, Martha	65	LONG, Mary	92
LESSELL, Mary	65	LONG, Sarah	30
LESTER	4	LONG, William	30
LEVY, Eliza R	75	LOTT, Casselia	54
LEVY, John	75	LOTT, Elizabeth	18
LEVY, Samuel	75	Louisa	81
LEWIS, Benjamin E	33	LOVE, Falba	68
LEWIS, E. H	82	LOVE, Josephus	68
LEWIS, Elizabeth	17	LOVETT, Thomas 4	35
LEWIS, Horace	94	LOWRY, John R	3
LEWIS, Isabella	17	LUCIUS, Barboam E	27
LEWIS, J. C	82	LUCIUS, Catherine	27
LEWIS, Lucy C	82	LUCIUS, E. C.	27
LEWIS, Lucy J	5	LUCIUS, J	27
LEWIS, M. A	82	LUCIUS, J. B.	27

LUCIUS, Lucinda	. . . .	25
LUCIUS, Lucinda C	. . . .	27
LUCIUS, Martha A	. . . .	27
LUCIUS, Sarah E	. . . .	27
LUCIUS, Thomas J	. . . .	27
LUCKEY, Wm	. . . .	94
LUCUS, John	. . . .	36
LUCUS, Nancy	. . . .	36
LUCUS, William	. . . .	36
LUMBLEY, Joseph S	. . . .	5
LUMLEY, Joseph S	. . . .	1
LUMLEY, William W	. . . . . .	5
LUSE, Alexander	. . . .	67
LUSE, Alice	. . . .	66
LUSE, Ann E	 66,	67
LUSE, Calvin	. . . .	67
LUSE, Clementina	. . . .	67
LUSE, Edwin	. . . .	66
LUSE, Henry	. . . .	46
LUSE, Hester Ann	. . . . . .	24
LUSE, James N	. . . .	46
LUSE, Mary Berlinda	. . . . .	66
LUSE, Nathan	. . . .	22
LUSE, Nathan H	. . . .	22
LUSE, Nathan K	. . . .	67
LUSE, Olivia	. . . .	46
LUSE, Richard H. M.	. . . . . .	21
LUSE, Sally A	. . . .	46
LUSE, Stephen	. . . .	46
LUSE, Thaddeus	. . . .	46
LUSK, Elizabeth	. . . .	45
LUSK, Francis	. . . .	45
LUSK, Hiram	. . . .	45
LUSK, James	. . . .	45
LUSK, John	. . . .	45
LYLE, Harriet S	. . . .	8
LYLE, Susan	. . . .	6
LYLE, William H	. . . .	6
LYNCH, A	. . . .	80
LYSELL, Louisiana	. . . . . .	66
MABIN, Andrew S	. . . .	10
MABIN, Benjamin F	. . . . . .	10
MABIN, Charity	. . . .	10
MABIN, Elizabeth	. . . . . .	10
MABIN, Joseph W	. . . .	9
MABIN, Lauretta A	. . . . . .	10
MABIN, Mary A	. . . .	10
MABIN, Mary E	. . . .	10
MABIN, Mary J	. . . .	10
MABIN, Nancy A	. . . .	10
MABIN, Robert M	. . . .	10
MABIN, Thomas S	. . . .	10
MABIN, Warren I	. . . .	10
MABIN, William	. . . .	10
MAIER, Moses	. . . .	91
MALONE, Margarett	. . . . . .	82

MALONE, Michael	. . . .	83
MALONE, Thomas	. . . .	82
MALONY, And.	. . . .	93
MALONY, Andy	. . . .	77
MANGUM, Catherine	. . . . . .	48
MANGUM, Frances	. . . . . .	48
MANGUM, Louisa	. . . . . .	48
MANGUM, Martha C	. . . . . .	48
MANGUM, William H	. . . . . .	48
MANGUM, William W	. . . . . .	48
MANN, C. T	. . . .	79
MANNING, Charles	. . . . . .	47
MANNING, Emily	. . . . . .	43
MANNING, Henry E	. . . . . .	47
MANNING, Mary A	. . . . . .	47
MANNING, Richard E	. . . . .	47
MANNING, Susan	. . . . . .	47
MANOR, Evelina C	. . . . . .	38
MANSFIELD, S	. . . .	96
MANSFIELD, S.	. . . .	96
MANSFIELD, S. J	. . . . . .	96
MANSFIELD, William A	. . . . .	1
MANSFIELD, Wm	. . . .	96
MARBLE, B.F.	. . . .	6
MARBLE, Elizabeth	. . . . . .	27
MARBLE, Rinaldo D	 6,	15
MARBLE, S. M	. . . .	84
MARCHBANKS, C. W.	. . . . . .	4
MARCHBANKS, Elizabeth	. . . .	4
MARKHAM, Elizabeth M	. . . .	95
MARKHAM, Frances	. . . . . .	79
MARKHAM, Frances M	. . . . .	95
MARKS, Isaac	. . . .	89
MARKS, Susan Ann	. . . . . .	89
MARLEY, Amelia	. . . . . .	9
MARLEY, Mary R	. . . . . .	9
MARLEY, Nancy	. . . .	9
MARLEY, Nancy C	. . . . . .	9
MARLEY, Robert H	. . . . . .	9
MARLEY, Samuel	. . . . . .	9
MARLEY, Samuel P	. . . . . .	9
MARLEY, Walter S	. . . . . .	9
MARLEY, Wesley A.	. . . . . .	9
MARSHALL, Charles	. . . . . .	19
MARSHALL, Frances	. . . . . .	19
MARSHALL, Henry	. . . . . .	90
MARSHALL, Milley	. . . . . .	19
MARSHALL, Octavia H	. . . . .	50
MARSHALL, Thomas S	. . . . .	19
MARSHALL, William	. . . . . .	19
MARTIN, Benjamin F	. . . . . .	5
MARTIN, Caroline	 26,	35
MARTIN, Elisha A	. . . . . .	5
MARTIN, Isaac	. . . .	56
MARTIN, Isaac W	. . . . . .	5
MARTIN, James	. . . .	2

MARTIN, James W	5	McCANN, Emma	36
MARTIN, Jesse W	5	McCANN, James	36
MARTIN, John	84	McCANN, Martha J	36
MARTIN, Joseph J	5	McCANN, Mary	36
MARTIN, Louisa	35	McCANN, Patrick N	36
MARTIN, Lucretia	2	McCANN, Rachel N	36
MARTIN, Martha	35	McCANN, Robert	36
MARTIN, Mary	2	McCANN, Susan	36
MARTIN, Mary Allison	53	McCARTY, C. J. T	69
MARTIN, Nancy C	5	McCARTY, Catherine	22
MARTIN, Nancy Catherine	1	McCARTY, Elizabeth	69
MARTIN, Rebecca	5, 35	McCARTY, Matilda	22
MARTIN, Sampson A	5	McCARTY, T.C.R	22
MARTIN, Susan I	5	McCLEARY, J. A	90
MARTIN, Susannah	5	McCLOUD, G. A	82
MARTIN, William	5	McCLURE, Anne	5
MARTIN, William A	2	McCLURE, John	5
MARTIN, William P	5	McCLURE, Thomas	5
MARTIN,? Adeline C?	87	McCOMBS, Mary D	80
MASSEY, S. T	88	McCORKNEY, Eveline	35
MATHEWS, Emila	85	McCORKNEY, George	35
MATHEWS, Nancy	60	McCORKNEY, J. D.	35
MATHEWS, Sam'l	85	McCORKNEY, Jesse	35
Mathis Day	60	McCORKNEY, Julia	35
MATHIS, Lucy	31	McCORKNEY, Maben	35
MATHIS, Mary A	30	McCORKNEY, Sarah J	35
MATHIS, W. F.	30	McCORMACK, Joseph	19
MATIAR, William B	10	McCORMACK, Almira	18
MATTHEWS, Elizabeth	59	McCORMACK, Amanda	19
MATTHEWS, Sophia	63	McCORMACK, Benjamin T	18
MATTINGLY, J. R	79	McCORMACK, Elizabeth	19
MAULDING, Wm	83	McCORMACK, Franklin	19
MAXEY, Celia	57	McCORMACK, George	19
MAXEY, Eliza	57	McCORMACK, James C	19
MAXEY, James	57	McCORMACK, John C	19
MAXEY, Martha	57	McCORMACK, John D	63
MAXEY, W. G. W	57	McCORMACK, John H	19
MAXEY, William	57	McCORMACK, Margaret	63
MAY, Berry	67	McCORMACK, Robert	19
MAY, Elizabeth	78	McCORMACK, Robert P	19
MAY, L. B.	67	McCORMACK, Sarah A	19
MAY, Mary	50	McCORMACK, Sarah L. J.	63
MAY, Michajah	78	McCUTCHEN, Elizabeth	76
MAY, Thomas	67	McCUTCHEN, James P	76
MAY, William	67	McCUTCHEN, John H	76
MAYNARD, M. C	79	McCUTCHEN, L. E	76
MAYNER, John	38	McCUTCHEN, Mary E	71
MAYNER, Lavina	38	McCUTCHEN, T? N	76
MAYNER, Levi	38	McCUTCHEN, Wm. R	76
MAYNER, Margaret	38	McDOWELL, A. J	42
MAYNER, Sanders	38	McDOWELL, Dealia	42
MAYNER, Thomas	38	McDOWELL, Ezelia	42
MAYNER, William	38	McDOWELL, Harriet	42
MAYS, Frances E	50	McDOWELL, Harrison	42
MAYS, Laura A	24	McDOWELL, Sarah	42
McCAFFREY, Catherine M	27	McDOWELL, William T.M.	42

McDUFFIE, John 35	MEYER, James 41
McDUFFIE, Martha J 35	MEYER, July 41
McDUFFIE, Mrs. Mary 39	MEYER, Massa? 41
McDUFFIE, Norman L 39	MEYER, Phillip 41
McEACHEN, John A 71	MEYER, Thomas 41
McEACHEN, Lucretia 71	MICHIE, John J 90
McEACHEN, Peter 71	MIKIE, Patrick 75
McELEVEE, Elvy 86	MILES, Deut H 6
McELEVEE, John 86	MILES, Elizabeth 6
McELEVEE, Martha 86	MILES, Mary J 6
McFARLAND, Andrew 3	MILES, Mary Jane 80
McFARLAND, John 91	MILES, Sheridan 6
McGEE, Emily 18	MILES, Virginia 6, 8
McGEE, Louisiana Indiana 35	MILLER, Caroline 81
McGEHEE, Augustus 24	MILLER, Delilah 65
McGEHEE, Edward S 24	MILLER, Eveline V 65
McGEHEE, James E 24	MILLER, F. E 82
McGEHEE, Nancy 24	MILLER, Henry C 65
McGIBONEY, James 15	MILLER, James M 65
McGIBONEY, Mary 15	MILLER, Joseph 90
McGRATH, Patrick 83	MILLER, Joshua 14
McKEE, Anna R 3	MILLER, Mary F 65
McKEE, Copeland 3	MILLER, Thos. P 93
McKEE, Edward C 45	MILLER, William D 65
McKEE, Edward G 45	MILLS, Buford B 36
McKEE, Isabel E 45	MILLS, Harriet B 73
McKEE, Maria 45	MILLS, Henry C 73
McKENNA, Ann 83	MILLS, William 73
McLAIN, Alfred 12	MILLS, William J 73
McLEOD, Alexander 8	MITCHELL, E. A 86
McLEOD, Cordelia 8	MITCHELL, Edward 80
McLEOD, Emma J 8	MITCHELL, Martha E 93
McLEOD, Jane M 8	MITCHELL, Priscilla 7
McLEOD, Nancy 8	MITCHELL, S. V 86
McLEOD, Richmond 8	MOBLEY, Adeliza 46
McMASTERS, Jefferson 41	MOBLEY, Edward G 46
McMASTERS, John 41	MOBLEY, Eugena 46
McNEIL, Daniel N 64	MOBLEY, Gertrude 46
McNEIL, Matthew M 64	MOBLEY, Jane 46
McNIEL, William A. J. 56	MOBLEY, M. R 79
McQUISTTON, Amanda 94	MOBLY, Benjamin A 66
McQUISTTON, M. P 94	MOORE, Casandra 58
MEAD, Horace D 75	MOORE, Elizabeth 37, 39
MEEK, Anna 57	MOORE, Ezekiel 37, 62
MEEK, Harriet 57	MOORE, Ezekiel, Jr 37
MEEK, James 57	MOORE, Harrison 55
MEEK, Mary 57	MOORE, J. W 92
MEEK, Thomas 57	MOORE, James A 55
MELLEN, Mary 93	MOORE, Jane 37, 74
MERCHANT, Alfred 41	MOORE, Joseph G 55
MERCHANT, William 41, 84	MOORE, Lewis 55
METZLER, J. T 83	MOORE, Lewy 55
METZLER, M. A 83	MOORE, Martha 58
METZLER, Thomas 83	MOORE, Mary 55, 59, 61
MEYER, Alexander 41	MOORE, Mary A 37
MEYER, Harrison 41	MOORE, William J 37

MOORIS, Mary	31	NEWBAKER, Lucinda	11
MOREY, William S	19	NEWBAKER, Marshall H	11
MORGAN, J. M	84	NEWBAKER, Martha	8, 11
MORRIS, Joseph F. M.	47	NEWBAKER, Mary	8, 11
MORRIS, M	85	NEWBAKER, Mary A	13
MORTON, Alexander	40	NEWBAKER, Penimia	11
MORTON, Alice L	40	NEWBAKER, Thomas	11
MORTON, Augustine	40	NEWBERRY, Elizabeth	86
MORTON, Catherine	17	NEWSOM, David	57
MORTON, Catherine L	40	NEWSOM, Nancy	57
MORTON, Cornelia	40	NICEMAN, Peter	83
MORTON, Elenor H	40	NICHOLS, Daniel	26
MORTON, Ellen S	40	NICHOLS, Eliza A	26
MORTON, Fanny E	32	NICHOLS, James	26
MORTON, Joseph W	32	NICHOLS, Lydia	88
MORTON, Louisa	48	NICHOLS, William	26, 88
MORTON, William	40	NILES, E. A	87
MOSELY, Ann E	34	NILES, J. W. J	87
MOSELY, Edwin	34	NILES, S. L. G	87
MOSELY, Joseph R	34	NILEY, Alonzo	84
MOSELY, Josephine	34	NILEY, John	84
MOSELY, Lucina? J	34	NILEY, Margaret	84
MOSELY, Peter	45	NILEY, Mary	84
MOSELY, Sarah	45	NILEY, Perry	84
MURPHEE, Elizabeth	70	NOBLE, Amanda M	59
MURPHEE, John	70	NOLAN, Elizabeth	50
MURRAY, Robert	34	NOLAN, James H	50
MURRAY, Wm	86	NOLAN, Maria L	23, 50
MURRY, Thomas	86	NOLAN, Tilman	50
MYERS, Elizabeth	85	NOONAN, Thomas	24
MYERS, John	77	NORMAN, Andrew J	29
NEEL, Sarah Jane	55	NORMAN, Elizabeth	71
NEELY, Emily	38	NORMAN, James A	71
NEELY, Jane T	38	NORMAN, James F	71
NEELY, Martha	38	NORMAN, James R	29
NEELY, Minerva	38	NORMAN, Lavina	29
NEELY, Nancy S	38	NORMAN, Mary G	71
NEELY, Susan	38	NORMAN, Nancy L	29
NEELY, William	38	NORMAN, William D	29
NEIL, Henry	67	NUNNALLY, H. A	79
NEIL, Matthew	67	NUNNIMAN, Joseph	14
NELSMIRTH, Catherine	82	NYE, D. J	90
NELSON, A. Louisa	95	NYE, L. A	90
NELSON, Bernard H	23	NYE, N. G	90
NELSON, Elizabeth E	23	NYE, S. E	90
NELSON, Elzira	23	NYE, W. H. H	90
NELSON, Franklin H	23	O'BRIEN, Henry	67
NELSON, T. J. L	23	O'CONNER, James	81, 86
NESBITT, Moses E	32	O'DONALDSON, Mary	18
NEWBAKER, Benson	11	O'DONNELL, P	79
NEWBAKER, Catherine	11	O'FERRELL, John	96
NEWBAKER, David S	11	O'NEAL, Eveline	38
NEWBAKER, James	13	O'NEAL, Joab	38
NEWBAKER, James Jr.	13	O'NEAL, Mary	30, 38
NEWBAKER, John	11	O'QUINN, David	69
NEWBAKER, John W	13	O'QUINN, Elizabeth	69

O'QUINN, James	69	PEARSALL, Charlotte	86
O'QUINN, Martha	69	PEASE, John B	89
O'QUINN, Nancy	69	PEASTER, Alfred	65
O'QUINN, Sarah E	69	PEASTER, Cynthia	65
O'QUINN, Teresa	69	PEASTER, Delilah	65
O'QUINN, Z. E	69	PEASTER, Elizabeth	65
O'REILLY	23	PEASTER, James	65
O'REILLY, J. E	79	PEASTER, James H	49
O'REILLY, Kate	51	PEASTER, Jane	65
O'REILLY, Mary	51	PEASTER, Leonidas	49
O'REILLY, Sarah	51	PEASTER, Lucinda	49
O'REILLY, Thomas	82	PEASTER, Mary	65
O'ROURKER, David	81	PEASTER, Michael	65
OGDEN, Benjamin	68	PEASTER, Samuel	49
OGDEN, Elizabeth	69	PEASTER, Sarah	49
OGDEN, Elnora	68	PEASTER, Tapley H	65
OGDEN, George	69	PEASTER, William	65
OGDEN, George W	56	PEERS, Catherine	3
OGDEN, Harrison	68	PEERS, Elizabeth	3
OGDEN, Henry	68	PEERS, John W	3
OGDEN, Louisa	68	PEERS, Marion	3
OGDEN, Lucy W	69	PEERS, Mary	1
OGDEN, Mary Ann	56	PEERS, Mary E	3
OGDEN, Mary J	69	PEERS, Minerva	3
OGDEN, Rebecca	12	PEERS, Nancy A	3
OGDEN, Rebecca Irion	21	PEERS, Samuel	3
OGDEN, Theophilus	69	PEERS, Samuel P	3
OGDEN, Wm. D	68	PEERS, Sarah A	3
OLDHAM OR WILLIAMS, E. C	12	PEERS, William	3
OLDHAM, James	12	PEERS, William N	3
OLDHAM, John	12	PEIRCE, Lewis	80
OLDHAM, Minerva	12	PENDER, Amanda	14
OLDHAM, Moses	12	PENDER, Celab	14
OLDHAM, Sarah A	12	PENDER, Gabriel	96
OLIVER, Octavia	60	PENDER, Helen	14
OWENS, Charlotte	32	PENDER, James W	14
OWENS, William F	48	PENDER, John	14
PAGE, Anderson	84	PENDER, Nancy	14, 96
PAGE, Elizabeth C	84	PENDER, Nancy Ann	40
PAGE, J. A. W	84	PENDER, William B	14
PARASOT, Amandus	89	PENNY, Eliza	60
PARASOTT, Sherman	80	PENNY, Elizabeth	60
PARISH, Anderson	19	PENNY, George W	31
PARISH, Archibald A	19	PENNY, James	83
PARISH, Harriet	10	PENNY, John A	60
PARKER, James	94	PENNY, John W	60
PARKS, Margaret	6	PENNY, Mary	60
PARMER, B. H	96	PENNY, Mary E	22
PARNELL, Samuel	74	PENNY, Rachel	60
PARRISOT, Josephine	89	PENSTER, William	65
PATTERSON, Alexander	83	PEPPER, Ambrose	61
PAUL, John S	73	PEPPER, Bruce	61
PAUL, O. S	73	PEPPER, E. B	63
PAUL, Sarah J	73	PEPPER, Elisha	63
PEARCE, Stephen D	75	PEPPER, Elizabeth	63
PEARL, Alice	45	PEPPER, Franklin	63

PEPPER, Freelove	63	PHIPPS, R.	45
PEPPER, James	61	PICKETT, Eliza	50
PEPPER, Jesse	61	PICKETT, Georgeana	87
PEPPER, John	61	PICKETT, J. M	87
PEPPER, John J	63	PICKETT, James M	52
PEPPER, Rachel	61, 63	PICKETT, Jane E	52
PEPPER, Sarah	61	PICKETT, John	50
PEPPER, William	61, 63	PICKETT, Louisa	52
PEPPER, Zedikiah	61	PICKETT, Mary	87
PEPPER, Zedikiah Jr	61	PICKETT, Mary E	50
PERKINS, A. S	84	PICKETT, Micajah	52
PERKINS, Amanda	16	PICKETT, R. K	87
PERKINS, Charles	16	PICKETT, S. C	87
PERKINS, Cornelia	94	PICKETT, Sarah	52
PERKINS, F. M	84	PICKETT, Susan	50
PERKINS, Judith N	16	PICKETT, William	50
PERKINS, Julia	16	PICKETT, Wm	87
PERKINS, Kate	16	PIERSON, John J	62
PERKINS, Lucy	16	PIERSON, Joseph J	62
PERKINS, M. V. F	84	PIERSON, Louisiana	62
PERKINS, Martha	16	PIERSON, William	62
PERKINS, Mary	16	PINKLESON, John	62
PERKINS, Robert S. G	16	PINKSTON, Anderson	21
PERKINS, Susan	16	PINKSTON, Elizabeth	21
PERKINS? Mary	44	PINKSTON, Feliz G	21
PERRY, A. L	95	PINKSTON, John S	21
PERRY, Ann	1	PINKSTON, Margaret	21
PERRY, Eliza	77	PINKSTON, Mary J	21
PERRY, Elizabeth	95	PINKSTON, Susan	21
PERRY, Emanuel	77	PITMAN, Mary	86
PERRY, James Jr	18	PITTMAN?, Nancy	31
PERRY, John	95	PLUNKETT, Benjamin	42
PERRY, L. A	90	PLUNKETT, Eveline	42
PERRY, Mary	18, 78	POND, Sidney A	1
PERRY, Nat	95	POND, Thomas	1
PERRY, Nat. N	95	POND, Walter A	1
PERRY, Nathaniel	18	POOL, Elizabeth P	13
PERRY, Pauline	91	POPE, Emina	80
PERRY, Sarah	95	POPE, Irene	80
PETER, Emeline W	33	POPE, Ophelia	80
PEYTON, William H	7	POPE, P. B	80
PHILLIPS, Benj	77	POPE, S. G	80
PHILLIPS, F. R	77	POPE, W. C	80
PHILLIPS, Haywood	77	POTTER, Annie M	1
PHILLIPS, J. R. W.	77	POTTER, Caleb	1
PHILLIPS, Jane	74	POTTER, Cynthia	1
PHILLIPS, Joseph	84	POTTER, Elizabeth	1
PHILLIPS, Martha Jerusha	91	POTTER, James	1
PHILLIPS, Peter	77	POTTER, John	1
PHILLIPS, S. E	77	POTTER, John C	1
PHILLIPS, Ther	77	POTTER, John Jr.	1
PHILLIPS, W. E	77	POTTER, Joseph	1
PHILLIPS, Wm	77	POTTER, Polly	1
PHIPPS, Fanny E	32	POTTER, Sarah Ann	4
PHIPPS, M. B.	38	POTTER, Thomas	1
PHIPPS, Mary Pauline	30	POTTS, R. E	80

POTTS, Z. W	80	QUINNE, William	21
POTTS? Ellen J	80	RABB, Harriet J	24
POWELL, Alice C	15	RABB, Hester J	24
POWELL, B. F	80	RABB, Matilda	24
POWELL, Edward B	15	RABB, Rachel	24
POWELL, G. M	79	RABB, William	24
POWELL, J. J	62	RABB, William F	24
POWELL, M. J.	15	RAMMELSBERG, Hugo	81
POWELL, Martha A	15	RANDOLPH, L. W	82
POWELL, Richard B	15	RANDOLPH, Mary T	84
POWELL, Susan	27	RASPBERRY, John T	74
POWERS, Benjamin	40	RASPBERRY, Mary A	74
POWERS, C.A	32	RASPBERRY, Patience A	74
POWERS, Cynthia A	40	RASPBERRY, William G	74
PRESTRIDGE, Mary	50	RATCLIFF, Calvin	78
PRESTRIDGE, William A	50	RATCLIFF, J. N	86
PRICE, Amos	28	RATCLIFF, Nancy	78
PRIMM, A. R	87	RATCLIFF, Sam'l H	78
PRIMM, C. H	87	RATCLIFF, Sam'l N	78
PRIMM, John B	87	RAWLINGS, Caroline H	16
PRIMM, Lucy	87	RAWLINGS, Daniel	16
PRIMM, Mary A	87	RAWLINGS, Emma J	16
PRIMM, W. J	87	RAY, Elijah	16
PRITCHARD, Theophilus P	70	RAY, Emily	16
PRITCHETT, Georganna	7	RAY, Frances M	16
PRITCHETT, Henry M	7	RAY, George N	16
PRITCHETT, Robert J S	7	RAY, Hernando D	16
PRITCHETT, Sarah M	7	RAY, James J	16
PRITCHETT, William P	7	RAY, Martha M	67
PUCKETT, Robert	59	RAY, Mary J	16
PUGH, Henry G	93	REAGAN, Thomas J	6
PUGH, Martha E	93	REAVES, Jane	12
PUGH, N. T.	93	REDDING, Amanda	94
PUGH, Wm. D	93	REDDING, Eliz	94
PUGH, Wm. E.	93	REDDING, James	94
PURVIS, Dorothy	95	REDDING, John	94
PURVIS, Edward W	20	REDDING, Mary	94
PURVIS, Eliza. E	95	REDDISH, Elisha	55
PURVIS, Eveline	20	REECE, Emma	40
PURVIS, Henry A	20	REED, J. M	84
PURVIS, James R	20	REED, Jane	13
PURVIS, John J	95	REED, John	13
PURVIS, John R	95	REED, Mary A	13
PURVIS, John W	20	REED, Matthew	13
PURVIS, Philip G	20	REED, Virginia	13
PURVIS, Purlina L	95	REESE, John	18
PURVIS, Sarah	20	REGAN, Mary A	14
PURVIS, Sarah F	20	REGAN, William	14
PYLES, Milton	44	REGAN, William L	14
QUACKENBOSS, Eliza C	93	REICE, Harriett Elizabeth	6
QUACKENBOSS, Emma	93	REIMAN, Lency	88
QUACKENBOSS, F. W	93	REIMAN, Morris	88
QUACKENBOSS, H. M	93	REVELL, James	15
QUACKENBOSS, J. A. Q	93	REYNOLDS, E R M	11
QUACKENBOSS, Mary P	93	REYNOLDS, James C J	11
QUIGLEY, Edward	81	REYNOLDS, John R	11

REYNOLDS, Lucy R	11	ROBERTS, Levi R	23
REYNOLDS, Mary C	11	ROBERTS, Lewis R	23
REYNOLDS, Wiliam H H	11	ROBERTS, M. J	85
REYNONS, Henry	94	ROBERTS, Martha	23
REYNONS, John	94	ROBERTS, Mary	23
REYNONS, Michael	94	ROBERTS, Mary A	74
RICE, Cornelius A	2	ROBERTS, Medora	85
RICE, Joel C	2	ROBERTS, Ophelia	48
RICE, Joel W	2	ROBERTS, Orville R	23
RICE, Lewelyn	2	ROBERTS, Ransom	48
RICE, Noland S	2	ROBERTS, Sarah C	70
RICHARDS, B. G	89	ROBERTS, Thomas B	23
RICHARDS, J. R	89	ROBERTS, Thomas G	70
RICHARDS, James P	78	ROBERTS, William	23
RICHARDS, S. P	89	ROBINETT, Catherine	30
RICHARDSON, Amelia C	46	ROBINETT, Elizabeth	30
RICHARDSON, Catherine	82	ROBINETT, Jane	30
RICHARDSON, Frances	46	ROBINETT, John	30
RICHARDSON, Frances E	25	ROBINETT, John R	35
RICHARDSON, George W	25, 46	ROBINETT, Lewis	30
RICHARDSON, Joseph S	25	ROBINETT, Margaret	30
RICHARDSON, Robert J	25	ROBINETT, Margaret R	35
RICHARDSON, Sarah	46	ROBINETT, Martha	30, 78
RICHARDSON, Sarah J	25	ROBINETT, Nathan	30
RICHARDSON, Thomas C	25	ROBINETT, Susan	30
RICHARDSON, William J	25	ROBINETT, William	30
RICHARDSON, Winston B	25	ROBINSON, Catherine	42
RICHMOND, George O	32	ROBINSON, Cynthia E	42
RICHMOND, Joseph J?	32	ROBINSON, Helen B	42
RICHMOND, Martha H	32	ROBINSON, James H	3
RICHMOND, Mary Ann	32	ROBINSON, John W	43
RICKELLS, Adeline	56	ROBINSON, Lewis M	42
RICKETTS, Adeline	53	ROBINSON, Lucy	6
RICKETTS, James	53	ROBINSON, Lucy Jane	42
RICKETTS, Temperance	53	ROBINSON, Maria	42
RIDEGAN, Edmund	83	ROBINSON, Mary	42
RIDLEY, Sara Vincent	53	ROBINSON, Mary E	3
RILEY, Harriet E	6	ROBINSON, Noah	74
RILEY, Martha P. A	6	ROBINSON, Thomas	92
RILEY, Robert	19	ROCHILD, Fanny	85
RILEY, William E	6	ROCK, George	82
RILEY, William W	6	RODGERS, Frances A	30
ROBERTS, Buttain P	51	RODGERS, Francis M	3
ROBERTS, C. D	85	RODGERS, G. W	88
ROBERTS, Carolina	74	RODGERS, Martha A	30
ROBERTS, Charles W	23	RODGERS, Moses H	30
ROBERTS, Elizabeth	70	RODGERS, S. M. R	96
ROBERTS, Ellen	74	RODGERS, Sarah E	30
ROBERTS, Elmira M	23	RODGERS, Theron H	30
ROBERTS, Franklin P	70	ROGILLIO, William	43
ROBERTS, George Q	74	ROOK, Benj	76
ROBERTS, George W	23	ROOK, E. A	76
ROBERTS, Georgiana	74	ROOK, James W	76
ROBERTS, James	71	ROOK, Joseph	76
ROBERTS, John W	23	ROOK, S. A	76
ROBERTS, Leroy	85	Rosalie O	92

ROSE, James	34	RUSSELL, Margaret E	21
ROSEMEYER, Fred	83	RUSSELL, Mary	39
ROSS, Alexander	45	RUSSELL, Mary A	7
ROSS, Daniel H	45	RUSSELL, Mary F	14
ROSS, Elizabeth	23	RUSSELL, Mary W	51
ROSS, John P	23	RUSSELL, Napoleon B	39
ROSS, Lewis G	45	RUSSELL, Nixon	21
ROSS, Martha	45	RUSSELL, Reuben	14
ROSS, Mary L	23	RUSSELL, Reuben C	39
ROSS, Richard	23	RUSSELL, Sarah A	25, 39
ROSS, Thomas J	23	RUSSELL, Sarah Ann	25
ROSS, William K	23	RUSSELL, Sarah C	17
ROSSI, Charles	81	RUSSELL, Susanna	21
ROWE, Elizabeth	15	RUSSELL, William G	39
ROWE, Sarah	15	RUSSELL, William J	17
ROWLEY, Cornelia	27	RUSSELL, Zachary F	21
ROWLEY, John R	27	RYAN, Bridget	93
ROWLEY, Matilda	27	SALE, Eveline R	16
ROWLEY, Ophelia	27	SAMPLE, Isaac N	55
ROYALL, J. ?	79	SAMPLE, Margaret J	55
ROYALL, J. M	79	SAMPLE, Martha M. D. A	55
ROYALL, L. E	79	Sarah E	91
ROYALL, Louisianna E	79	SAUCER, Christopher	69
ROYSTER, E. J	80	SAUCER, John S	69
ROYSTER, Nathaniel	80	SAUCER, Letitia	69
RUCKER, Amanda	53	SAUCER, Martha	69
RUCKER, Ann M	53	SAUCER, Nancy	69
RUCKER, Catherine	53	SAUCER, Wm	69
RUCKER, Eliza J	53	SAYRE, Sarah	2
RUCKER, Ellen	53	SAYRE, William K	2
RUCKER, Joanna	53	SCANLAND, Michael	81
RUCKER, John W	53	SCANTLING, William	55
RUCKER, Maria M	53	SCHAFER, J.	6
RUCKER, Sarah F	53	SCHAFER, N	81
RUCKER, William	53	SCHOULTER, J. H	88
RUNDELL, E. A	80	SCHULTZ, Henry	89
RUNDELL, E. B	80	SCONYER, John	74
RUNDELL, H. J	80	SCOTT, Burnwell	36
RUNDELL, Phebe E	12	SCOTT, F. E	76
RUNDELL, Sally	2	SCOTT, F. M	76
RUNNELLS, Henry	82	SCOTT, Lewis	61
RUPERT, P. J	79	SCOTT, Mary	36
RUSSELL, Abner	17	SCOTT, W. P	76
RUSSELL, Abner R	14	SCREWS, Archibald	4
RUSSELL, Ann A	21	SCREWS, Celia A	4
RUSSELL, Catherine	48	SCREWS, James	4
RUSSELL, Columbus	39	SCREWS, James H	4
RUSSELL, Cornelia C	25	SCREWS, John	4
RUSSELL, Elijah	14	SCREWS, Latitia	4
RUSSELL, Eliza	6, 14	SEAGER, James P	3
RUSSELL, Elizabeth	39	SECRIST, Francis	26
RUSSELL, Elizabeth F	73	SELSER, Hiram	23
RUSSELL, Gaton D	17	SELSER, Margaret	23
RUSSELL, George W	25	SHACKELFORD, John	70
RUSSELL, J. T. Jr	79	SHAFER, Jacob	1
RUSSELL, James D	21	SHANDS, A. C	92

SHARP, Ann L	53	SIMMONS, John N. B.	49
SHARP, Elizabeth R	53	SIMMONS, M. C.	66
SHARP, John M	53	SIMMONS, Margaret S	49
SHARP, Mary	53	SIMMONS, Mary A	49
SHAW, E. D	95	SIMMONS, Susan E	49
SHELL, Emily	20	SIMMS, Rebecca	13
SHELL, George H	20	SISIL, Mary Ann	29, 37
SHELL, Ira B	20	SISSON, Annes E	13
SHELL, Maria C	20	SISSON, Henry	13
SHELL, Mary	20	SISSON, James E	13
SHELL, Peter J	20	SISSON, Mary J	13
SHELL, Sarah	21	SISSON, Oliver	13
SHELL, Thomas H	20	SLADE, Ed	96
SHELL, Thomas W	20	SLATER, Launer M	10
SHEPPARD, Eliza	25	SLATER, Mississippi	10
SHERRARD, Benjamin	18	SLATER, T. A.	12
SHERRARD, Elinore	18	SLATER, The. A.	10
SHERRARD, Emily	18	SLAUGHTER, Nat. G	94
SHERRARD, Frances V	18	SMALLY, J. B.	54
SHERRARD, Joel	18	SMITH, Abigail	8
SHERRARD, Joel Jr.	18	SMITH, Alex	87
SHERRARD, John L	18	SMITH, Alphonso	59
SHERRARD, John R	18	SMITH, Ann E	59
SHERRARD, Martha	18	SMITH, Ann L	12
SHERRARD, Mary E	18	SMITH, Arnold	63
SHERRARD, Minerva	18	SMITH, Austin P	1
SHERRARD, Richard	18	SMITH, Benjamin	12
SHERRARD, Sarah	18	SMITH, C. E	85
SHERRARD, Thomas W	18	SMITH, Catherine	61
SHERRARD, William	18	SMITH, Celia A	3
SHERRARD, William Jr	18	SMITH, Cyntha	5
SHIRLEY, John	14	SMITH, Edward H	12
SHIRLEY, Martha A	14	SMITH, Elinora	59
SHIRLEY, Robert	14	SMITH, Eliza	49
SHIRLEY, Thomas	14	SMITH, Emeline	63
SHIRLEY, William	14	SMITH, F. M. E	87
SHORTER, Susan	1	SMITH, Francis A	52
SHROPSHIRE, A. M	89	SMITH, George E	1
SHROPSHIRE, Emily	89	SMITH, H. H	85
SHROPSHIRE, James	89	SMITH, Henry	85
SHROPSHIRE, John E	89	SMITH, James	1, 3, 63
SHROPSHIRE, M. H	89	SMITH, James M	12
SHROPSHIRE, M. J	89	SMITH, Jane	71
SHROPSHIRE, M. V	89	SMITH, John	48
SHROPSHIRE, S. C	89	SMITH, John L	48
SIBLEY, Asa	6	SMITH, Joseph B	12
SIBLEY, Elizabeth	5	SMITH, Leonidas	63
SIBLEY, John C	6	SMITH, Louisa	59, 77
SIBLEY, Mary A.M.	6	SMITH, Louisa H	12
SIBLEY, Mrs. Mariah Ann	94	SMITH, Malissa E	1
SIBLEY, Nancy G	6	SMITH, Martin	59
SIBLEY, Samuel W	6	SMITH, Mary	48
SIBLEY, Susan A	6	SMITH, Mary Margaret	62
SIBLEY, William H.H.	6	SMITH, Mary R	12
SIDDON, Charlotte	72	SMITH, Nancy	13
SIMMONS, Benjamin G	49	SMITH, Nathaniel T	52

SMITH, Sarah C.	1	SPIARS, Sidney	37
SMITH, Susan A	12	SPIARS, Theophilus O	25
SMITH, Tennesse	12	SPIARS, William	7
SMITH, Theophilus	1	SPIERMAN, Elizabeth	51
SMITH, Thomas	63	SPIERS, Martha Jane	8
SMITH, Wellington	61	SRICRES? John	77
SMITH, William B	12	STAMM, Eliza	92
SMITH, William M	59	STAMM, Henry	92
SMITH, William Z.	1	STAMPLEY, Abbygen	8
SMITH?, Elizabeth B	52	STAMPLEY, Absalom	8
SNIDER, J	41	STAMPLEY, David	8
SOJOURNER, Mary	22	STAMPLEY, Harriet S	8
SORELLLS, Nancy	42	STAMPLEY, Jefferson	8
SORELLLS, Samuel	42	STAMPLEY, Jesse S	8
SORRELLS, A. C	85	STAMPLEY, John	8
SORRELLS, Allen	85	STAMPLEY, John S	8
SORRELLS, E. A	85	STAMPLEY, Leonidas	8
SORRELLS, Henry	42	STAMPLEY, Malvinia	8
SORRELLS, Henry Jr	85	STAMPLEY, Richard	8
SORRELLS, Henry Sr	85	STAMPLEY, Sarah	8
SORRELLS, James	85	STAMPLEY, Sarah A	8
SORRELLS, Mila	85	STARK, Jane	30
SORRELLS, S. J	85	STEIN, Eliza A	51
SORRELLS, Sam'l	85	STEIN, Elizabeth	51
SORRELS, John L	20	STEIN, Jane	51
SOUTHARD, Joseph	45	STEIN, Jefferson	51
SPAIN, Cordelia	8	STEIN, Margaret	51
SPANE, Nancy	8	STEIN, Thomas C	51
SPELL, Ann	22	STEIN, Thomas C, Jr	51
SPELLS, Martha	22	STEPHENS, Ann S	78
SPELLS, Mary E	29	STEPHENS, Elizabeth	78
SPELLS, Z.D.	29	STEPHENS, Rebecca	78
SPENCER, Alzira	70	STEPHENS, Richard S	78
SPENCER, Isaac	70	STEPHENS, Robert	78
SPENCER, J. W.	41	STEPHENS, Thomas	78
SPENCER, Lycurgus	70	STERLING, Isaac F	61
SPENCER, Marshall G	70	STERLING, Josiah	61
SPENCER, Saphronia N	96	STERLING, Octavia	61
SPENCER, Sim F	70	STEVENS, A. P	88
SPENCER, William O	70	STEVENS, Benjamin F	50
SPIARS, Charles C	25	STEVENS, C. A	88
SPIARS, Frances A	7	STEVENS, C. E	88
SPIARS, Gracy	7, 25	STEVENS, Elizabeth	20
SPIARS, James	7	STEVENS, James A	88
SPIARS, John	7, 25	STEVENS, James F	20
SPIARS, John C	7	STEVENS, Lewis	50
SPIARS, John W	25	STEVENS, Martha	20
SPIARS, Levi	7	STEVENS, Martha A	45
SPIARS, Lydia	25	STEVENS, Rebecca	72
SPIARS, Mary Ann	69	STEVENS, Robert H	20
SPIARS, Mary C	7	STEVENS, S. F	88
SPIARS, Polly	55	STEVENS, Theodore	88
SPIARS, Robert	7, 25	STEVENS, Tolbert	20
SPIARS, Robert F	7	STEWART, Adeline	39
SPIARS, Robert K P	7	STEWART, Andrew M	39
SPIARS, Sarah	25	STEWART, Charles	39

STEWART, Felix G	39	STURDIVANT, Mary A	3
STEWART, Hannah	39	STURDIVANT, Mary E?	3
STEWART, Hiel	41	STURDIVANT, Ransom	3
STEWART, James	39, 41	STURDIVANT, Sarah Ann	3
STEWART, Margaret E	39	SULLIVAN, Kezah	85
STEWART, Mary A	41	SUMNER, Franz	83
STEWART, Mary M	39	SUMNER, Henry	83
STEWART, Nancy A	39, 41	SUMNER, Mary	83
STEWART, Rosana	41	SUMNER, Mary J	83
STEWART, Samuel G	39	SWAIN, Margaret J	38
STEWART, Samuel V	39	SWAYZE, Agnes	22
STEWART, Seth	39	SWAYZE, Alfred	21
STEWART, Washington D	39	SWAYZE, Belinda	22
STIGLER, James	48	SWAYZE, Budd	21
STILLEY, J. H	81	SWAYZE, Charles	40
STILLEY, M. M	81	SWAYZE, Clara E	40
STILLY, Ellen J	80	SWAYZE, Emily	22
STILLY, M	80	SWAYZE, Emma	22
STINER, Sophia	74	SWAYZE, Frances	22
STINNETT, James L	14	SWAYZE, Gabriel	67
STINSON, Robt	77	SWAYZE, H. A.	40
STOWER, Laura	9	SWAYZE, Hardy	22
STRANE, E. F	94	SWAYZE, Hirum O	67
STRANE, M. S	94	SWAYZE, J. A.	67
STREET, David	35	SWAYZE, Mary	22, 67
STREET, Eliza A	34	SWAYZE, Mary A	22
STREET, Francis M	34	SWAYZE, Missouri	22
STREET, James A	34	SWAYZE, Nancy A	40
STREET, John	35	SWAYZE, Octavia S	21
STREET, John P	34	SWAYZE, Orange	22
STREET, John W. F.	34	SWAYZE, Prentiss	22
STREET, Malissa A	35	SWAYZE, Richard	16, 22
STREET, Martha	35	SWAYZE, Sina	21
STREET, Mary	35	SWAYZE, Solomon	22
STREET, Samuel A	34	SWAYZE, Virginia	22
STREET, William	35	SWAYZE, William	22
STRODE, M. C	96	SWISHER, Elizabeth J	86
STROMP, Jacob	44	TAMBORNINE, D	80
STROUP, Baruch	96	TANIER, C.	41
STROUP, Soloman	96	TAYLOR, George W	29
STUBBLEFIELD, Almira	18	TAYLOR, Green B	29
STUBBLEFIELD, Amanda	62	TAYLOR, Mary	29
STUBBLEFIELD, Aurora	62	TAYLOR, William L	29
STUBBLEFIELD, Calvin	62	TERBERVILLE, M. J	90
STUBBLEFIELD, David A	8	TERRILL, Francis	58
STUBBLEFIELD, Eliza P	6	TERRILL, James F	58
STUBBLEFIELD, Elizabeth	62	TERRILL, John	58
STUBBLEFIELD, Jane	62	TERRILL, Martha	58
STUBBLEFIELD, Marlin	18	TERRILL, Mary E	58
STUBBLEFIELD, Mary	62	TERRY, Mary A	74
STUBBLEFIELD, Sarah A	18	TERRY, Thomas B	74
STUBBLEFIELD, Simon P	62	THAMES, Elizabeth	27
STUBBLEFIELD, Stephen P	6	THAMES, Redding	27
STUBBLEFIELD, William	62	THAMES, Virginia	27
STURDIVANT, Ann E	3	THARP, Abraham	29, 37
STURDIVANT, Henry	4	THARP, Adelade	90

THARP, Caroline E	79	VANCLEVE, Thos. V	87
THARP, Emma	90	VANGHAN, Emma	40
THARP, James	90	VANGHAN, Frances	40
THARP, James W	90	VAUGHAN, Alice A	40
THARP, John W	37	VAUGHAN, Ann	43
THARP, Margaret	37	VAUGHAN, Charles B	40
THARP, Mary A	29, 37	VAUGHAN, Edwin	43
THARP, Mary P	90	VAUGHAN, Elizabeth	43
THARP, one infant	90	VAUGHAN, Emma M	40
THINS, Margarie	37	VAUGHAN, Henry	40
THOMAS	27	VAUGHAN, Hugh R	40
THOMAS, H. J.	72	VAUGHAN, James	40
THOMASSON, Eliza	77	VAUGHAN, James W	43
THOMASSON, John	77	VAUGHAN, Joseph	43
THOMASSON, Ulysses	77	VAUGHAN, Margaret A	40
THOMASSON, Virginia	77	VAUGHAN, Maria	43
THOMASSON, W. B	77	VAUGHAN, Mary S	40
THOMASSON, W. H.	77	VAUGHAN, Pamela	43
THOMPSON, Amanda	29	VAUGHAN, Priscilla	93
THOMPSON, E. W	89	VAUGHAN, Sarah	43
THOMPSON, Jane	29	VEIRNN, Joseph	80
THOMPSON, Levi	37	VINCENT, Francis	80
THOMPSON, Mary	37	VINCENT, Virginia	80
THOMPSON, Mary J	37	WADLINGTON, Ferdinand	9
THOMPSON, Oliver G	37	WALDO, C. M	79
THOMPSON, Preston S	29	WALKER, Alfred	17
THOMPSON, R. N	89	WALKER, Alfred Jr.	17
THOMSON, Mary Ann	14	WALKER, Asa	17
THORN, Albert C	88	WALKER, D	88
THORN, Eliz	95	WALKER, E. W	88
THORN, Estha	95	WALKER, Edward	26
THORN, John	95	WALKER, Frances	26
THORNTON, Albert	93	WALKER, J. A	88
TIDWELL, M. A. E.	74	WALKER, John	83
TIDWELL, Saunders	74	WALKER, John L	26
TIDWELL, Wiley	74	WALKER, Laurentina Ophelia	88
TIDWELL, William H	74	WALKER, Lucretia M	73
TILLAYE, Sophia	93	WALKER, Lucy	69
TILLEY, Calvin	41	WALKER, Margaret	44
TILLEY, Nancy	41	WALKER, Mary J	17
TILLEY, Sarah	41	WALKER, Moses E. N.	17
TRANER, Anna M	94	WALKER, R. S	88
TRANER, Terence	94	WALKER, Robert F. M	17
TRIBBLE, Ann	67	WALKER, Samuel	44
TRUNK, Catherine	26	WALKER, Sarah	17
TRUNK, John	26	WALKER, Semitha	9
TRUNK, Rosina	26	WALKER, Sherwood	26
TUCKER, Catherine	51	WALKER, Thompson	44
TWINER, John T	78	WALKER, William O	23
TYLER, Henry C	94	WALLACE, California	62
USHER, Catherine S	4	WALLACE, Charles	89
USHER, Charlotte L Hinds	4	WALLACE, Elvira	11
UTLEY, John W	9	WALLACE, Helen	62
UTLEY, Louisa	9	WALLACE, Hiram F	62
VANCE, Rachel	26	WALLACE, Nancy	62
VANCLEAVE, Jonathan	8	WALLACE, Nicholas	62

WALLACE, Phillip	62	WATERS, Susan	66
WALLACE, Richardson	62	WATLINGTON, Elizabeth	56
WALLER, Casilla	54	WATLINGTON, Frances E	63
WALLER, Elizabeth	20	WATLINGTON, Francis	56
WALLER, James S	20	WATLINGTON, Henry	56
WALLER, John C	54	WATLINGTON, Julius	56
WALLER, Lafayette	54	WATLINGTON, Keziah	56
WALLER, Susan	20	WATLINGTON, William	56
WALLER, William	20, 54	WATLINGTON, William F	56
WALLINGTON, Martha	60	WEDEKIND, C	81
WALLIS, A. L	83	WEDEKIND, Mary	81
WALLIS, F. J	83	WEDELL, John B	87
WALLIS, P. C	83	WEIMS, John	42
WALLIS, V. E	83	WEIMS, Martha	42
WARE, Helen	70	WEIMS, Sarah M	42
WARE, James	70	WEIMS, William C	42
WARE, Julian	70	WEIR, Amelia C	46
WARE, Mary	70	WELLS, Adeline	69
WARE, Virginia C	70	WELLS, Ann	69
WARMACK, Apolonia	38	WELLS, John	69
WARMACK, Bennet	38	WELLS, Medora	69
WARMACK, Effie J	38	WELLS, Rebecca	69
WARMACK, Jeanot	38	WELLS, Soloman	69
WARMACK, Mary A	38	WESLING, John H	81
WARREN, Belinda	56	WESLING, Mary A	81
WARREN, John	93	WESSELL, Catherine	26
WARREN, John S	56	WESSELL, John	42
WARREN, Mary A	56	WESSELL, Mary K	42
WARREN, Moses	56	WEST, Augustus	34
WARREN, Reuben	56	WEST, E. D	89
WARREN, Sarah E	56	WEST, James R	89
WARREN, Susan	56	WEST, L. D	89
WARRICK, Robert	96	WEST, Sarah Rachel	63
WASHBURN, A. W.	14	WEST, T. S	89
WASHBURN, George W	14	WHELENBERG, Herman	81
WASHBURN, Leonora	14	WHELESS, Ada	6
WASKUM, Eliza	68	WHELESS, Elizabeth A	6
WASKUM, Griffin	68	WHELESS, Falba	6
WASKUM, James M	68	WHELESS, Frederick W	6
WASKUM, John	68	WHELESS, Kossuth	6
WASKUM, Mary E	68	WHELESS, Quesney	6
WASKUM, Thomas	68	WHITCOMB, C. S.	44
WASSON, Elihu	1	WHITCOMB, John H	44
WASSON, Lucius E	1	WHITCOMB, Jonas D	44
WASSON, Sarah T	1	WHITCOMB, Pamela	44
WATERMAN, Henry	77	WHITCOMB, Sarah M	44
WATERS, Adamson	66	WHITE, B. F. L	76
WATERS, Alma	66	WHITE, B. G. S	91
WATERS, Glycerian	66	WHITE, Bartholemew	42
WATERS, John	66	WHITE, Emily	24
WATERS, John W	19	WHITE, Francis E	33
WATERS, Joseph	66	WHITE, Greenup	42, 91
WATERS, Laura	66	WHITE, H. R. W	76
WATERS, Lucinda	19	WHITE, Harriet	42
WATERS, Mary	66	WHITE, J. J. B	76
WATERS, Needham	19	WHITE, James J. B	76

WHITE, John 24	WILLIAMS, Sarah E 37
WHITE, L. B 76	WILLIAMS, Susan 36
WHITE, Louisa 24	WILLIAMS, Susan D 52
WHITE, Louisianna 33	WILLIAMS, Tabitha J 37
WHITE, M. B 76	WILLIAMS, Tuy? 34
WHITE, Margaret 42, 91	WILLIAMS, W. Cicero 52
WHITE, Mercy Leonard 32	WILLIAMS, William M . . . 38, 52
WHITE, Nancy 42	WILLIAMS, Wm 77
WHITE, Nathan H 33	WILLIAMSON, R. R 82
WHITE, Phebe Jane 34	WILMORE, Elizabeth 56
WHITE, Rebecca 33	WILSON, A. C 87
WHITE, Rebecca S 76	WILSON, David 91
WHITE, Wm. V 91	WILSON, Henry S 93
WHITMAN, Charles 93	WILSON, John 60
WHITMAN, Mary 93	WILSON, John C 91
WHITMAN, Mary Frances 93	WILSON, John F 91
WHITMAN, Nostrand 93	WILSON, John I 91
WHITMAN, Sophia 93	WILSON, L. L. S 87
WHITMAN, Ulysis 93	WILSON, Margaret 6
WHITTAKER, Aaron N 75	WILSON, Martha J 91
WHITTEN, Eliza 16	WILSON, Mary F 93
WILBORN, Elizabeth 65	WILSON, Nat. N 91
WILBORN, James 65	WILSON, Pauline 91
WILBORN, Joseph 8	WILSON, Pauline A 91
WILBORN, W. Wyche 65	WILSON, R. B 91
WILDY, H 9	WILSON, Robert 6
WILDY, Laurena 9	WILSON, Robt. C 91
WILDY, Matilda 9	WILSON, Sam'l H 93
WILDY, Sally 9	WILSON, T. J 87
WILDY, William W 9	WILSON, Talbot 79
WILES, Elizabeth L 3	WINCAUGH 90
WILES, Morris G 3	WINDHAM, William 1
WILES, W W 3	WINN, C. V 79
WILKINSON, Albert 31	WINN, E. B 79, 81
WILKINSON, Benjamin R 49	WINN, E. S. 79
WILKINSON, Carey H 49	WINN, J. B 79
WILKINSON, Cornelia 94	WINN, K 79
WILKINSON, Edward C 94	WINN, L 79
WILKINSON, Eliza C 49, 94	WINN, M. E 81
WILKINSON, G. B 94	WINN, O 81
WILKINSON?, Nancy 92	WINN, R. M. 79
WILLIAMS, Amanda M 58	WINN, R. M. Jr 79
WILLIAMS, B. R. 30	WINN, S. D 81
WILLIAMS, Benjamin F 58	WINN, W. S 81
WILLIAMS, Christopher C 52	WINSTED, Frances A 66
WILLIAMS, David F 38	WITHERS, Martha J 89
WILLIAMS, Elizabeth 52, 75	WOMACK, E J 44
WILLIAMS, Frances A 58	WOOD, Clarissa R 31
WILLIAMS, James 84	WOOD, Mary P 45
WILLIAMS, Jemima 38	WOOD, William W 45
WILLIAMS, John 58, 64	WOODARD, Frances 1
WILLIAMS, Joseph N 52	WOODARD, Margaret C 1
WILLIAMS, Martha J 58	WOODBERRY, George W 8
WILLIAMS, Nancy A 58	WOODBERRY, Robert S 8
WILLIAMS, Parham 52	WOOLDRIDGE, Thomas 74
WILLIAMS, Samuel H 58	WOOLFOLK, Dudley 76

WOOLFOLK, John H	76	YARBOROUGH, Minerva C	55
WOOLFOLK, Sarah	76	YARBOROUGH, Thomas G	67
WORD, Adelia	30	YORK, John B	22
WORD, Elizabeth	30	YOUNG, Anderson J	93
WORD, Mary P	30	YOUNG, Augusta W	47
WORD, William M	30	YOUNG, Catherine	47
WORMACK, John	46	YOUNG, Henry	66
WORMACK, John F	46	YOUNG, Isaac	93
WORMACK, Sarah M	46	YOUNG, John C	93
WORMACK, Sarah V	46	YOUNG, Joseph	2
WORMACK, William Q	46	YOUNG, Joseph A	47
WORTHINGTON, Eliza	40	YOUNG, Julia	47
WORTHINGTON, George H	23	YOUNG, Keziah	19
WORTHY, Benjamin F	71	YOUNG, Laura	35, 93
WORTHY, Rebeckah	71	YOUNG, Lavina	19
WORTHY, Seaborn J. F	71	YOUNG, M. A	93
WRENN, C. S	75	YOUNG, Mary	47
WRENN, Catherine	15	YOUNG, Mary A	19
WRENN, Robert	15	YOUNG, Ophelia	47
WRENN, William	15	YOUNG, Rachel	19
WRENN, William R	15	YOUNG, Robert A	47
WRIGHT, A. S	82	YOUNG, Samuel	19
WRIGHT, Delphine	40	YOUNG, Thomas	47
WRIGHT, J. M	92	YOUNG, Thomas D	19
WRIGHT, J. M.	28	YOUNG, Virginia	47
WRIGHT, John M	82	YOUNG, William	47
WRIGHT, M. A	82	ZEIGLER, James	52
WRIGHT, M. C. S	82	ZEIGLER, Matilda	52
WRIGHT, M. F	82		
WRIGHT, Mary S	92		
WRIGHT, Rebecca E	82		
WRIGHT, Robert	37		
WRIGHT, S. S	92		
WRIGHT, William	82		
WRIGHT, Wm. Sl.	82		
WYMAN, Wm	90		
YANDELL, Burton	24		
YANDELL, Ellnora	73		
YANDELL, Emma A	73		
YANDELL, John S	73		
YANDELL, Malvina	24		
YANDELL, Susan J	73		
YANDELL, William M	73		
YANDELL, Wilson	73		
YANKEY, Edney C	12		
YANKEY, Jonathan	12		
YANKEY, Mary E	12		
YANKEY, Mary J	12		
YANKEY, William A	12		
YARBOROUGH, Alfred	55		
YARBOROUGH, James H	55		
YARBOROUGH, Jane	67		
YARBOROUGH, John	67		
YARBOROUGH, Lydia A	67		
YARBOROUGH, Melissa	55		
YARBOROUGH, Micajah	55